EDP
ADMINISTRATION
AND CONTROL

EDP ADMINISTRATION AND CONTROL

William E. Perry
CPA, CIA, CISA

Prentice-Hall, Inc.
Englewood Cliffs, N.J. 07632

Library of Congress Cataloging in Publication Data

Perry, William E.
  EDP administration and control.

  Includes index.
  1. Electronic data processing departments—Management
I. Title. II. Title: E.D.P. administration and control.
HF5548.2.P47283 1984   648.054   83-24750
ISBN 0-13-235649-X

Editorial/production supervision
  and interior design: **Aliza Greenblatt**
Cover design: **Wanda Lubelska**
Manufacturing buyer: **Gordon Osbourne**

Printed in the United States of America
10 9 8 7 6 5 4 3 2 1

ISBN 0-13-235649-X 01

PRENTICE-HALL INTERNATIONAL, INC., *London*
PRENTICE-HALL OF AUSTRALIA PTY. LIMITED, *Sydney*
EDITORA PRENTICE-HALL DO BRASIL, LTDA., *Rio de Janeiro*
PRENTICE-HALL CANADA INC., *Toronto*
PRENTICE-HALL OF INDIA PRIVATE LIMITED, *New Delhi*
PRENTICE-HALL OF JAPAN, INC. *Tokyo*
PRENTICE-HALL OF SOUTHEAST ASIA PTE. LTD., *Singapore*
WHITEHALL BOOKS LIMITED, *Wellington, New Zealand*

To Karl Karlstrom,
whose untiring effort in orchestrating
publications in the data processing
field has contributed to the professional
advancement of that field.

Contents

Preface

Good data processing administration and control are necessary for success. Projects that are successfully administered and controlled succeed. Projects with poor administration and control are frequently overbudget, behind schedule, and undergo extensive maintenance.

EDP administration and control is often the elephant's graveyard of data processing. Putting the poorer people into administration is the equivalent of putting the future of data processing in the hands of those who are against automation. Many managers who are unsuccessful in the technical areas of data processing are moved into administration—administration being the punishment for mediocrity in the technical areas.

Administration and control are two of the building blocks of an effective EDP function. Administration is the lifeline of information within the data processing department. Control is the mechanism that ensures that the function is performing in an effective, efficient, and economical manner, in accordance with the intent of management, and meeting the requirements of users.

This book was designed to provide immediately implementable solutions to many of the problems occurring in data processing. The processes proposed do not increase the cost of data processing but rather, decrease it. It is far more economical to do it right the first time with good administrative and control practices than to pay to correct systems after they have been implemented improperly.

EDP ADMINISTRATION AND CONTROL

ORGANIZING AN EFFECTIVE ADMINISTRATIVE FUNCTION

Just as one should not embark on a long trip without a map, neither should administration plan to build an effective function without a plan of action.

Chapter

1

EDP Administration
and Control:
An Elephant's Graveyard

In too many organizations, EDP administration detracts from productivity. Administration can be a bane or a boon to the management of data processing. Properly established, it can improve the credibility and productivity of the function as well as ensure that the function's mission is accomplished. Poorly structured, everything bad that people say about EDP happens.

EDP administration is another data processing project. It has requirements, must be designed and implemented, placed into operation, and then maintained and evaluated. In a successfully administered project the cost of administration should provide a return on investment to the department.

This book is designed to assist organizations in building and evaluating an effective EDP administration function. The book is designed to provide immediately implementable solutions to today's administrative challenges. The book is based on the administrative practices of several hundred corporations and is structured to explain in a step-by-step format how to get the most administration for the fewest resources.

The author has taken the privilege of codifying administrative practice into guidelines for the practice of EDP administration. These basic principles are the building blocks of an effective administration function. Those who believe and follow these guidelines should achieve success far greater than those who think they can tangle with the way the world was meant to be—and win!

EDP ADMINISTRATIVE GUIDELINE 1
Whatever can go wrong in EDP will go wrong—and at exactly the worst moment.

Some of the questions that need to be pondered about your EDP administration function are:

1. Would the functioning of the data processing department be adversely affected if all the administrative procedures, rules, and practices were eliminated?
2. Does the administrative information presented to management assist them in making decisions, or are the critical data collected by other means?
3. Does the administrative staff recommend meaningful suggestions on how to improve the development and operation of information systems?
4. Does the data processing staff complement the administration function by helping them get their job done more effectively, efficiently, and economically?
5. Is EDP administration in step with corporate administration, or do they operate solely within DP?

If you answered *no* to any of these questions, you may need to make some significant changes in your administration function.

WHAT AND WHO ARE EDP ADMINISTRATION?

To administer means to furnish help, to be of service, and to manage. In EDP, administration deals with all aspects, from the personal computer on the lower end of the continuum to large integrated data base data communication systems at the sophisticated end of the continuum.

Administration is people. It must include the personal needs and desires of people, as well as make things happen in a corporate culture. Administration is everybody's responsibility, yet without central guidance and direction, things that should happen may not, or may happen poorly. The goal of administration should be to make things happen through people, and to make them happen right the first time.

EDP ADMINISTRATION AND THE SHOEMAKER'S SON

Data processing professionals are the change makers of the world. Within a tiny time span in the history of humankind, data processors have revolutionized the way business is conducted. However, like the shoemaker's son, many data processing departments have provided their users with the most up-to-date, sophisticated administrative systems, yet have neglected their own internal housekeeping.

Here are the types of problems that a good EDP administration function must address:

- The average data processing department has a three-year backlog of work growing at a rate of 10 percent per year.
- Faced with this backlog, many organizations are freezing or reducing EDP budgets.
- One group of experts say that there is a programmer shortage, whereas another says there is not. Regardless, it is almost universally agreed there is a shortage of good systems analysts/programmers.
- Project management systems can track the resources expended much more accurately than they can the progress of the project work.
- Few EDP departments have effective long-range plans, and those that do rarely integrate them into the plans for the organization.
- Estimating and scheduling is more of a black art than a science.
- A commonly held belief by organization management is that data processing professionals are not team players and thus show more allegiance to their profession than the organization by which they are employed.
- Administration can measure neither the effectiveness of the data processing function nor the return on investment to the data processing department by the administration function.

DP administration is the glue that should hold together the individual segments of the data processing function. Administration is the lifeblood of the DP department. Without proper administration the individual pieces will not be molded into a cohesive, effective function.

THE CONCEPT OF FIT

The person responsible for EDP administration may find himself or herself in the position of a parent trying to put together a child's toy without directions. The EDP administrator must put together some diverse segments, both within and without the EDP department. There are no ideal set of instructions on how to build an effective administrative function. The EDP administrator has a box of tasks, tools, and talents to manage for the purposes of accomplishing the department's mission.

The bottom-line task of EDP administration is to "fit" data processing into the goals and objectives of the organization. Data processing cannot be just another service function, like the mail room, and be effective. Information systems must complement the characteristics of the organizations they serve. If the data processing systems and services fail to "fit" their organization's needs, data processing will be inhibited from reaching its full potential. Administration must assure that the proper fit occurs.

The concept of fitting data processing into the organizational structure is illustrated in Figure 1. The four aspects of data processing that must be fit into a cohesive working strategy are:

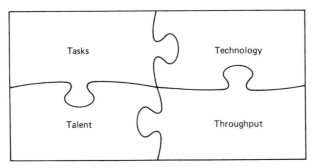

Figure 1   *Concept of Fit*

1. *Tasks:*   The requirements assigned to the data processing function for completion
2. *Talent:*   The effective use of personnel in the accomplishment of those tasks
3. *Technology:*   The matching of technology to the needs of the organization
4. *Throughput:*   The satisfaction of the requirements in an adequate quantity and on a timely basis

The task of administration is to interface these four aspects of data processing into an effective, highly productive unit. If the segments are managed independently, a department's talents may not be applied to the appropriate tasks, nor may the technology meet the business throughput and information needs. The proper fitting of these four segments ensures the improved credibility and productivity of the data processing function.

EDP ADMINISTRATIVE GUIDELINE 2

The concept of fit is like teamwork; when all forces pull together in the same direction, the company wins.

EDP administration is a subset of the administration of the organization. It cannot function effectively in an isolated environment. EDP management must be apprised of the plans and objectives of their organization so that they can integrate those needs into the plans of data processing. The administration function is the vehicle for this integration.

THE IMPEDIMENTS TO EFFECTIVE ADMINISTRATION

In this book, the DP administrators are the good guys, whereas the data processing staff is the enemy. A war can never be won until you understand who the enemy is. However, the real enemy is the lack of understanding of how the objectives of administration fit into accomplishing the DP mission.

The fulfillment of the data processing mission involves requirements, resources, schedules, and administration. Let us look at these attributes of any project in order to put administration in the proper perspective. It will also illustrate the impediments faced in attempting to implement an effective administration program.

To simplify the discussion, let us assume that the data processing department has been asked to develop a project. The characteristics of that project can be expressed in terms of the project's requirements, schedule, resources, and administration. Whereas administration is a constant, the other three are established by management for each project.

When data processing accepts a project for implementation, the requirements are established by the user of that project. The user may be within or outside the data processing department. When the requirements have been defined, a schedule is established for implementing that project. Knowing the requirements and the schedule, the resources needed can be determined. These are illustrated in Figure 2 as dials set by management. The fourth dial represents the integration, or the "fit" of the project into the overall data processing mission for the organization. At this point, the dials are set and the project commences.

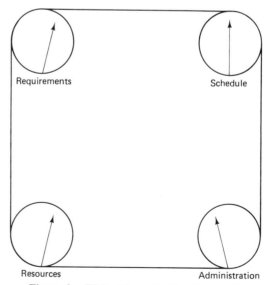

Figure 2   *EDP Administration Perspective*

EDP administration includes the following tasks:

- Developing people
- Ensuring the quality of the project
- Ensuring data and processing consistency with other projects
- Following administrative procedures and standards
- Optimizing technology

As the project commences, requirements frequently change. This necessitates that the requirements dial be moved. At the same time, management frequently holds the schedule and resources dial firm. As the project characteristics are interrelated, the movement of one dial must be reflected in one of the other three areas. If schedule and resources are held firm, then administration must move, and frequently it degrades. For example, standards may not be followed, or project personnel adequately supervised and trained to incorporate the new requirements into the project. Later, an experienced programmer may be replaced with a trainee, having the net effect of lowering the available resources. If management holds the requirements and schedule dials firm, administration will again degrade (i.e., policies, procedures, and standards will not be followed).

The problem with administration is that it frequently takes a back seat to the accomplishment of the department's mission. Administration may be viewed as a time-consuming, redundant, and often an unnecessary part of the achievement of the data processing mission. It is this attitude that is one of the major impediments to building and operating a successful EDP administration function. It is only when the project personnel fully understand how administration improves project productivity that the "administration dial" will be held firm by management, so that a change in one of the other three dials must be reflected among those dials, and not allowed to degrade the project administration.

THE TECHNOLOGICAL COMMUNICATION GAP

A problem that has plagued data processing from the early days of computer technology is communication. The vocabulary used to describe the computer, its uses, and its problems has been foreign to noncomputer personnel. The problem, data processing personnel have said, will resolve itself when users and senior management learn the computer basics.

In the early 1960s, the use of the computer grew dramatically in many corporations. From a fraction of a percent of sales, the resources expended for computer services grew to 1 percent, 2 percent, and higher in many corporations. The projected growth rate for computer services was such that, unless checked, it would shortly consume all of the organizational revenue.

Senior management could not speak computer terminology, and the computer personnel were unable to communicate their position. When senior management is unable to develop a solution to a problem, they normally implement one of the following two controls:

1. *Capping expenditures:* Senior management restricts funding or personnel to the current level and makes the organizational unit work out the best possible solution to their work situation within that resource cap.

2. *Cost justification:* Each expenditure in the unit must be cost-justified prior to resources being expended.

In the data processing industry, the cost-justification method was chosen. Many data processing organizations were forced to charge out their services to users, and at the same time cost-justify any new projects. The net effect of the approach was a significant reduction in the growth of resources being expended on data processing services.

Twenty years later, the technological communication gap still exists (see Figure 3). Even in those organizations where senior management has been exposed to computer systems, they still have difficulty communicating with many of their data processing personnel. Unfortunately, many data processing personnel still put the blame for the communication gap on senior management.

Senior management has been saying for 20 years that the language with which they want to communicate about data processing is the language of accounting and economics. Senior management chose 20 years ago not to discuss data processing in technical terminology, they do not choose to do so

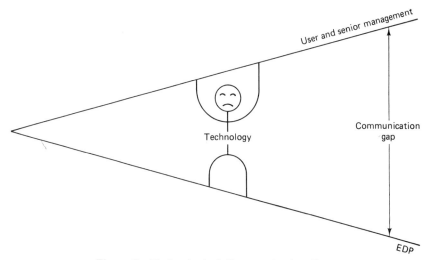

Figure 3   *Technological Communication Gap*

today, and they will probably choose not to do so 20 years from now. The solution to the technological communication gap resides with the data processing profession.

Users normally speak basically the same language as senior management. A study[1] by the American Petroleum Institute in the mid-1970s showed that the two major user priorities for data processing services, in order of priority, are:

1. The economic feasibility of their systems
2. Conformity to user specifications

At the same time, the data processing personnel viewed their two most important priorities to be:

1. Completeness of the documentation
2. Conformity of the systems and programs to data processing standards and practices

EDP administration has an opportunity to help close the technological communication gap. The administration function should conform to the type and tone of communication desired by their users and senior management. Administration should help define the type of analysis and justification provided to senior management and users about the work currently being performed and proposed. The communication gap solution must be resolved within the data processing function because data processing personnel should not expect senior management to learn EDP—after all, senior management is not trying to be promoted into EDP.

EDP ADMINISTRATIVE GUIDELINE 3
Learn the language of senior management and then discuss EDP in that language.

THE RESPONSIBILITIES OF EDP ADMINISTRATION

There is little uniformity in the data processing profession about the responsibilities of EDP administration, how to staff it, or where it should be located. In some organizations, administration exists as a separate function within data processing, whereas in other organizations it is spread among all segments of the data processing organization. In some companies it is staffed

---

[1] "The EDP Quality Assurance Function," *EDPACS,* January 1977, p. 6.

with people who long ago reached their potential, whereas in other organizations it is staffed with bright, young management candidates riding the crest of a wave toward management.

Administration is that part of management which administers or manages the affairs of the data processing department. Normally, the EDP administration function develops for management the policies and procedures of their organization, and then oversees the execution of those policies and procedures.

Among the responsibilities that are normally associated with EDP administration are:

- Assisting in the development of EDP policies
- Developing EDP procedures
- Managing or directing the implementation and execution of those policies and procedures
- Acting as office manager for the department and, as such, having responsibility for:

  Office services such as mail and telephone
  Disseminating and overseeing company policies and procedures
  Physical location and layout of office
  Acquiring and maintaining office equipment and supplies

- Assisting departmental personnel in interpreting and following policies and procedures
- Compiling budgets
- Maintaining departmental accounting records
- Maintaining departmental personnel records
- Personnel acquisition and management

In a small data processing department, much of the administrative work load will be performed by the data processing manager or an assistant manager. As a department gets larger, the manager usually acquires a staff assistant for administration, and in very large data processing organizations, administration might be handled by a special staff group.

Some of the functional names of the groups responsible for EDP administration include:

- System support
- Data processing comptroller
- Data processing administration
- Data processing services

PERRY'S PRINCIPLES OF EDP ADMINISTRATION

Certain inalienable truths in the practice of administration must be observed. There is an infinite variety of approaches to EDP administration. The organizational location of administration must be situated based on the managerial philosophy of the function. The skills and background of the staff can vary significantly. However, a violation of one of the basic principles of administration will adversely affect the success of that function.

Most disciplines acknowledge the principles on which that discipline is founded. Accounting is based on generally accepted accounting procedures. Engineering works with strength of materials, and the stress placed on those materials according to the type of construction. The sciences are based on the laws of nature. The principles of EDP administration have been codified by the author to assist administrators in determining whether or not the policies and procedures will work. For example, an engineer, through engineering principles, can determine what is needed to sustain a bridge or tall building. Similarly, Perry's Principles of EDP Administration are that body of knowledge against which administrative practices and procedures can be measured to determine whether or not they will work.

The 10 principles of EDP administration are the success factors for administration. They are summarized briefly in Figure 4 and described individually below (in later chapters we discuss how to achieve these principles).

Principle	Description
1. Establish objectives	Know what is wanted
2. Assign ownership	Make people feel a part of their work
3. Define completion	Know what must be done before a project is ended
4. Develop plans	Determine how to get what is needed to be accomplished
5. Limit alternatives	Select the best alternatives (limit of five) before investigations
6. Assign accountability	Make people responsible for their work
7. Respect leadership	Do not challenge management's right to run the organization
8. Obtain tools	Do the job using the best tools and techniques
9. Criticize product	Direct advice and criticism to the product—not the person
10. Discard the obsolete	Discard the outdated and ineffective

Figure 4 *Perry's Principles of EDP Administration*

Administrative Principle 1. *Establish Objectives*

Administration, like any other part of data processing, must operate from clearly established objectives. If administration does not have objectives, the mission of the function will not be clear to those within the function. Administration objectives, such as developing reporting procedures that reasonably reflect the actual status of projects, are necessary both to utilize the function effectively and to measure the performance of the function.

Administrative Principle 2. *Assign Ownership*

People only do well that which they believe is theirs. Effective administration uses policies and procedures that have been "bought into" by the data processing personnel. If the policy and procedure is theirs, they will like it, follow it, and enforce it. If the administrative policy and procedure is dictated, it may not work. For example, a time-reporting system developed by the data processing staff will supply meaningful information, but one dictated and not fully understood by the staff may only account for an individual's workweek.

Administrative Principle 3. *Define Completion*

The deliverables or expectation from each task performed by the administration function must be defined. Open-ended tasks are time-wasters and may not achieve satisfactory results. People must be able to know that they have completed a task. Although there is need for some research and exploratory tasks, these should be the exception and not the rule.

Administrative Principle 4. *Develop Plans*

Once the objectives and completion specifications have been determined, a plan should be developed for accomplishing the administration objectives. Planning is necessary to ensure both that the objectives will be accomplished, and that they will be accomplished with minimum resources. In a function where the results are frequently elusive, plans are essential to the effective performance of the function.

Administrative Principle 5. *Limit Alternatives*

The "rule of five" is applicable to evaluating alternative courses of administrative action. For example, there are literally hundreds of ways to collect people's status and time information, to cost-justify projects, and to prepare annual budgets. However, if the number of alternatives are not quickly limited to the best four or five alternatives, the studies consume excessive time. In any administrative decision process, the alternatives should quickly be limited to the best few, and then only those investigated.

Administrative Principle 6.   *Assign Accountability*

One person must be accountable for each administrative task. This is true not only within the administrative function, but within the entire department. For example, if standards manuals are to be updated, one person must be accountable for updating each manual. Administrative tasks should not be assigned to projects, committees, or functions but rather, assigned to specific people, with each person accountable for the administrative action.

Administrative Principle 7.   *Respect Leadership*

Administration should not challenge leadership but rather, should work with people in responsible positions. Administration does not work well when it threatens a project leader or manager's right to perform or not perform a certain act. Threatening people, or challenging their authority, will not produce the type of administrative results necessary to improve the productivity of the data processing function. The indirect pressures are far more effective in the execution of administrative procedures than the direct confrontation between administrators and line managers.

Administrative Principle 8.   *Obtain Tools*

EDP administration stands in the middle of a highly automated organizational function. Unfortunately, too many administrators perform their function with pencil and paper. Administration, like any other function, should be automated wherever practical. EDP administration should know the tools available to facilitate administration and use those tools wherever appropriate.

Administrative Principle 9.   *Criticize the Product, Not the Person*

In the course of the administration function, problems will occur both within the function and within the data processing department. It will be the responsibility of administration to bring those problems to the attention of management. If the criticism is about the product or the process, the situation is usually remedied quickly; on the other hand, if the criticism is directed at an individual, a defensive posture may occur. The person being attacked may feel it necessary to defend his or her position and thus the needed administrative progress is delayed or may not occur at all.

Administrative Principle 10.   *Discard the Obsolete*

Technological advances in hardware have made it possible to retain obsolete and outdated software systems in many organizations. This is because the inefficiencies of design are overcome by huge increases in hardware speed and reduction in hardware costs. This philosophy has carried over to administrative practices. The administration function must continually challenge the efficiency of administrative practices and discard or replace the obsolete procedures and methods.

EDP ADMINISTRATIVE GUIDELINE 4
Poor administrative practices comprise one of the greatest obstacles to improving productivity within the data processing function.

EDP ADMINISTRATION AS A PROFIT CENTER

EDP administration is not a necessary evil but rather, a function that should pay its own way. Administration too frequently has been viewed as a support function, a record-keeping function, the bean counters, and so on. Part of the objective of this book is to remake both the image and the concept of EDP administration.

Data processing needs to be viewed by senior management as a profit center. If a function cannot justify itself, it is likely to be reduced in size or eliminated. Administration should be a profit center within data processing.

Management views with favor those functions that return a profit to the organization. On the other hand, the cost centers are not contributors to the bottom line, and thus in the eyes of many managers do not provide a very valuable function. Necessary, perhaps, but not valuable. As economic times get hard, it is the cost centers that get cut, not the profit centers.

Following is the age-old accounting formula used to measure the profitability of an organization:

Revenue (from sales, operations, or budgets)	$XXX.XX
Less cost of operations	– XXX.XX
Gross operating profit	$ XX.XX

This formula shows how we derive the gross profit from operations. Those functions that contribute to the revenue line are frequently referred to as profit centers; those that contribute to the cost line are cost centers. However, this formula does not show the cost of inefficiency and ineffectiveness. If this cost is not known, it cannot be controlled.

The EDP administration function becomes a profit center when it attempts to control the inefficiencies and ineffectiveness occurring within the data processing function. Let us rewrite our formula for gross profit as follows:

Revenue (from sales, operations, or budgets)	$XXX.XX
Less cost of operations	− XXX.XX
Less cost due to inefficiency and ineffectiveness	− XX.XX
Gross operating profit	$ XX.XX

In this accounting formula, we see the cost of inefficiency and ineffectiveness. It has been estimated that in many organizations these costs account for 30 or 40 percent of the cost of operations. Within the data processing organization, these costs cover the following areas:

- Nonproductive time
- Correcting system flaws
- Computer reruns
- Discarded projects that fail to achieve user needs
- Correcting problems not performed properly the first time
- Unnecessary paperwork
- Delays due to the inability to obtain a decision on a timely basis (within and outside the EDP function)
- Others

The administration function has two opportunities to improve the productivity of the data processing organization. The first is to reduce the incidence of failure and waste in the performance of the data processing mission. The second is to improve the productivity of the administration function. Both of these measures of productivity are definable and measurable. In later chapters in the book we explain how to define and measure administrative productivity.

The project approach enables the benefits of administration to be stated and measured. If the resources allocated to administrative services are less than the benefits, administration becomes a profit center (see Figure 5). When the benefits exceed the resources, administrative services provide a positive return on investment for the data processing function.

The profit center concept for data processing can be implemented in one of two ways. First, the costs and benefits can be determined using accounting methods. This is the preferred method, as it is factual. Unfortunately, it may be practical only in larger organizations whose senior management is profit-center oriented. Second, profit centers can be a mental challenging of each task and function. Zero-based budgeting is this type of concept. No task or function is continued unless its benefits can be shown (not necessarily numerically) to exceed the costs.

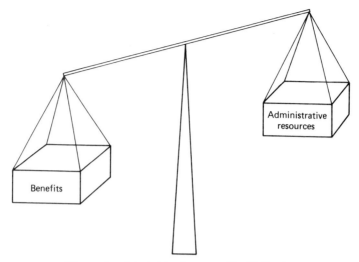

Figure 5   *Administration as a Profit Center*

A ROAD MAP THROUGH THE BOOK

There are four basic managerial responsibilities: organizing, planning, directing, and controlling. Each requires administrative support.

This book is divided into four sections. The sections are organized to address these four managerial responsibilities: organizing, planning, directing, and controlling. The sections are described below. The intended audience for each part of the book, together with the chapter titles, are listed in Figure 6.

Section I: Organizing an Effective Administrative Function

This section describes the administrative challenge and responsibilities, explains how to identify current weaknesses, and culminates in an administrative plan of action. The section assumes that the data processing function already has an administrative function and thus it is not so much a problem of organizing but rather, of redirecting the administrative process. This chapter has attempted to put administration into the proper perspective in a data processing department. Chapter 2 provides a self-assessment exercise used to probe and identify administrative weaknesses. Chapter 3 provides a step-by-step plan of action for revitalizing and redirecting an organization's administrative function.

	Intended Audience[a]				
Chapter Name	Senior Mgt.	User Mgt.	DP Senior Mgt.	DP Admin.	DP Line Mgt.
Section I: Organizing an Effective Administrative Function					
1 EDP Administration and Control: An Elephant's Graveyard	S	S	P	S	
2 How Are We Doing? Establishing an Administrative Baseline			P	S	
3 An Administrative Plan of Action	S		P	S	S
Section II: Administrative Planning					
4 Administrative Planning			S	P	S
5 Estimating and Budgeting			S	P	S
6 Scheduling and Status Reporting			S	P	S
7 People Management			S	P	S
Section III: Directing Administration					
8 Administration of Computer Center Operations			S	P	S
9 Systems Administration			S	P	S
10 User Administration		S	S	P	
11 Vendor Administration			S	P	
Section IV: Controlling Administration					
12 The Quality of Administration	S	S	P	S	S
13 Controlling and Measuring the Administrative Function			S	P	

[a]P, primary audience; S, secondary audience.

Figure 6 *Road Map through the Book*

Section II: Administrative Planning

Effective administration is normally the result of good planning. Administrative activities include planning for the data processing function, budgeting and scheduling activities, and people management. Chapter 4 provides planning procedures for a data processing department and describes how to create and administer those plans effectively. Chapter 5 explains methods for estimating and budgeting. The chapter also discusses budgetary reporting methods. Chapter 6 addresses the scheduling of activities and the reporting of status against those schedules. Chapter 7 addresses the people aspect of data processing. The chapter attempts to address the communication problems between and among all parties involved within data processing and then suggests methods to integrate data processing personnel more effectively into the organization.

Section III: Directing Administration

The majority of the work of the administrative function is in handling day-to-day activities. It is through these activities that the productivity incorporated into the plan is achieved. Chapter 8 addresses the administration of technology and the day-to-day production requirements of the department. Chapter 9 provides a plan for administering system development and maintenance projects. Chapter 10 describes the changing activities of users as they get more involved in interfacing with automated applications and operating mini- and microcomputers in their own area. Chapter 11 describes effective ways for interacting with vendors of computer products and services.

Section IV: Controlling Administration

Controls must ensure that administrative activities are in place and working. However, this two-edged sword must address both the quality and productivity of administrative activities. Productivity without quality is a nonproductive use of administrative resources. Chapter 12 explains how to define and measure the quality of administrative activities. Chapter 13 explains how to control and measure the administrative activity. The thrust of this section is on measuring and improving the productivity and quality of the data processing function through effective administrative activities.

Chapter

2

How Are We Doing?
Establishing
an Administrative
Baseline

Administrative improvements should be planned and measured. This requires a knowledge of "how we are doing" to determine what needs to be improved and then to determine how much improvement has occurred. How we are doing can be developed by taking an administrative self-assessment.

A self-assessment of the EDP administration function involves taking a hard and critical look at the process. This chapter describes a method of performing that self-assessment. The recommended process is to "baseline" the current administrative process. The recommended baseline is both factual and attitudinal. The results from the baseline study can be used to plan and monitor changes to the EDP administrative process.

THE NEED FOR SELF-ASSESSMENT

Self-assessment is an important part of any process. Most self-assessments are informal, but they occur. For example, while watching our television set we examine the quality of the picture, the decor of the cabinet, and the type of problems we have incurred in maintaining the set. Based on this analysis, we will decide to keep or replace the television set.

The end product of most of these informal self-assessments is to keep the status quo. In our television-set example, the television set works. Therefore, the question arises as to why one should replace or change something that works. Many informal self-assessments of the EDP administration function come to the same conclusion. What is continually overlooked in this type of thinking is the "rat hole theory." The rat hole theory states that any resources expended on a project are down the rat hole, and thus should be ignored in any future consideration. (Note: Accountants call these sunk costs.) In our television-set example, let us assume that six months ago we had the television set repaired for $87. Then three months ago another repair cost $129, and today the television set is in the service shop and they tell us that it will cost $93 to be repaired. Using the rat hole theory, we ignore all past costs and consider whether or not we will spend $93 to have the set repaired, or $500 to buy a new set. The answer according to the rat hole theorists is to have the set repaired. On the other hand, if we had done a good self-assessment of our television set, we would know that during the last six months we have already spent $216, and if we add the $93, our six-month cost will come to $309 for the year. A good self-assessment would tell us that it is cheaper to buy a new set than to keep the old set. Thus, in any administrative self-assessment we must ignore the rat hole theory and take a good, hard look at the process.

Self-assessment of the EDP administration function attempts to determine the economy, effectiveness, and efficiency of data processing administration. The process must define what administration is, and then evaluate the performance of the function. The concept of self-assessment means that the administrative personnel assess themselves and the performance of their work.

Alternatives are available to self-assessment. An EDP quality assurance function, internal auditors, or consultants could perform the review. Although there are advantages to having an independent party perform the assessment, it is recommended that if the administrative group has a manager, the manager should perform the self-assessment. This is because the manager will then believe the findings and be more willing to take action based on the results of the self-assessment.

Attributes of a Self-Assessment

A good self-assessment process involves the following four attributes:

1. Administrative management desires self-assessment.
2. The administration function can be defined.
3. Self-assessment must be described in quantitative terms.
4. The data for measurement must be attainable.

Of the four self-assessment attributes, the first is the most important. Self-assessment means self-criticism. It is difficult for many managers, first, to want to be criticized, and second, to make that criticism known to their superiors. Unfortunately, a good self-assessment tends to be critical, and should be made available to data processing senior management.

Self-assessment must be viewed by all levels of data processing management as a normal part of the administrative process. The desire to improve administration should be rewarded regardless of the self-assessment findings. Any action by senior data processing management should be directed at improving identified deficiencies, not to reprimand people because of those deficiencies.

EDP administration management is counseled to discuss the self-assessment process with senior data processing management. The remainder of this chapter will provide a basis for those discussions. The outcome of these meetings should be twofold:

1. A plan to collect and analyze self-assessment information
2. A plan as to how to use the results of the self-assessment

DEFINITION OF ADMINISTRATIVE ACTIVITIES

A self-assessment exercise is impossible until the area of self-assessment is defined. Although the general area of administration is well known, the specifics of the area may be elusive. Unfortunately, until the specific administrative process is defined, self-assessment is impractical.

Self-assessment begins with a definition of the administrative process. This should include all of the tasks within the department relating to administration. It is recognized that these tasks will vary from organization to organization. What is important is that administration be defined specifically so that a measurable assessment process can occur. Also, this information will be used to improve the administrative tasks after the self-assessment process.

The recommended framework for defining the EDP administrative process is twofold. The first step is to divide administration into nine general areas. The second is to identify the controllable tasks within those nine areas.

The nine administrative areas are described briefly below; and listed with the controllable tasks within those areas in Figure 7.

1. *Administrative planning:* The process of establishing short- and long-term objectives, together with determining how those objectives are to be accomplished. Planning also includes determining better methods of performing the administrative process.
2. *Estimating and budgeting:* Includes the development of procedures to estimate and budget data processing projects, together with the collection and presentation of that information. The area includes the develop-

Area	Task	Include in Assessment?	
		Yes	No
Administrative planning	Annual work planning Long-range planning Steering committees Organizational planning Establishing objectives Automating administration Interfacing with organizational planning Improving EDP credibility		
Estimating and budgeting	Estimating procedures Budgeting procedures Chargeable procedures Accounting for DP resources Maintenance of estimates and budgets Accounting data collection process Risk analysis Automation of scheduling and estimating		
Scheduling and status	Setting priorities Scheduling projects Status reporting within EDP Scheduling people Status reporting to users Automation of scheduling Status data collection process Maintenance of schedules		
People management	Staffing and recruiting Career development/motivation Performance evaluation Salary administration Developing skills/training Personnel regulations and policies Communication with staff Technical suport management		
Operations administration	Library management Contingency planning Security and privacy—physical Record retention/backup Computer operations/data entry User-controlled operations Recovery Job scheduling/conversions		

(continued)

Figure 7   *Controllable Administrative Tasks*

Area	Task	Include in Assessment?	
		Yes	**No**
Systems administration	Project administration Standards program Documentation program Risks and controls Security and privacy—logical System change requests Proposals/feasibility studies Data administration		
User administration	Information center Administration reports Complaint procedures Auditors' relationships Communications with users User input/output Senior management communications User-owned computer resources		
Vendor administration	Software acquisition Hardware acquisition Contract negotiations/bidding Contract management Service bureaus Using consultants Vendor evaluations Maintaining vendor-developed/purchased products		
Quality of administration	Administrative response time Accuracy of output Timeliness of output Response to problems Attitude and cooperativeness Meeting schedules Usefulness of output Distribution of output		

Figure 7 *continued*

ment of procedures and the methods for collecting and recording account-ing-type information. In some administrative organizations, this is performed by a data processing comptroller.

3. *Scheduling and status:* This area is closely allied with estimating and bud-geting. It involves setting priorities and developing schedules that can accomplish the departmental objectives with the allocated resources.

4. *People management:* Includes obtaining, training, and maintaining an adequate staff of skilled data processing professionals. Administrative procedures should be designed to motivate personnel through appropriate communication, salary administration, and career planning. However, the process must ensure that the personnel policies of data processing are in compliance with organizational policies and governmental regulations.

5. *Operations administration:* The prime objective of data processing is to provide the desired results from automated systems. This involves computer operations and all of the support activities that ensure the timeliness and reliability of operations. Operation administration also includes the security and privacy of the jobs run in operations.

6. *Systems administration:* Involves the procedures, standards, guidelines, and methods necessary to develop and maintain computer applications. Administration includes maintaining the development support software and other programs designed to improve the performance and usefulness of the developmental projects.

7. *User administration:* Includes much of the interaction between the users of data processing services and the data processing department. Included within the users group are senior management and auditors. User administration also includes oversight of user-owned computer resources and the operation of an information center, either formal or informal, needed to provide users with technical assistance in the development, maintenance, and operation of automated systems.

8. *Vendor administration:* Includes interaction and oversight with outside contractors. Includes hardware and software vendors as well as other outside services and consultants. The process includes contract negotiations, contract management, and evaluating the services provided by vendors.

9. *Quality of administration:* The previous areas have addressed the specific tasks that are performed by the administration function. This area describes the quality of the overall administration function. The assessment of the quality of administration is a key area because although the tasks may be performed very well, the perception of the value of those tasks to the users (i.e., quality) may be poor.

The definition of a controllable task is one that can be installed, operated, and evaluated independently of all other tasks. It is unimportant whether the task is performed by a single organizational entity, or whether the completion of the task involves several organizational units. For example, the first administrative planning task is the development of an annual work plan. Although most of data processing management is involved in this task, the task itself can be viewed as a stand-alone task—and thus a controllable task.

USING AN ADMINISTRATIVE BASELINE

A baseline is a snapshot of the administrative process at a given point in time. The snapshot should show the following types of information:

- What type of administrative work is being performed
- The amount of resources consumed by the administrative process
- The effectiveness of the administrative process as measured
    By management and staff attitudes
    As a percent of resources consumed for administrative purposes

The baseline information should be composed of both factual and attitudinal information. The data collected for the baseline will be from administrative personnel, administrative records, and users of the administrative processes. The extensiveness of the baseline study will depend on the areas to be covered and the uses to be made of the baseline information.

Baseline information can be used for any or all of the following objectives:

1. Determination of "how we are doing" in the administrative process at a given point in time
2. Identification of administrative areas in need of improvement
3. Identification of specific administrative tasks that require improvement
4. Determination of the attitudes of personnel using administrative services about the performance of those services
5. Provision of a basis for discussion between administrative personnel and users of administrative services as to how to improve the services

A baseline is a report card against which progress can be measured. The baseline provides the grades and basis for evaluation of administrative services. It reduces subjective judgment to quantitative measures. Quantitative evaluations can be discussed intellectually without the emotion included in most subjective judgments. Rather than shouts of "I don't agree with you," the argument shifts to the specific evaluation of measurable tasks.

A baseline is a tool that can be used to evaluate and improve administrative services. It is not a high-precision measurement tool but rather, one designed to identify areas needing improvement and to measure attitudes about the service. If it can be accepted that baselining provides information that must be subject to analysis and judgment, it is a very useful tool. On the other hand, if the baseline numbers are taken as absolute, it is easy to misuse the baselining tool.

EDP ADMINISTRATIVE GUIDELINE 5

Administrative improvements are rare when based on generalities, but common when based on specifics.

HOW TO PERFORM A BASELINE STUDY

An administrative baseline study should be conducted by the administrative manager of a data processing function. Like other studies, objectives must be established and then a plan developed to achieve those objectives. The following sections discuss the what, who, when, and how of a baseline study.

What to Include in the Study

Five general objectives of a baseline study have been discussed. Determining which of those objectives are to form the basis of the study determines what the study is to accomplish. Obviously, the author recommends that all five objectives be accepted.

The baseline study can involve collecting facts, collecting attitudes, and can involve users of administrative services. Which of these elements of the study should be included will be determined by which of the five baseline objectives are accepted as the objectives of the study. Figure 8 cross-references the baseline objectives to the elements of the study. The check marks in the figure indicate which elements of the study should be included in the study.

Baseline Objective	Element of the Study		
	Collect Facts	Collect Attitudes	Involve Users
1. Determine "how we are doing" in the administrative process at a given point in time	✔	✔	✔
2. Identify administrative areas in need of improvement	✔	✔	
3. Identify specific administrative tasks that require improvement	✔	✔	
4. Determine the attitudes of personnel using administrative services about the performance of those services	✔	✔	
5. Provide a basis for discussion between administrative personnel and users of administrative services about how to improve the services			✔

Figure 8   *What to Include in the Study*

Who Should Be Involved in the Study

If the Figure 8 matrix indicates that users of administrative services should be involved in the study, then the question "which users?" must be answered. The following list represents the most common users of EDP administrative services:

- Data processing senior management
- Project management
- Systems analysts/programmers
- Computer operations management
- Technical support services (e.g., system programmers, data librarian, data base administrator, etc.)
- User management (i.e., departments using computer services)
- Organizational senior management
- Auditors
- Security personnel

Each one of the users listed above should be analyzed individually. The determination of whether or not to include them in the study should be based on:

- The amount of administrative services utilized by the person
- The value of involving that person in a baseline study
- The contribution that person might make to either the baseline study or the uses of the baseline results

When to Conduct the Study

The baseline study should be conducted at a time when both administrative management and senior data processing management are willing to expend resources to improve administrative services. The study can have a negative impact if no changes are made at the conclusion of the study. However, the three elements of the study can be conducted at different times as follows:

1. *Collect facts.* Most of the facts to be collected are based on information supplied by accounting systems. The accounting systems used should be ones already in place. Many organizations have accounting systems that collect time and job status from individuals; computer operations job accounting systems (many are automated); corporate budgeting systems; and departmental status reports.

Facts should be collected at the end of an accounting period. Normally, the best information is collected at the end of a quarter, and therefore it is recommended that the facts be collected for a full calendar year ending at one of the four quarters (i.e., March 31, June 30, September 30, or December 31).

2. *Collect attitudes.* Attitudes can be collected any time that it is convenient for both the party collecting and the party providing the attitudinal information. However, it is best to do it as close as possible to the end of the baseline study.

3. *Involve users.* Involving users in an EDP administrative baseline study takes time of both the administrative group and the user group. The administrative group must train and assist the user in completing the necessary baseline forms. The user must expend the time to provide meaningful information for the baseline study. Therefore, it is best to select times that are the low periods in the production cycle for users and administrative personnel so that the appropriate time can be allocated to the baseline study.

How to Conduct the Study

The baseline study consists of two parts: first, the collection of factual information, and second, the accumulation of attitudinal information. The methods for collecting the two types of baseline data are different.

Baseline facts are just that—facts. If they exist, they can be collected. They are nonargumentative and pose no threat as such to people. The collection of facts focuses on the following areas:

- Location of the facts
- Collection of the facts
- Consolidation of the facts

Collection of attitudinal information poses a more difficult collection process. It is important in the process to collect the true attitudes about administrative services. However, people are frequently reluctant to provide negative criticism, or criticism to which their name is attached. Therefore, collection must focus on the following:

- Identification of specific people to be queried
- Explanation of the objectives of the study
- Elimination of bias from the study (i.e., people answering positively or negatively based on criteria other than the one being sought)
- Secretive versus open responses (i.e., signed responses versus unsigned responses)

The specific forms and methods for collecting factual and attitudinal baseline information are discussed individually in the following sections.

Collecting Baseline Facts

The collection of baseline facts is a four-step process, as follows:

Step 1.   Identify Facts to Collect

The type of factual information to be collected should be based on (1) the types of information needed to analyze the administrative process and (2) types of information that are currently being collected. It is generally impractical in a baseline study to collect information that is not easily available. This does not mean that the information must be centrally located but rather, that the information must be collectible at nominal cost. However, the process begins by identifying how the administrative function can best be evaluated, and then determining what information is needed to perform that evaluation. The suggested baseline factual information is outlined in Figure 9.

Step 2.   Identify the Source of Factual Information

Each item of data wanted should be listed on a worksheet. For each item of data, the source of information for that data should be listed. The most common sources of information are:

- Departmental time reporting system
- Departmental project reporting system
- Automated job accounting system (normally these systems are automated such as IBM's Systems Management Facility)
- Information currently available in the administrative function
- Information currently available from projects
- Departmental accounting system

Step 3.   Collect Factual Information

The needed factual information should be collected from the identified source. For example, if the information is on a job accounting log, the necessary software query should be developed to list that information in a report format. If the information is available in an accounting system, the person responsible for that system should be instructed to provide a special report for baseline purposes. On the other hand, if the information is maintained at the project level, special forms may need to be developed to gather that information from the project leaders.

Step 4.   *Record Factual Information on the Baseline Fact Worksheet*

The information collected should be recorded on the baseline fact worksheet (Figure 9). In many instances, the information will have to be consolidated, stratified, or analyzed prior to being recorded on the worksheet. For example, item F on the worksheet is a stratification of the completion of a project versus the scheduled completion date. In order to record the information under item F, it would have to be stratified according to the "closeness to schedule" criteria provided on the worksheet for item F.

When all the collected information has been recorded, the baseline fact worksheet will be completed. Note that administrators may wish to collect additional information or delete some of the information on the worksheet. This decision should be made based on how the factual information will be utilized. Administrators are cautioned not to collect information "just to have" that information. If a specific purpose of the information cannot be determined in step 1, that information should not be collected. On the other hand, if information is needed that is not included on the baseline fact worksheet, the worksheet should be extended and that information collected.

Figure 9 *Baseline Fact Worksheet*

Date of Baseline _____

A. Number of employees   _____
B. Number of professional employees   _____
C. Number of administrative employees   _____
D. Total departmental budget   _____
E. Total administrative costs   _____
F. Annual project schedule analysis

Number of Projects	Closeness to Schedule
	More than 3 months early
	2 + –3 months early
	1 + –2 months early
	1 week to 1 month early
	On time
	1 week to 1 month late
	1 + –2 months late
	2 + –3 months late
	More than 3 months late

G. Annual project budget analysis

Number of Projects	Percent Over/Under Budget
	More than 25% under budget
	20–24.9% under budget
	15–19.9% under budget
	10–14.9% under budget
	5–9.9% under budget
	Within budget
	5–9.9% over budget
	10–14.9% over budget
	15–19.9% over budget
	20–25% over budget

H. Annual department schedule and budget analysis
Percent of planned projects complete _____
Percent over/under annual budget   _____

I. Production data

Number of Jobs	Closeness to Schedule
	More than 1 day late
	16–24 hours late
	8–15.9 hours late
	2–7.9 hours late
	0.5–1.9 hours late
	On time
	0.5–1.9 hours early
	2–7.9 hours early
	8–15.9 hours early
	16–24 hours early
	More than 1 day early

J. Contracts analysis

Name of Contract	Percent Over/Under Budget	Days Over/Under Schedule

K. Departmental administrative tasks (forms)

Name of Form	Number of Forms Used/Year	Average Hours to Complete	Average Days to Process

Collecting Baseline Attitudes

The evaluation of administration by personnel should be based on criteria that are predictive of the desired result. For example, if you were to evaluate the performance of a television repairperson, you would want to select criteria such as completed on time, completed on budget, set works satisfactorily after repair, cabinet not damaged, and so on. It is these types of criteria that would be indicative of good performance in the television service area.

The attitude of people toward administration can be rated in nine areas of administration. The persons performing the rating should be familiar with the results of administration in those nine areas. Within the nine areas should be a representative number of items which when rated would provide a reasonable evaluation of EDP administration.

Administrative evaluation checklists are provided for each of the nine administrative areas. The items included on each of these checklists have been taken from data processing literature and from the personal experience of the author within data processing and as a consultant and teacher of data processing topics.

The administrative evaluation checklist should be given to those persons selected for rating administrative services. They should rate each item on the checklist as follows:

$$5 = \text{exceptional}$$

$$4 = \text{highly satisfactory}$$

$$3 = \text{good}$$

$$2 = \text{poor}$$

$$1 = \text{unsatisfactory}$$

$$\text{N/A} = \text{not applicable to the area being rated}$$

The checklist can be completed anonymously, or the person completing it can indicate his or her name or job function. If there is to be a follow-up or response, it is highly desirable to have the person's name included on the checklist. If no direct response is to be made to the person performing the evaluation, it may only be necessary to indicate whether it has been completed by someone within the administrative function, the data processing department, or a user department.

The nine administrative evaluation checklists are included as Figure 10. The area to which the items apply is indicated at the head of each worksheet. Each checklist should be scored using the attitude scoring worksheet (Figure 11). The scoring worksheet should indicate the area evaluated, the evaluator, and the date. The worksheet should contain the number of items that were rated in each of the five rating categories. The N/A category should be ig-

Figure 10 *Administrative Evaluation Checklist*

Area: Administrative planning   **Completed by** _____   **Date** _____

	Item	Evaluation Rating					
		5	4	3	2	1	N/A
1.	Is an annual work plan prepared for the data processing department for new projects?						
2.	Are the resources allocated to maintenance in the work plan allocated for specific enhancements and work?						
3.	Is a long-range plan prepared for the data processing department (normally for five years)?						
4.	Is a steering committee comprised of senior corporate executives established to identify and set priorities for data processing work?						
5.	Is a sponsor identified for each project that is to be implemented?						
6.	Is an administrative process established to ensure that the organizational structure is realistic for the departmental mission, and if not, are procedures established for changing the organizational structure?						
7.	Are procedures in place and working that require each area to establish objectives for accomplishment by the area? (Note that this should include the administrative function.)						
8.	Is the administrative process studied at least annually to determine areas that shoud be automated, and then appropriate plans made to automate that part of administration?						
9.	Are procedures established to ensure that both the annual and long-range data processing plans are consistent and in support of the organizational plans?						
10.	Are procedures established to measure the credibility of EDP in the organization and to make improvements where needed?						

Evaluation Rating Interpretation

5 = Exceptional	4 = Highly satisfactory	3 = Good
2 = Poor	1 = Unsatisfactory	N/A = Not applicable

		Evaluation Rating					
	Item	**5**	**4**	**3**	**2**	**1**	**N/A**
1.	Are standardized procedures established for estimating EDP projects?						
2.	Are procedures established to ensure that the estimating process is consistent from project to project?						
3.	Are standardized procedures established for estimating the cost (i.e., budget) for new projects?						
4.	Has a formal or informal procedure been established to charge users for the data processing services they consume, or inform them of the cost of those services?						
5.	Are procedures established to make people accountable for the resources they use?						
6.	Are procedures established to update estimates in the event that project requirements or available resources change?						
7.	Are procedures established to change budgets as requirements or available resources change?						
8.	Is a formalized process in place to collect accounting data?						
9.	Are risk analysis procedures used to identify the degree of risk of projects so that estimates and budgets can be appropriately adjusted?						
10.	Is the scheduling and estimating process reviewed periodically to determine where the process could be automated?						

Evaluation Rating Interpretation

5 = Exceptional	4 = Highly satisfactory	3 = Good
2 = Poor	1 = Unsatisfactory	N/A = Not applicable

	Item	5	4	3	2	1	N/A
		Evaluation Rating					
1.	Is a formal process established for setting priorities for implementing data processing projects?						
2.	Is a formalized process established for setting priorities for maintenance work?						
3.	Is a formalized process established for scheduling the implementation of data processing work?						
4.	Are maintenance changes installed on a "release" concept rather than installed periodically?						
5.	Is a formalized process established for reporting the status of work within the data processing department?						
6.	Is a formal process established for scheduling people which takes into account the needs of both the project and the person?						
7.	Has a formalized process been established for reporting progress to users?						
8.	Is the scheduling and status project periodically reviewed to determine where it can be improved and/or automated?						
9.	Is a formal process established for collecting the status of projects from data processing personnel?						
10.	Is a formalized process established to change schedules when requirements or resources allocated to the project change?						

Evaluation Rating Interpretation

5 = Exceptional   4 = Highly satisfactory   3 = Good
2 = Poor   1 = Unsatisfactory   N/A = Not applicable **37**

Area: People management   **Completed by** _____   **Date** _____

	Item	Evaluation Rating					
		5	4	3	2	1	N/A
1.	Is a formalized process established for recruiting personnel from both within and outside the company to staff the data processing department?						
2.	Is a formal carer development program established to help staff personnel develop and achieve career plans?						
3.	Are formal procedures established to improve the motivation of personnel within the data processing department?						
4.	Is a formal performance evaluation process established and in place?						
5.	Is a formal salary administration process established within the data processing department?						
6.	Is a formal process developed to identify missing or needed skills of staff members and then work with them to acquire the needed skills?						
7.	Is a formalized training program established which is coordinated with the department's mission, work plan, and the skill requirements of the EDP staff?						
8.	Are the personnel policies reviewed to ensure they are in compliance with governmental regulations and organizational personnel policies?						
9.	Has a formalized method been established to communicate between data processing management and the EDP staff?						
10.	Have administrative procedures been established to manage and coordinate the work of the technical staff with the systems development staff?						

Evaluation Rating Interpretation

5 = Exceptional   4 = Highly satisfactory   3 = Good
2 = Poor   1 = Unsatisfactory   N/A = Not applicable

		Evaluation Rating					
	Item	**5**	**4**	**3**	**2**	**1**	**N/A**
1.	Are administrative procedures established to ensure that the data processing libraries contain only needed programs, JCL, etc.?						
2.	Has a formal contingency plan been established?						
3.	Have the security and privacy operation needs been established and procedures installed to satisfy those needs?						
4.	Are the security measures and contingency plans tested periodically?						
5.	Is a formal record-retention program established which includes the necessary data to back up computer operations?						
6.	Have formal procedures been established for entering jobs into computer operations and disseminating output to users?						
7.	Are administrative procedures established to assist users in controlling those parts of operations that are under their jurisdiction?						
8.	Have formal administrative procedures been estblished for recovering operations in the event of loss of integrity of processing?						
9.	Has a formalized job scheduling process been established for operations which takes into account a change of job priorities in the event of computer problems?						
10.	Is a formalized administrative procedure established for converting from one version of software to another or for installing a new application?						

Evaluation Rating Interpretation

5 = Exceptional	4 = Highly satisfactory	3 = Good
2 = Poor	1 = Unsatisfactory	N/A = Not applicable

Area: Systems administration   Completed by _____   Date _____

Item	Evaluation Rating					
	5	4	3	2	1	N/A
1. Has a formalized process been established for administering projects from their inception through completion?						
2. Has a formalized program been established for developing and approving EDP standards?						
3. Has a formalized program been developed to specify application system documentation?						
4. Has a formalized process been established to identify security and privacy risks and take the necessary action to reduce those risks to an acceptable level?						
5. Have formalized procedures been established to identify application system risks and to develop the appropriate system of internal controls to reduce those risks to an acceptable level?						
6. Has a formalized procedure been established to integrate changes into application systems which takes into account any impact on previously established budgets and schedules?						
7. Has a formalized process been established for proposing new systems which includes the information that it is necessary to collect during the feasibility study?						
8. Has the process for administering data been formalized?						
9. Have procedures been established to oversee and enforce system development policies, procedures, and standards?						
10. Has a formalized procedure been established to record administrative problems?						

Evaluation Rating Interpretation

5 = Exceptional   4 = Highly satisfactory   3 = Good
2 = Poor   1 = Unsatisfactory   N/A = Not applicable

Area: User administration   Completed by _____   Date _____

	Item	5	4	3	2	1	N/A
		Evaluation Rating					
1.	Has a formal or informal information center been established to assist users in performing data processing activities.						
2.	Is a formalized procedure established to provide users with the necessary administrative information needed to evaluate and adjust data processing activities?						
3.	Has a formalized procedure been established to receive and act on user complaints?						
4.	Has a formalized procedure been established for interfacing with auditors?						
5.	Has a formalized procedure been established for conducting communications between data processing personnel and users?						
6.	Are users periodically surveyed, either formally or informally, to determine their satisfaction with data processing services?						
7.	Has a formal procedure been established to log input from users and ensure that outputs are received by users?						
8.	Has a formalized process been established for conducting communications between the organization's senior management and the data processing department?						
9.	Have administrative procedures been established regarding users' acquiring computer resources for use within their own organization?						
10.	Are formal procedures established to enable users to gain training about data processing concepts and insight into the policies and procedures of the data processing department?						

Evaluation Rating Interpretation

5 = Exceptional	4 = Highly satisfactory	3 = Good
2 = Poor	1 = Unsatisfactory	N/A = Not applicable

		Evaluation Rating					
	Item	**5**	**4**	**3**	**2**	**1**	**N/A**
1.	Are formal procedures established for use in acquiring software?						
2.	Are formal procedures established for use in acquiring hardware?						
3.	Are formal procedures established for negotiating contracts between outside vendors and the data processing department?						
4.	Where appropriate, is open bidding used to ensure that the best possible product is acquired at the lowest price?						
5.	Are formal procedures established to oversee and manage contracts during the execution phase of contracts?						
6.	Are formal procedures established explaining when and how to use service bureau facilities?						
7.	Are formal procedures established defining how and when to use the services of consultants?						
8.	Are formal procedures established which evaluate the performance of outside vendors?						
9.	Is a departmental policy established which governs the maintenance of vendor-produced software?						
10.	Are formal procedures established which indicate how to proceed in the event of problems in vendor products and how to maintain those products during the duration of their useful life?						

Evaluation Rating Interpretation

5 = Exceptional   4 = Highly satisfactory   3 = Good
2 = Poor   1 = Unsatisfactory   N/A = Not applicable

Area: Quality of administration   **Completed by** _____   **Date** _____

Item	Evaluation Rating					
	5	**4**	**3**	**2**	**1**	**N/A**
1. Are the administrative responses to requests reasonable?						
2. Are the administrative reports accurate and complete?						
3. Are administrative reports issued on a timely basis?						
4. Is the administrative function responsive to problems brought to their attention?						
5. Are administrative personnel cooperative and have a positive attitude when dealing with users of the services?						
6. Are administrative projects completed on schedule?						
7. Is the information included in administrative reports useful in the performance of your function?						
8. Are administrative reports distributed to the appropriate people?						
9. Does the administrative service function contribute to the completion of your projects?						
10. Is the process of collecting administrative information optimized so that it takes a minimal amount of project resources to gather and record that information?						

Evaluation Rating Interpretation

5 = Exceptional   4 = Highly satisfactory   3 = Good
2 = Poor   1 = Unsatisfactory   N/A = Not applicable

Area Evaluated _____

Evaluator _____ **Date** _____

Number of Items Rated		Multiply by:	Score
No.	Rating		
A	Totals	B	

	B	÷	A	=	Individual Score
		÷		=	

Figure 11 *Attitude Scoring Worksheet*

nored on the scoring worksheet. The number of items rated should then be totaled. In each of the five rating categories the number of items rated should be multiplied by the counts on the worksheet. For example, if three items have been rated as exceptional (a rating of 5), that should be multiplied by the constant 5 to produce a score of 15. After each of the five multiplications have been completed, the numbers in the score column should be accumulated. The total score should be divided by the number of items rated to produce an individual score. The individual score will be in the range of 1 through 5 and can be evaluated by the rating interpretation. For example, if the individual score was calculated as a 3, it would be interpreted as a "good" score.

DEVELOPING A BASELINE

Two baselines should be developed for the administrative services area. The first is a factual baseline and the second is an attitudinal baseline. Both should be considered raw information subject to interpretation.

A factual baseline should be developed using the factual information recorded on the baseline fact worksheet (Figure 9). The attitudinal baseline information should be developed from the information contained on the attitude scoring worksheet (Figure 11).

An abbreviated administrative factual baseline is provided in Figure 12. This figure shows where on the factual worksheet the information can be obtained. For example, two percentages are shown in evaluating administrative employment. The first shows the relationship between total employment and administrative employment, and the second the relationship between professional employment and administrative employment. As in all of the data collected, these are raw data and thus subject to interpretation.

The eight administrative factual baseline items for the period of data collected can be obtained from the information on Figure 9. When completed, the information can be listed on the report shown in Figure 12, or it can be put into graphical form. For example, the administrative employee analysis

---

For the period: _____

1. Administrative employees percent

   Admin. (C)   Prof.   (B)
   Emp. _____ = _____ %   Emp. _____ = _____ %

   Total   Admin.
   Emp.   (A)   Emp.   (C)

2. Administrative budget percent

   Admin.
   Budget (E) = _____ %

   Total
   Budget (D)

3. Projects completed on schedule (use Schedule F)
   Jobs completed early _____ %   On time _____ %   Late _____ %

4. Projects completed within budget (use Schedule G)
   Jobs completed under _____ %   Within _____ %   Over _____ %   budget

5. Percent of planned projects complete _____ %
   Status annual expenditure _____ %   Over/under budget (use Schedule H)

6. Production jobs completed (use Schedule I)
   Early _____ %   On time _____ %   Late _____ %

7. EDP contract performance (use Schedule J)
   (a) Percent completed: Early _____ %   On time _____ %   Late _____ %
   (b) Budget: Under _____ %   Within _____ %   Over _____ %

8. Administrative procedures (use Schedule K)
   Number of administrative forms used   _____
   Average hours to complete a form   _____
   Average days to process a form   _____
   Total administrative hours completing forms _____

Figure 12 *Administrative Factual Baseline*

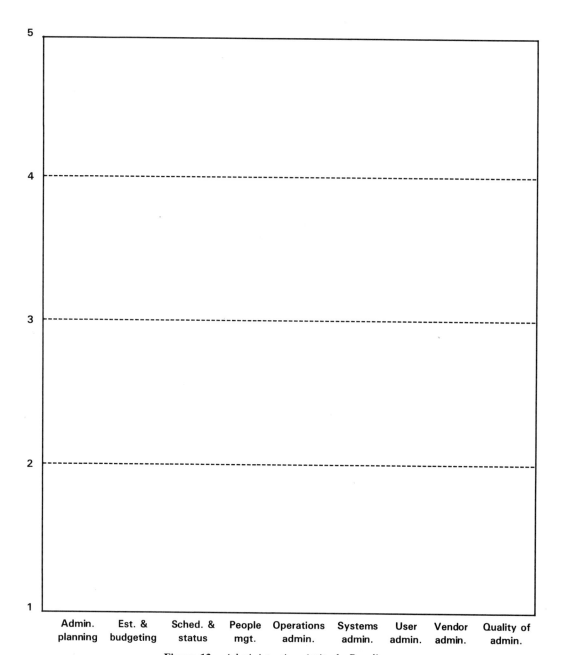

Figure 13 *Administrative Attitude Baseline*

can be shown as a bar chart showing the two percentages as a bar on the chart. All of the percentage items could be shown on the same bar chart if clearly labeled.

The administrative attitude baseline can be presented on the chart shown in Figure 13. This provides space to show the following for each of the nine administrative areas:

1. *Average evaluation of all people who evaluated each area:* For example, if the average of all the evaluations for administrative planning were a 3, then a 3 would be indicated on Figure 13 as an × in the 3 line above the administrative planning heading. Each of the nine areas should be shown on the chart. The × should be located in the approximate position of the arithmetic average for the evaluators.
2. *The high and low score for that area by individual evaluators:* Again, periods or dashes can be shown to indicate the numerical average of the high score for that area and the low score for the area.

WHAT A GOOD BASELINE IS

National averages are not available for baseline comparison purposes. Quality assurance studies under the Department of Defense are developing such figures, but they are not yet available. Therefore, how does one know how he or she is doing?

The two most common methods are:

1. Establish objectives and then compare results against those objectives.
2. Exchange criteria with other organizations.

Both methods are reasonable. However, the object of a baseline is to establish a starting point for improvement, not to develop a number to compare to a norm. Administration, by its nature, is customized to management style. This lends itself to improvement by setting objectives as opposed to comparison to other organizations.

USING BASELINE DATA

Many people question the value of answering seemingly subjective questions and filling out more forms. These are the same people who say, "We have tried it all before," and then tell you why new ideas will not work. They may be right except for one thing—the objective of the proposed baseline is to involve the people in the study who are responsible for taking action.

Before change occurs, two conditions must exist:

1. *People must believe action should occur.* This will happen if they collect the facts personally.
2. *The recommendation for change is theirs.* This will happen if they interpret the facts and propose action.

Note that nowhere in the conditions listed above does it say that the facts must be indisputable, absolutely correct, or complete. All that is needed is that the information collected identify problems.

The collection of baseline data provides the basis to evaluate current administrative practices, and to measure improvement. The analysis and development of a plan for areas of improvement is presented in Chapter 3. The specifics for establishing good administrative procedures for each of the nine areas is included in Chapters 4 through 12. The process for conducting future baseline studies and measuring improvement in administrative services is covered in Chapter 13. All of these chapters will make use of the information collected in establishing the administrative baseline.

Chapter

3

An Administrative
Plan of Action

An administrative plan of action is a blueprint for improving the administrative process. It is not an annual work plan. The plan of action should be developed through a careful study of the problems in administration for the purpose of developing administrative solutions to those problems. We are talking about a one-time plan.

Planning is the inspiration of action. But the thing done is what counts—not the thing planned. The world is full of starters, but there are few finishers. Therefore, the administrative plan of action must have both a start and a strong finish—particularly the finish.

This chapter describes how to develop a plan of action that has a high probability of being finished. Administration touches the job functions of all parties involved in data processing. Dictatorial administration rarely works. The process outlined in this chapter utilizes rational problem-solving skills to develop the best possible plan of action for improving the administrative function.

MANAGEMENT INVOLVEMENT IN ADMINISTRATION

Technical people generally dislike administration. EDP is a technical area often managed by technicians. This can pose a problem in obtaining management support for the function in general, and specifically for any proposal that may "smell" of additional administrative work.

The key to successful administration is management support. The key to management support is the involvement of management in the establishment of administrative policies and strategies.

Involvement begins by sitting down with management and getting their answers to questions such as:

1.   What information does management want for decision-making purposes?
2.   What type of information do they want to collect from and to make available to their staff?
3.   What is this information worth?
4.   How do they want to use administrative practices to help accomplish the department's mission?

The answers to these questions are not as important as having management devote time and effort to administrative concerns, which may be neglected to make more time available for the more enjoyable technical challenges. These types of questions help involve management in the development of and support for an administrative plan of action.

THE NEED FOR A PLAN OF ACTION

People's minds are full of many brilliant ideas, but few of these ideas ever see the light of day. They are represented primarily by much talk and little action. Not only must a plan of action be initiated, but action must be sustained to be effective.

EDP ADMINISTRATIVE GUIDELINE 6

Lack of action is the direct cause of most failures. It is the predominant error made by people in every walk of life.

It is unusual when an operation cannot be improved. However, improvement can occur only when problems are recognized. The objective of baselining the administrative function was to help identify those problem areas.

Changes in the administrative process should not be confused with improvements. Improvements are designed to permit people to perform the process more effectively, economically, efficiently, or to satisfy more fully an administrative need. Changes in the process are frequently made arbitrarily and often for the convenience of the administrator rather than for the purpose of improving the process.

Many administrative procedures appear to the staff to benefit primarily management. Therefore, to gain acceptance to change so that management's needs are met and productivity is improved, it is important to:

*   Indicate the desire to reduce the administrative burden of the data processing staff
*   Indicate to the staff that the administrative process is not rigid but can be continually changed

- Solicit suggestions from the staff for improvement
- Demonstrate that the administrative process is in synchronization with the current needs of data processing management

INTRODUCING CHANGE CONSISTENT
WITH ADMINISTRATIVE STRATEGY

Data processing departments utilize administrative strategies. Strategies, by definition, are thoughtfully conceived plans of action. Unfortunately, many of these strategies exist but are not planned. Regardless, the deviation from commonly accepted strategy represents a significant shift in administrative approach and needs the endorsement of management prior to making such a change. On the other hand, administrative improvements occurring within the existing administrative strategy are normally easy to implement and get accepted by the staff.

Four major areas requiring administrative strategies are:

1. *Staff size:* The number of staff assigned to the administrative function (both full- and part-time staff)
2. *Administrative data collection methods:* The process by which administrative data are collected
3. *Administrative direction:* The thrust of the administrative process (i.e., task oriented or people oriented)
4. *Administrative systems:* The degree of automation utilized in the administrative process

The types of strategies that an organization could use in any one of these four areas vary significantly. Each of these four strategies can be presented as a continuum (see Figure 14). The continuum shows the range of methods, from the most desirable to the least desirable, used to incorporate an administration strategy.

The strategies need to be established by data processing management. The most desirable administrative strategies observed by the author are those in organizations that appear to have very productive administrative functions. The least desirable strategies are those observed in organizations where there appears to be a high degree of unhappiness in administrative methods.

The most desirable administrative strategies are:

- *Minimal staff:* The fewest possible number of people are assigned to the administrative function.
- *Data collected as a work by-product:* The information needed for administration is collected as a part of the normal course of doing work

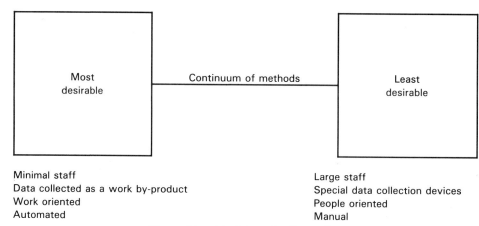

Minimal staff
Data collected as a work by-product
Work oriented
Automated

Large staff
Special data collection devices
People oriented
Manual

Figure 14   *Administrative Strategies*

and thus does not require any extra effort on the part of the data processing staff.

- *Work oriented:* Administration is aimed at controlling tasks, not people.
- *Automated:* The administration function should be automated in order to use the power of the organization's computer to reduce the burden on people.

The least desirable administrative strategies are:

- *Large staff:* Parkinson's Law prevails and the administrative staff grows in size regardless of the work load.
- *Special data collection devices:* The administrative group develops special forms, systems, and so on, to collect the data needed for administrative purposes.
- *People oriented:* Administration is directed at controlling people as opposed to controlling the work performed.
- *Manual:* The administrative methods are primarily manual methods.

Rarely does an organization fall into either the most desirable or least desirable category as to the method employed for implementing administrative strategies. For example, part of the administrative process may be automated, part manual; part of the data collected may be about tasks and part about people. What is important is whether the strategy is to automate, collect data about tasks, and so on, or is to perform the administration process manually and have it directed at monitoring people's activities.

It is recommended that when making changes or improvements:

1. *Strategy changes are made by management.* For example, if the data to be collected are to be shifted from people oriented to task oriented, management should make that decision.

2. *Improvements within the accepted strategy can be made by the administrative function.* For example, if the process is to collect information as a work by-product, the collection of this information (as long as it *is* a by-product) can be achieved by the administrative function.

EDP ADMINISTRATIVE GUIDELINE 7

Do not neglect to involve senior data processing management in administrative strategy decisions.

STEPS IN THE DEVELOPMENT OF AN ADMINISTRATIVE PLAN OF ACTION

Administration affects every member in the data processing department and many of the users. An administrative plan of action that involves the key parties in the development of the plan will have a higher probability of success than one that is developed solely within the administrative function. This occurs because good administrative processes require high-quality information, which requires the cooperation and support of the people providing that information.

The development of the administrative plan of action is the responsibility of the administrative manager in the data processing function. That person should not delegate the responsibility for the plan to a committee or task force. What the administrative manager should do is use rational problem-solving techniques to develop the framework for an administrative plan of action. Prior to this, the administrative manager has identified the problems, and following the rational problem-solving techniques, will develop the final administrative plan of action.

The process used to develop an administrative plan of action is comprised of three parts:

1. *Define problems.* This is the responsibility of the administrative manager and is performed in conjunction with the administrative baseline study. These are the problems uncovered by conducting the baseline study— for example, some difficult-to-use forms.
2. *Develop solutions to problems.* The nine-step rational problem-solving exercise involving persons associated with the administrative function.

This approach, explained below, attempts to get a consensus solution to a problem.

3.   *Develop a plan of action.* The pulling together of the solution into a cohesive plan of action. This is the responsibility of the administrative manager.

This three-part process for developing an administrative plan of action incorporates the following nine problem-solving steps (see Figure 15, which illustrates that the latter steps are built on a base established by completing the earlier steps).

1.   Identify administrative problems/needs.
2.   Determine the magnitude of effort required to solve the administrative problems.
3.   Establish the administrative objectives to be considered in an administrative plan of action.

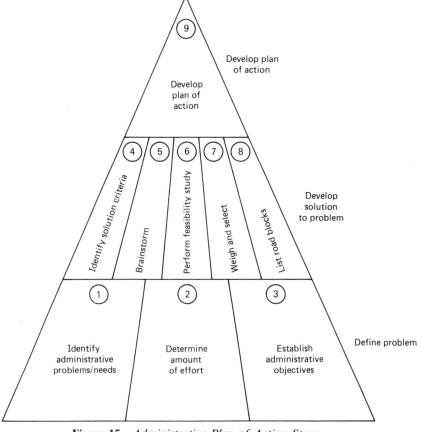

Figure 15   *Administrative Plan of Action Steps*

4. Identify the solution criteria which if met will be indicative that the problem has been solved.
5. Conduct sufficient brainstorming so that all involved parties have an opportunity to contribute to the solution.
6. Perform a minifeasibility study on each of the most probable solutions for the administrative objectives.
7. Weigh the reasonableness of each of the alternatives developed during the feasibility study and through a formal method select what appears to be the best solution to achieve the administrative objective.
8. List all of the possible roadblocks for preventing the solution from being implemented. If the roadblocks are formidable, select another alternative and repeat this step until an alternative is selected that appears to have a high probability of success.
9. Draw together a durable set of administrative objectives and solutions and work them into both short-range and long-range administrative plans of action.

Each of these steps is discussed individually, together with any tools, checklists, or aids that are valuable for use in completing the step.

Part 1: Define Problems

This part of the plan of action is designed to produce administrative action objectives. These can be thought of as the needs of the administrative function. However, all of the needs need not be included in either the short-term or the long-term plan of action. The purpose of defining objectives is to identify the needs that should be considered in developing the plan of action. This process involves the first three plan-of-action steps.

Step 1. *Identify Administrative Problems/Needs*

An administrative problem can be defined as a dissatisfaction with part or all of an administrative service. For example, if the administrative group is responsible for collecting and reporting staff time, the problem could be with the entire system, or with only a part of it, such as the data collection form. The dissatisfaction can be with data processing management, user management, data processing staff, or the administrative staff.

Administrative problems can be identified through any or all of the following four methods:

Baseline Study

The baseline study has documented "what is." From this, an analysis must be made to determine whether "what is" is what is wanted. For example, if the timeliness of administrative reports is rated unsatisfactory by the users, that would be an obvious candidate for improvement in the administrative function. Properly performed, the baseline study highlights administrative problems.

Three baseline aids that should prove helpful in identifying administrative problems are:

- Baseline worksheet (Figure 9)
- Administrative factual baseline (Figure 12)
- Administrative attitude baseline (Figure 13)

Administrative Survey

The administrative group can identify problems by surveying personnel involved with administrative activities. These people can include:

- Systems analysts/programmers
- Data processing management
- Senior management
- User management
- Computer operations management

The surveys can be structured in one of two ways. First, they can be open-ended, in which general questions are asked such as "What administrative services have not met your expectations?" and "What areas in the administrative function do you feel could be improved?" and "What administrative services should be deleted or added?" This is a probing type of survey and is more concerned with attitude than with facts.

The second type of administrative survey is more specific and is directed toward uncovering specific types of information. This type of survey normally identifies specific administrative services and asks for a reaction to those services. For example, if there was an administrative time report, the survey would ask specifically about that report. Obviously, in this second type of survey the questions are directed toward the person involved with the service. For example, users would not get the same survey as that given to data processing systems analysts/programmers.

Administrative Complaints

In the course of doing business, users of any service tend to be vocal about those services that displease them. Some administrative service groups have formalized the process of documenting these complaints. The method is usually internal within the administrative function. The member of the function who receives the complaint documents it on an internal administrative complaint form.

Administrative groups should be alert to external complaints. Some are given informally, whereas others may be formal. Some users may take the time and effort to construct an internal memo or comment formally about the inadequacy of a procedure or recommend areas of improvement. It behooves administrative groups to collect and analyze these periodically in order to improve the administrative process.

EDP ADMINISTRATIVE GUIDELINE 8

The administrative group that ignores the complaints and suggestions of users may find itself ignored by senior data processing management.

Problem Identification Task Force

The administration function can call together those persons who they believe could contribute to administration problem identification. The session is not designed to be solution oriented but rather, to be one of problem identification. The session should be a brainstorming type of session. However, administrative personnel should lead the group through the entire series of services provided by the administrative function so that problems can be identified with specific services. In addition, some open ended time should be given to brainstorming general problems, including areas that may not be currently provided by the administrative function.

DETERMINE THE MAGNITUDE OF PROBLEMS IDENTIFIED

After the problems have been identified, a determination must be made regarding the magnitude of the problem. You would not hire a tractor-trailer to move a box of paper clips. Insignificant problems should be discarded so that the limited administrative resources are directed toward solving significant problems.

It is recommended that problems be categorized into those of high and of low priority. High-priority problems are those exhibiting the following characteristics:

- Affect more than one group of people
- Consume more than 15 minutes' time per week to execute
- Fail to provide the appropriate information needed to make management decisions
- Cause aggravation on the part of the person completing the task
- Are considered of little value to the groups involved with the activity
- Delay rather than facilitate an activity

Note that high-priority items *must* be put into a business perspective, meaning that lack of action would have a negative impact on the business. If the problem does not meet the criteria listed above, it would be considered a low-priority problem. As such, it should not be considered for immediate action.

Step 2. Determine Magnitude of Effort

Determining the magnitude of effort required to solve a problem frequently is the deciding factor as to whether or not to perform a task. For example, if the benefits are very great and the effort very little, the decision will normally be made to perform the task. On the other hand, if the effort is very great and the benefits very little, the task will rarely be performed. It is only those decisions where there is uncertainty as to whether the effort or the benefits will be greater for which additional studies need to be made.

The estimate of effort made at this time is for planning purposes only. It is not intended to be a high-precision estimate but rather, a "ballpark" estimate. The detailed estimate will be calculated in the administrative planning process, which will be performed after the plan of action is developed.

It is recommended that the amount of effort required to solve a problem be categorized into high or low effort. The amount of effort needed to cause a problem to be considered of high effort would vary from organization to organization. For example, a very large data processing organization may not consider two or three months of effort high, whereas for a small organization that may be considered very high. Therefore, it is suggested that as a general rule of thumb, any effort that requires less than 1 percent of the total administrative resources be considered low and an effort requiring greater than 3 percent of administrative resources be considered high. Obviously, some judgment should be used when making this determination.

Step 3. Establish Administrative Objectives

An administrative objective is a positive problem-resolution statement. The objective indicates the desired problem improvement. For example, if the problem is that the estimating procedure is resulting in an average project variance of 15 percent, an administrative objective may be to develop an estimating procedure that will produce estimates accurate within plus or minus 5 percent of actual costs.

Administrative objectives should be stated as specifically as possible. A later step in the development of a plan of action will require the identification of the solution criteria for each objective. This is possible only when objectives are specifically stated. As a general rule, an objective should be stated in sufficient detail so that its completion can be measured mathematically. Our previously stated estimating objective meets that criterion.

The defined objectives from this step become the input to developing a plan of action. The totality of the list of administrative objectives defines the maximum scope of the plan of action. However, all of the objectives may not be included in the plan of action.

An administrative objective worksheet (see Figure 16) is provided for the purpose of recording the objectives. The worksheet contains the type of information needed in developing a plan of action. The worksheet contains the example of improving the estimating process noted above. The following discussion explains how to complete each part of the worksheet:

- *Number (column):* Each objective should be sequentially numbered. This provides for easy identification of each objective.
- *Administrative objective:* List each objective in a clear and measurable format.
- *Source:* State the origin of the problem that was used to create the objective. For example, if it came from the baseline, the appropriate worksheet could be referenced. This is useful in obtaining background information on the objective for use in developing the work plan.
- *Magnitude of problem:* From the previous analysis, indicate by a check mark (✓) whether it is a high- or low-magnitude problem.
- *Amount of effort:* From the previous analysis, indicate through the use of a check mark (✓) whether the effort required to achieve the objective is high or low.
- *Priority:* Give a preliminary estimate of the importance to the organization for achieving each objective. The prioritization process should be based on the return on investment to the organization. Administration is a project, and it is suggested that the administrative function be considered a profit center. If the administration expends their resources on a project with little or no return on investment, it will affect the overall profitability of the administration function.

The process for selecting a priority for each objective is outlined in Figure 17. This matrix utilizes the magnitude of the problem in the amount of effort to solve the problem. From the administrative objective worksheet (Figure 16), the magnitude of the problem and the amount of effort for that objective should be noted (e.g., high or low). The appropriate columns should then be identified in the objective priority matrix (Figure 17) and the intersection within the matrix will indicate the priority. For example, if the magnitude of the problem is high and the amount of effort required to solve that problem is low, the matrix indicates that the objective should be given a high priority. Note that the letter to put on the administrative worksheet is indicated in parentheses in the matrix intersection. The reasoning behind this is that a high-magnitude problem that requires only minimal effort should produce a high return on investment. The same logic is utilized for all four prioritizations.

Number	Administrative Objective	Source	Magnitude of Problem		Amount of Effort		Priority
			High	Low	High	Low	
1	Improve the project estimating process through the acquisition of estimating software such that estimating on the average will be accurate within ±5%	Department accounting system shows that the estimates are off by 15% or greater than 63% of the time	✓			✓	High

Figure 16 *Administrative Objective Worksheet*

Amount of Effort

		High	Low
Magnitude of the Problem	**High**	Medium-priority objective (M)	High-priority objective (H)
	Low	Probably should not be considered (N/A)	Low-priority objective (L)

Figure 17   *Objective Priority Matrix*

At the conclusion of this step, the administrative problem definition part of the process is complete.

EDP ADMINISTRATIVE GUIDELINE 9

Establishing administrative priorities based on the return on investment will also return a credibility dividend to the administrative function.

Part 2: Develop Solutions to Problems

Two processes can be followed to develop a proposed solution to administrative problems. First, the administrative function can analyze the problem and develop a solution consistent with the administrative objective. Second, rational problem-solving techniques can be used which incorporate the "team" concepts of problem solving. The recommended approach is to use the five-step rational problem-solving method described in this part of the plan-of-action process as follows:

Step 4. Identify Solution Criteria

Much effort is expended on problem solving without knowing what the solution must accomplish. This is normally attributable to the fact that there is inadequate problem definition. The cause of this major problem-solving dilemma is not knowing the criteria for a successful solution.

Solution criteria are defined as those criteria which when satisfied will convince the parties involved that the problem has been solved satisfactorily. In our previous example (see Figure 16) of setting an objective—to reduce the variance between estimates and actual from 15 to 5 percent—the solution criteria are included. In this instance, the estimating process must be such that there will be reasonable assurance that the estimates produced will be accurate within plus or minus 5 percent. However, in solving other objectives, the solution criteria may not be included in the objective.

The purpose of defining the criteria in the problem-solving part is two-fold. First, as stated previously, it outlines ways in which a successful solution can be determined. Second, and equally important, it orients the problem-solving team toward working on a solution to meet common criteria. The solution criteria should have the following characteristics:

- Indicate what results or behavior changes are required to satisfy the administrative objective
- Identify a time frame for providing those results
- Define the system and persons affected

The information gathered during the rational problem solving step should be documented. An administrative objective plan-of-action worksheet (Figure 18) is provided for this purpose. One of these worksheets should be completed for each administrative objective analyzed. The worksheet is started in this step and completed in step 8. The example used is the one started in Figure 16.

One worksheet is used for each administrative objective. The objective and the priority of the objective are included at the top of the worksheet. Note that the priority may change as the process continues and more information and insight into the objective are gathered.

At the end of this step, the solution criteria should be documented on the worksheet. Again, these criteria should be as specific as possible. It is the combination of the stated objective plus the solution criteria that will provide the input for the remainder of the plan-of-action process.

Step 5. Conduct Brainstorming

Brainstorming should follow the identification of the solution criteria and precede any feasibility study for two reasons. First, at this point people's minds

Objective:
Improve the project estimating process through the acquisition of estimating software such that estimating on the average will be accurate within ±5%.

Priority:
High

Solution Criteria:
Estimates developed by this system should be accurate within ±5%, 90% of the time.

Alternative Solution	Selection Criteria				
	Effectiveness	Resources	Completion Date	Quality	Total Score
1. Acquire Estimax software system	3	4	4	3	14
2. Hire consultant to develop new method	3	3	3	3	12
3. Appoint a departmental task force to develop a new method	3	1	2	4	10

Selected Solution 1 Roadblocks:
1. Acceptance by staff of an automated package
2. Acceptance by staff of a new method

[X] Acceptable   ☐ Unacceptable

Figure 18 *Administrative Objective Plan of Action Worksheet*

are usually open and receptive to a wide variety of solutions. Second, it enables everyone to have an opportunity to offer suggestions prior to one or two good ideas being selected. Once the group feels that some good alternatives have been put forward, they may be inhibited from making a suggestion, when, in fact, the suggestion may be the best method.

The objective of brainstorming thus is twofold: first, to bring out a wide variety of potential solutions, and second to give everyone an opportunity to speak. It is frequently the second objective that makes brainstorming so valuable. Once people believe that their ideas have been heard and analyzed, they are much happier with the group solution than with a solution forced on them by management.

Brainstorming, sometimes called green-lighting, should include the key decision makers involved in the administrative area. These are the people who generally have the respect of the organization in setting direction. They need not be management-level people, but should be the acknowledged leaders of the organization, not the followers. Normally, these persons are well known and easy to select. Once this group has been convinced that a certain decision is correct, the others will normally accept it or the leaders can convince the followers that the decision made was the correct decision.

The rules that must be followed in brainstorming are:

1. There is no leader but rather, a moderator or facilitator to ensure that the proper subjects are addressed and that the general ground rules of brainstorming are followed.
2. No one can criticize another's idea.
3. Everyone in the group must be given an opportunity to speak.
4. All ideas generated should be recorded.
5. At the conclusion of the idea-generation part, the ideas should be summarized and consolidated to avoid duplication and overlap (note that the facilitator should take an active role in this summarization process).
6. The group should prioritize or select the best three or four ideas for further study. If four ideas are to be selected, each member of the group can vote for four and the ideas receiving the most votes are considered for further study. Note that attempting to do a feasibility study on too many ideas is generally a waste of time.

EDP ADMINISTRATIVE GUIDELINE 10

Limit alternatives considered to no more than four choices; rarely will anyone ask for more.

The best alternative solutions should be listed on the administrative objective plan-of-action worksheet. The solutions should be sequentially numbered to facilitate the discussion. Note that the worksheet provides for only a brief description of each solution. The material gathered on each solution can be kept as a set of loose notes. However, it is advisable to number the notes with the alternative solution identification number.

Step 6. Perform Feasibility Study

The objective of the feasibility study step is to study the merits of implementing each alternative solution. Normally, each of the alternatives is evaluated individually. The process followed is similar to that in any other data processing feasibility study.

It is recommended that the feasibility study be a mini-cost/benefit evaluation. The benefits to be derived from each solution are determined. Next, the cost associated with each alternative solution is determined. The results provide an estimate of the potential return on investment for each potential solution.

The amount of time expended on the feasibility study should be equivalent to the importance and cost of the problem being addressed. If the costs are small, personal estimates may be used, whereas if costs are large, a more detailed and thorough data collection may be required in order to develop good estimates.

Note that the purpose of this feasibility study is to produce an administrative plan of action. It is assumed that once in the plan of action, additional planning and implementation effort will occur. During this time, feasibility can be restudied and adjustments made as necessary.

The purpose of the feasibility study is to gather sufficient information to make a decision about the feasibility of each of the alternative solutions. If the feasibility study should show that an alternative is not feasible, it should be eliminated from consideration. This can be accomplished by crossing out the alternatives on the worksheet. Those remaining as feasible solutions will be evaluated and the best-appearing solution be selected in the next step.

Step 7.   Weigh and Select

The objective of this step is to pick the apparent best solution from among the alternatives considered. The word "apparent" is used because the following step will challenge that decision.

The decision that goes into the plan of action will be selected from a three-part evaluation. The first part was the feasibility study (step 6), which was designed to eliminate infeasible solutions. This step is the second part of the selection process, which attempts to pick the best of the remaining solutions. The next step (step 8) provides a last opportunity to challenge the decision.

The selection process recommended is to evaluate each solution on the following four criteria:

1. *Effectiveness:* The proposed solution will satisfy the solution criteria and accomplish the objective.
2. *Resources required:* The amount of effort required to implement the solution.
3. *Completion date:* The length of the time span required to implement the solution.
4. *Quality:* The ability of the solution to achieve people's expectations. (Note: This is an estimate.)

For each one of the four criteria, those evaluating the solution should select one of the following four assessments for each of the four selection criteria:

1. *Effectiveness*
   - 4 = more than accomplishes the needs
   - 3 = fully accomplishes the needs
   - 2 = accomplishes most of the needs
   - 1 = fails to accomplish the basic needs

2. *Resources*
   - 4 = fully maximizes the use of resources
   - 3 = good use of resources
   - 2 = slight waste of resources
   - 1 = poor use of resources

3. *Completion date*
   - 4 = installed before needed
   - 3 = installed when needed
   - 2 = slightly misses date of need
   - 1 = late in meeting administrative needs

4. *Quality*
   - 4 = more than meets expectations
   - 3 = meets expectations
   - 2 = comes close to meeting expectations
   - 1 = fails to meet expectations

Each alternative solution should be evaluated and given the appropriate score in each of the four selection criteria. The scoring can be accomplished in two ways. First, the study group can develop a consensus score by looking at each solution individually and rating each of the four categories for that solution. The group would then go on to the next alternative solution and repeat the process until all alternatives have been considered. Second, each member of the study group can perform the rating individually and then the scores are accumulated and divided by the number of people in the group. For example, if there were three people in the group, each would score and the three scores would be totaled and then divided by 3 to get an average score for each selection criterion.

The four individual scores are accumulated to produce a total score for each alternative solution. Note that space is provided for recording the scores and accumulating the scores on the worksheet. The alternative solution with the highest score is normally considered the preferred solution for the accomplishment of the stated administrative objective.

If the total score for two or more alternatives is close, a further evaluation should be undertaken. The total score will be in the range 4 to 16. Sixteen would be the highest score representing the best solution, and 4 the lowest possible score, representing the worst solution. If the scores betwen two alternatives are within 10 percent, they should be considered a tie. In this case, the alternatives should be discussed and evaluated and the best solution picked by judgment rather than the score.

Step 8. List Roadblocks

The objective of this step is to identify why the selected solution will not work. Up to this point in the process, all of the effort has been positive in nature and directed toward finding the best solution. This step provides the opportunity to take a negative look at what appears to be the best solution to find out why it may not work.

This is another brainstorming type of step. Each member of the study group is provided an opportunity to attempt to identify why the solution selected may not work. It is important that the members of the group be very open in this step, because it is critical to the success of the administrative plan of action.

The step serves two purposes. First, if there are too many roadblocks, it may be better to eliminate this alternative and go back and pick the next best alternative solution. Second, if it is decided to go ahead with the solution after the roadblocks are identified, the implementers will know the problems before they start.

The type of roadblocks that should be considered for the selected alternative solutions are:

- Personal dislikes of management in other key personnel
- Resistance to change by certain people or areas
- Unavailability of necessary people resources to implement
- Unavailability of financial or other resources to implement
- Lack of management support
- Nonimplementation of required prerequisites

It is unlikely that this step will produce all of the possible roadblocks. However, by anticipating what might go wrong, steps can be taken to reduce the probability of a roadblock occurring. For example, if a potential roadblock is lack of management support, the study group might wish to raise a "trial balloon." The trial balloon gives management an opportunity to shoot down an idea before it progresses very far. For example, if the recommended solution to a scheduling problem was an automated scheduling system, it may be desirable to "trial-balloon" management with the idea to determine the receptivity to the concept. If the trial balloon is shot down, the roadblock is real, but on the other hand, if the trial balloon survives the flight, the roadblock may have been overcome by the trial ballooning, or it may have been a perceived but not real roadblock.

In identifying roadblocks, administrative management is cautioned that the existence of roadblocks should not necessarily eliminate a solution. The real question to be decided by this step is: Can the roadblocks be realistically overcome during the implementation process? If the answer to that is yes, the solution should be accepted.

The roadblocks for the selected solution should be listed on the worksheet. If the roadblocks are acceptable, the solution selected is acceptable and the acceptable box at the bottom of the worksheet should be checked. If the solution selected is unacceptable, the unacceptable box should be selected and the next-highest-scoring alternative evaluated from the perspective of roadblocks. The alternative solution that is accepted then becomes input to the development of the administrative plan of action.

Part 3: Develop a Plan of Action

A plan of action may be the single most important document leading to improving the administrative function. Action rarely occurs without a plan. In those instances where unplanned action occurs, it rarely succeeds because it takes determination and stamina to maintain action throughout. Without planning, action frequently ceases before the results are accomplished.

The administrative plan of action becomes the administrative blueprint for success. Such a plan should be developed at least annually. Once the objectives of the plan have been accomplished, a new plan of action should be developed and this cycle continued to ensure the increased productivity of the administrative function.

EDP ADMINISTRATIVE GUIDELINE 11
It takes fewer resources to do it right than to explain why you did not.

The selected objectives and solutions become the input into the plan of action. These must be ordered and put into a cohesive plan to ensure its effective implementation. The final plan of action must ensure that the individual objectives are consistent with one another and that there is no redundancy in the solutions. The plan must also match available resources to selection of the solution.

The development of an administrative plan of action is the full responsibility of administrative management. Other people can help set objectives, pick solutions, and so on. However, administrative management should not delegate their responsibilities to other groups in permitting them to write a plan of action for the function. This is a one-step process, as follows:

Step 9. *Develop a Plan of Action*

The administrative plan of action defines:

1. What must be done
2. Who must do it
3. When it must be done

The plan of action does not need to state how the objectives will be accomplished. However, the plan may include considerable insight into how the objective should be accomplished. Much of the work done during the feasibility study and the roadblock step should provide insight into how best to accomplish the objective.

The key concept that makes an administrative plan of action work is to acquire a sponsor for each objective. The concept of a sponsor is to make a single person accountable for the success or failure of accomplishment of each objective. The selection of a sponsor should be given careful thought.

EDP ADMINISTRATIVE GUIDELINE 12

People, not functions, accomplish objectives. Appointing a "sponsor" responsible for the accomplishment of administrative objectives improves significantly the probability of that objective being accomplished.

A sponsor for an administrative objective should have the following traits:

- Sufficient authority to accomplish the objective
- Access to the needed resources to accomplish the objective
- Respect by subordinates and superiors
- Adequate skills to accomplish the objective
- Desire to succeed (although this trait is listed last, it should be first in selection, because desire can overcome the absence of, or weakness in, the other traits)

The sponsor need not be a member of the administrative function. Remember that administration is everybody's responsibility. Therefore, it is not unusual or even undesirable to have a sponsor outside the formalized administration function. However, it is advisable to have the sponsor be a member of the data processing department.

The sponsor should accept the sponsorship of the objective voluntarily. If the sponsorship is forced on an individual, they may accept it reluctantly and not put the necessary energy into accomplishing the objective. It is most desirable to ask for sponsors to volunteer, but it is acceptable to discuss sponsorship with specific persons.

Number	Objective	Priority	Sponsor	Estimated Dates	
				Start	Stop
1	Acquire and install the Estimax software package	High	J. Jones, administrative manager	9/1	12/1

Figure 19 *Administrative Plan of Action for the Period 19XX*

The sponsor should agree to two other aspects of the administrative plan of action. First is the priority given to the objective. This is important so that the sponsor can orient the accomplishment of the objective within the sponsor's personal work load. Second, the sponsor must agree to the implementation time span: specifically, the start and stop dates for accomplishing the objective.

It is recommended that the administrative plan of action be established for a one-year period. Normally, the period selected should coincide with the fiscal or calendar year of the organization. This coincides with the administrative plan of action and with the budgeting process for the organization. It is also desirable to have a five-year administrative plan of action, for which the one-year plan is a subset.

The information above should be selected and recorded as the administrative plan of action. Figure 19 is presented for that purpose. (The form has been completed for the exercise illustrated in Figure 18.) When the plan of action has been recorded, the following questions should be asked about the plan and changes made according to the answers:

1. Are all of the objectives listed on the plan consistent with the missions of the data processing function?
2. Is the administrative plan of action consistent with the data processing department annual plan?
3. Are there sufficient resources to accomplish the objectives within the estimated time span?
4. Are the sponsors sufficiently committed to accomplishing the objectives?
5. Do the sponsors have sufficient time and resources to accomplish the objectives?

IMPLEMENTING THE ADMINISTRATIVE PLAN OF ACTION

The primary responsibility for the implementation of the plan of action is through the sponsors. Obviously, the plan must be approved by data processing management and incorporated into the data processing department plan. However, approval does not mean implementation. Implementation occurs through dedicated sponsors who are willing to put in the effort required to make the plan of action a reality. The administrative manager has the responsibility to ensure that the sponsors perform their job properly. If the sponsors fail to perform the tasks necessary to accomplish the objectives, the sponsors should either be encouraged to action or replaced. Obviously, it is best to get the original sponsor to implement the objective.

The administrative manager must recognize that the sponsors may have many pressures on them to accomplish work. The administrative manager's role is to provide sufficient pressure so that the administrative objectives are accomplished within the designated time span. Good sponsors closely monitored and encouraged produce good results.

EDP ADMINISTRATIVE GUIDELINE 13
There is no greater finale to a person's efforts than the simple words: "It is done and it works."

ADMINISTRATIVE PLANNING

No bird can soar too high if it flies with its own wings. Plans are the wings that carry administration to lofty organizational accomplishments.

Chapter

4

Administrative
Planning

The data processing function is a business within a business. In a medium-size to large corporation, the annual budget of the data processing function exceeds the gross revenue of many smaller organizations. Even in smaller organizations, the data processing budget may be a significant part of the total costs of operating the organization. The data processing manager has the responsibility of running the data processing business.

An important part of managing a business is planning. The administrative function normally has the responsibility for preparing data processing plans. The objective of this process is to explain how to run the data processing business so that it will provide a positive return on investment to the organization.

Data processing planning cannot be performed independently of the organization's planning. Data processing, although a business within a business, is still part of the total organization. This chapter provides a step-by-step approach to the development of an effective data processing plan.

ADMINISTRATION'S ROLE IN PLANNING

The role of administration in planning depends on the role and responsibility of administration in the data processing department. The role and responsibility will be related to the organizational placement of the administrative manager. Note that in larger organizations this may include a large staff, whereas in a small data processing shop, this may be a part-time position.

Accountability makes things work; thus it is necessary to make someone accountable for administration. A suggested organization structure is shown in Figure 20.

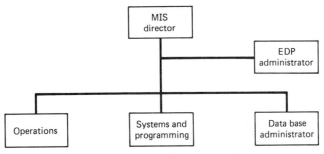

Figure 20 *Suggested Organization Structure*

The planning responsibility options for EDP administration are:

1. *Develop plan:* independently creates EDP plan.
2. *Contribute to plan:* provides administrative input to EDP plan.
3. *Orchestrate plan:* ensures that a good plan is developed.

The recommended planning role for EDP administration is option 3. Under this option, the entire EDP department is involved in the planning process, with administration providing guidance and direction. It also involves consolidating and presenting the proposed plan to senior EDP management.

MANAGING DATA PROCESSING AS A PLANNED BUSINESS

In many organizations, data processing management subscribes to the theory that data processing is a service organization. Some DP managers even proclaim that data processing is the in-house equivalent of a service bureau. It is a commodity that people purchase and use as required.

This philosophy ignores the responsibility of stewardship over the information processing resources of the organization. Although it is not the prerogative of data processing to run the organization, the function should not be subservient to other organizational units. Determining when to lead and when to follow has been a difficult decision for many data processing managers.

The solution to fitting data processing into the organizational mission is to establish clearly the role and responsibility of the data processing function. Once this has been established, plans can be developed to accomplish that mission. Unfortunately, plans not tied to a clearly established data processing role may lack the direction and purpose needed in an effective plan.

The role and responsibility of a DP function to today's information processing world should include:

1.   Use of personal computer
2.   Control over distributed system
3.   Interface of office automation and information processing system
4.   Negotiation and control over communication networks
5.   Administration of data base
6.   Central source of knowledge for information processing for the organization (sometimes called the information center concept)

EDP planning should involve all of the above.

Attributes of a Well-Planned Data Processing Function

The objective of planning is to permit data processing personnel to control their own destiny. Without plans, data processing may be reactive to the needs of others rather than providing the direction needed by the organization. Through planning, data processing is in a leadership position. For example, in an unplanned environment, data processing may have difficulty determining what work to accept and what work to reject. In a planned environment, this poses no problem to data processing management.

Data processing organizations must balance user requirements against data processing requirements. A data processing organization that fails to address the technological issues faces technological obsolescence. This occurs when data processing cannot properly balance the work load.

An unbalanced work load approach is illustrated in Figure 21a. This illustration shows that the work load flows into the data processing function to produce results. The results are sent to users, who perform an anlysis on the value of those results in accomplishing each user's mission. Based on this analysis, users develop new work requirements and feed them to data processing. In many organizations, users also select the priority of implementation, resulting in data processing being a subservient service organization. This concept is unbalanced in that data processing may not be able to do those functions deemed necessary to improve productivity and credibility, or to maintain technological currentness.

A balanced work load approach is illustrated in Figure 21b. This is the work load approach that results from administrative planning. In this approach, the work load is fed into a planning process prior to being performed by the data processing function. The work that is performed produces results which in this approach are analyzed by both the user and data processing. The user is evaluating the work with regard to accomplishing the user mission, and data processing is performing the analysis with regard to the accomplishment of the data processing mission.

In the balanced work load approach, both the user and DP develop new work requirements. These requirements are fed into the work load and through the planning process.

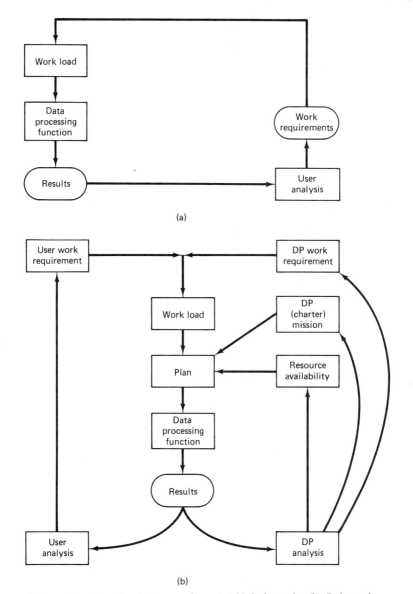

Figure 21 *Workload Approaches (a) Unbalanced (b) Balanced*

Planning has three inputs: the charter or mission of the data processing department, the projected work load, and resource availability. Planning must match the work load, with a mission, and then determine what tasks can be performed with the available resources. Without planning, the wrong work may be done, or done in a manner that minimizes the productivity of the data processing function.

We will discuss administrative planning from the following perspectives:

- *Input to planning:* The work load, the data processing mission, and the resource availability
- *Planning process:* The matching of resources to work load
- *Output:* The planning documents produced from the process

The types of tasks that need to be performed by the data processing department, for the data processing department, include:

- Technologically upgrading applications to increase the useful life and improve the productivity of those applications
- Studying, designing, and acquiring improved methods for developing, maintaining, and operating application systems
- Analyzing the working environment to identify areas of needed improvement
- Requesting, designing, and implementing systems for the operation of the data processing function

---

EDP ADMINISTRATIVE GUIDELINE 14

Planning is the function for which there never seems to be enough time—and there never will be unless the department plans ahead.

ADMINISTRATIVE PLANNING—AND OTHER TASKS THAT NOBODY CARES ABOUT

Planning is the task that everyone is involved in, yet nobody seems to care much about. Many people perform planning as if it were a perfunctory ritual, like turning the page on a calendar. The steps are performed, but few people seem to understand where the need for planning originates, who uses the plan, and who is measured against it.

There are three general approaches used for planning, as follows:

1. *Plan and ignore:* The plan is developed and approved, but after approval no one seems to be concerned with the plan, and work goes on as usual.
2. *Management by objective (MBO):* The plan includes some specific objectives for people to accomplish. As the plan is developed, people are measured against their ability to accomplish the objectives in the plan.
3. *Management by embarrassment (MBE):* The plan is used only to punish people by showing them how much they have fallen short of what is expected of them.

We need to look at where plans come from to understand the objective of planning. Next we must understand how to use the plan and how to measure performance against that plan without embarrassing the data processing staff. The basis for planning is illustrated in Figure 22. This shows how the data processing planning should parallel organization planning.

Corporations are formed through the development of articles of incorporation which state the broad objectives for forming the corporation. Federal, state, and local municipalities have equivalent constitutions or directives defining the role of the government. From these articles of incorporation come the broad objectives of individual units. The objectives for establishing the data processing function should be stated in its charter.

The organization must establish corporate objectives based on the articles of incorporation. For example, the articles of incorporation may state that the organization is established to do banking, and one of the objectives for the bank might be to handle the trusts and wills of their customers. Normally, these broad objectives are established by the organization's board of directors. Similarly, the data processing department will have a mission that will be a subset of those broad corporate objectives.

Organizations need a long-range plan to determine how they are going to accomplish the stated objectives. The annual corporate plan and budget will be a subset of this long-range plan. Similarly, the data processing department should have a long-range plan, which is a subset of the corporate long-range plan, and a short-range plan, which is a subset of the corporation's annual plan.

In other words, any planning performed by the data processing department should be consistent and part of the organization's plan. To develop a data processing plan that cannot be tied directly to the organization's plan is inconsistent with good planning principles and would lead senior management to believe that data processing is not a part of the organization, but rather, may be what some data processing people say it is—a service center owned by the organization.

Senior corporate managers have the primary responsibility for planning. The corporate plan, planning policies and procedures, and support for plan-

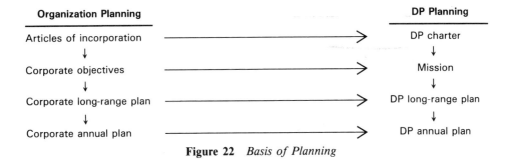

Figure 22 *Basis of Planning*

ning *must* originate with senior management. Data processing management should be included in corporate planning so that they can develop data processing plans consistent with both the objectives and intent of the corporate plans.

EDP ADMINISTRATIVE GUIDELINE 15

A good data processing plan is one that is in step with the organization's plan.

A good data processing plan should also answer the following five questions:

1. *Where do we want to be as a data processing department?* The plan must first define what is to be accomplished as a result of the plan. If data processing management cannot state where they want to be when the plan has been accomplished, they will have great difficulty developing the plan (i.e., the means to evaluate success).

2. *How do we get to where we want to go?* The plan should lay out step by step how the data processing department will accomplish the desired objectives. This chapter explains how to develop that part of the plan which explains how to accomplish the objectives.

3. *Who will be responsible for accomplishing the plan?* A good plan will make people accountable for the accomplishment of each part of the plan. It is not necessary to identify each person who will be involved in fulfilling the planned objectives, but it is important to assign responsibility for the accomplishment of each task in the plan.

4. *What will the plan cost?* Estimates must be made and budgets prepared defining the amount of resources required to accomplish the plan. This should be broken down by individual tasks. This topic is addressed in Chapter 5.

5. *When will the tasks be accomplished?* The final step of the planning process is the matching of the resources to the objectives to develop a schedule for accomplishing the plan. This includes establishing priorities as well as determining various staffing levels for each project. This topic is discussed in Chapter 6.

In answering these questions, this chapter presents planning in a step-by-step format. This chapter will discuss creating the tasks to be accomplished and ensuring that those tasks are supportive of the organization's plan. Chapters 5 and 6 explain how to estimate the resources required for each task and then how to develop a schedule for completing the plan.

Studies by the Harvard Business School[1] stated that the average data

---

[1]Keynote address by Dr. James Cash at the Second Annual DPMA Quality Assurance Symposium, March 1982.

processing work load is a three-year backlog. The study also indicated that the work load was growing at 10 percent per year. With a relatively static work force and productivity within data processing systems and programming rising at a rate of only 2 to 3 percent a year, data processing groups stand little chance of getting on top of their work load. An important solution for improving productivity is planning. Planning should be considered a major productivity tool.

THE ADMINISTRATIVE PLANNING PROCESS

The development of an administrative plan is an administrative project. It encompasses all of the attributes of any other project in the data processing department. The type of plan developed will depend on the time, attention, and resources devoted to the planning process.

Planners should recognize that there is a cycle of events that occurs in administrative planning (see Figure 23). The cycle commences with annual data gathering. During this ritual, those individuals and groups using and requesting services of data processing are contacted regarding future work

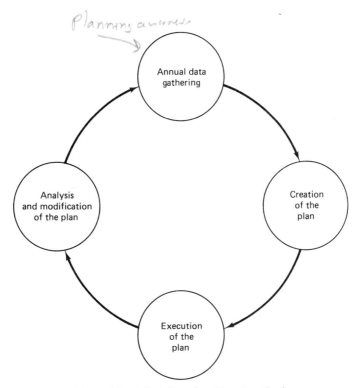

Figure 23 *Administrative Planning Cycle*

load. From the information gathered, a plan is created for the data processing function. Note that this may be both a long-term and a short-term plan.

The creation of the plan does not complete the planning cycle. Once approved, the plan must be placed into use to accomplish the tasks outlined in the plan. However, during the year, events change. Thus the plan must be subject to continual analysis and modification. Plans that are not kept current quickly fall into disuse, as does the entire planning process.

The plan as developed is the equivalent of documentation for a computer system. People rely on and use documentation as long as it maintains its currentness. However, as soon as the systems analysts and programmers fail to update documentation as they change the programs, the documentation can no longer be relied upon and is not used. The administrative plan must be subjected to the same maintenance standards as documentation if the plan is to maintain its usefulness throughout the year.

An important part of the planning cycle is the analysis of the work completed against the work planned. This analysis should evaluate:

- Percent of plan completed
- Frequency and extent of new requirements
- Correctness of information included within the plan
- Value of the plan to the function of the data processing department
- Weaknesses in the administrative planning process

The Administrative Planning Life Cycle

The planning process can be viewed as a set of phases that comprise an administrative planning life cycle (APLC). The APLC phases are similar to those of the system development life cycle (SDLC). We can look at the phases of both life cycles and see many similarities:

- *Planning requirements phase:* During this phase, planners must identify what the data processing department is to accomplish during the forthcoming planning period. All persons involved with the data processing function should be contacted to determine their needs. The planners must understand these requirements in order to develop a plan to accomplish the needs.
- *Planning design phase:* At the completion of requirements, the planners must convert those needs into an executable plan. The completion of the design phase is the equivalent of the specifications for the programmer.
- *Planning implementation phase:* During this phase, the planners will estimate the resources required to accomplish the design specifications, and then schedule those specified tasks utilizing any available resources, but

subject to constraints. Many planners use automated tools to help in this part of the process.

- *Planning test phase:* The planners must verify that the completed plan is reasonable, and that it is consistent with the company's plans.

- *Operation/maintenance phase:* Once approved, the plan must be put into execution; and maintained to reflect changes in both requirements and resources. Planning maintenance exhibits all the characteristics of systems maintenance. There are emergency changes, planned changes, and new requirements. Many of these requirements will cause the planners to rethink the design, implementation, and test phases of the APLC.

Administrative Planning Steps

EDP administration has responsibility for developing, implementing, and controlling the planning process. It is not administration's responsibility to determine what should be in the plan, or to judge on the merits of what has been proposed. However, this does not mean that administration personnel cannot question or assist other areas in planning.

The objective of planning is the effective utilization of data processing resources. This involves, first, identification of the task to be accomplished; second, prioritizing those tasks in conformance with the overall organization plan; and third, matching resources to accomplish the objectives in the most cost-effective manner.

The objectives of administering and controlling the planning are twofold: first, to minimize the resources expended in planning; and second, to administer and control a process designed to produce the best possible plan. In fulfilling these responsibilities, EDP administration must play an active role in the total planning process.

The effective administration and control of planning is a continuous process. Not only should administration be involved in creating the plan, but it should be involved in monitoring the implementation of the plan and recording the status of results. Through the analysis and evaluation of the process, improvements can be made.

The administration and control of the planning process is accomplishable through the following eight-step process (see Figure 24):

1. *Planning awareness:* Alert staff to planning requirements and build enthusiasm for the process. (Note: This may be initiated by senior corporate management.)

2. *Data gathering:* Collect as input for plans:

    Corporate plans
    DP long-range plan
    DP continuing requirements

Phase		Step	Purpose
Requirements	1.	Planning awareness	Alert the staff to planning requirements and build enthusiasm for the process
Requirements	2.	Data gathering	Collect as input for plans: Corporate plans DP long-range plan DP continuing requirements New user requirements New DP requirements
Requirements	3.	Definition of constraints	Determine the magnitude and limits placed on plans
Design	4.	Estimation of tasks	Identify the resources required to accomplish each task
Design	5.	Prioritization of tasks	Determine the sequence of the tasks
Implementation	6.	Scheduling of accomplishable work load	Create a plan to accomplish those tasks that can be accomplished with the resources proposed
Test	7.	Test plan	Evaluate plan for: Reasonableness Compliance to company plan Duplication
Operation/maintenance	8.	Approval and modification	Adjust plan based on company management–imposed limitations

Figure 24 *Administrative Planning Steps*

    New user requirements
    New DP requirements

3. *Definition of constraints:* Determine the magnitude and limits placed on plans.
4. *Estimation of tasks:* Identify the resources required to accomplish each task.
5. *Prioritization of tasks:* Determine the sequence of the tasks.
6. *Scheduling of accomplishable work load:* Create a plan to accomplish those tasks that can be accomplished with the resources proposed.
7. *Test plan:* Evaluate the plan for:

    Reasonableness
    Compliance to company plan
    Duplication

8.   *Approval and modification:* Adjust plan based on company management-imposed limitations.

These steps and the tools needed to accomplish the steps are discussed next.

Step 1.   *Planning Awareness*

Planning is not an everyday occurrence in the life of the data processing staff. On the other hand, it requires their time, attention, and allocation of resources to be effective.

One sure way to undermine the effectiveness of the planning process is to "spring" the need for a plan on the staff. Providing them with the forms and procedures and asking for a quick response normally results in a poor response. Planning takes time for analysis, consultation, and decision. A one-week planning process may only be worth the paper it is written on.

EDP administration must "market" the planning process. The marketing is designed, first, to alert the staff to the fact that they will be required to submit planning information, and second, to create an awareness of the importance of the information that will be provided. Unfortunately, few administrative groups put sufficient resources into this awareness program. As a result, many of the staff look at it as a perfunctory task and treat it accordingly.

Ask yourself about your own planning process:

1.   Have we trained our staff in how to do planning? (If not, should we expect good plans?)
2.   Have we explained the importance of EDP plans? (If not, should the staff think of planning as important?)
3.   Have we provided the staff with that part of the corporate plan that affects them? (If not, should we expect the DP plan to be a subset of the corporate plan?)
4.   Do we use and provide the staff status reports on the implementation of the plan? (If not, can we really expect them to believe that planning is more than an annual game?)

The best awareness method is one that continues throughout the year. Awareness of the importance of planning can best be accomplished by providing the creators of the plan with a regular status report on the results of implementing the plan. If the staff realizes that they are being measured on the performance of the plan, they will continue to be aware of the importance of the plan.

Effective awareness also occurs when the plan is changed when requirements change. If the creators of the plan must modify the plan when there is a significant change in requirements, they will be aware of the importance that management places on planning and the need to provide realistic planning information.

In presenting planning information, several counterproductive theories are used, as follows:

- *Double-cut theory:* The staff requests twice as much as they want, knowing that management will cut their request in half, so that they end up receiving what they need to do their job.
- *Rat hole theory:* The staff ignores all of the bad things that have happened in the past, assuming that those costs and problems are down the rat hole, and proposes the continuation or resurrection of ideas because when ignoring the past, it may seem economical to maintain an uneconomical system or process.
- *Trial balloon theory:* Not knowing what management wants, the staff includes a variety of "schemes" in the plan so that management can reject those things that they do not want, and accept what they do want.
- *Weasel-word theory:* Plans are worded such that almost any implementation would accomplish the plan. Using this theory, success is almost guaranteed, and completion of the plan assured.

The following awareness techniques may prove helpful in alerting the staff to the coming planning process in order to improve the reliability of the planning data and to minimize the impact of the counterproductive theories:

1. *Preplanning meeting/seminar:* The people who will be involved in planning are called together sufficiently in advance of planning to explain what is required, when it is required, why it is required, and how it will be used.
2. *Planning newsletter:* A short newsletter, usually one page, 8½ by 11 inches in size, with a planning masthead providing the same type of information that would be included in a planning meeting. The newsletter can include tips and techniques on how best to perform planning.
3. *Planning manual:* Well in advance of the planning process, a manual is issued that provides the worksheets and step-by-step procedures for people to following in planning. This explains what to do to get ready for the planning process. It is similar to the concept used by accounting firms to help taxpayers record the type of information that they will need when they prepare a person's tax return.
4. *Bulletin board notices:* General notices are prepared with slogans, cartoons, and other eye-catching artwork to alert people that planning is coming and to get ready for it.

Step 2.   *Data Gathering*

The best data-gathering method for planning is to provide the people who develop the plan with standardized forms and worksheets. This accomplishes two purposes: first, it defines the scope of information needed for planning; and second, it ensures that the information will be recorded in a standardized format.

People doing planning should be provided with the following three items:

1. Last year's plan, and preferably the current status of implementation of that plan
2. Instructions for preparing planning information
3. Documents/worksheets for recording planning information

A proposed worksheet for gathering planning information is illustrated in Figure 25. This form provides space to collect the type of information that is present in most data processing planning documents. The form is designed to minimize the planning process by:

*   Recording all needed data on one form.
*   Limiting space for recording data to minimize the information collected. It always possible to collect more information, but there is no way to recoup the time and effort expended in collecting unwanted information.

EDP ADMINISTRATIVE GUIDELINE 16

In deciding how much planning information to collect, make your error on the side of collecting too little information—time spent in collecting unwanted information is time lost forever.

The instructions for completing the planning requirements worksheet follow:

*   *Responsible area:* The area within the organization (e.g., payroll department) or within data processing responsible for the creation of the plan.
*   *Date:* The date on which the plan was developed or the planning period, whichever is most applicable.
*   *Originator:* The person accountable for the origination of the planning information.
*   *Approval:* The person who approved the planning item.
*   *Statement of need:* A single task that is to be considered for inclusion within the plan. A task is defined as a controllable and measurable item. For example, a task might be to create a new computer system, upgrade

Responsible Area: Administrative section	**Date:** 8/3/XX

Originator: J. Jones	**Approval:** W. Smith

Statement of Need:

Acquire estimating software system.

Reference to Company Plan: General EDP mission

Description of Need:

Identify and evaluate available estimating software and select the one most suitable.

Success Criteria:

Package should not exceed $25,000 purchase price, $25,000/year operation cost, and produce reliable estimates 90% of the time that are within ±5% of actual cost.

Date Needed: 1/1/XX	**Priority:** High

Constraints:

- Cannot be more effort for people than current estimating system
- Estimating criteria cannot exceed 25 in number

Effect on People:

- Should reduce people work load
- Requires training program to gain acceptance
- Requires training program to understand use

Effect on Systems:

None

Effect on Cost:

- Purchase price not to exceed $25,000
- Operation not to exceed $25,000 per year
- Net result should be no additional cost for estimating

To Be Completed by DP Administration

Estimate to Implement:

300 (one time) hours of administrative effort, and 4 hours (one time) per person for training in use.

DP Responsibility Area: Administration section

Dates: Start 9/1/XX	**Stop** 12/15/XX

Figure 25   *Planning Requirements Worksheet*

hardware capacity, acquire a new methodology, purchase an application software package, or perform maintenance on a specific application system. The size of the item is unimportant, but the ability to identify, measure, and control the implementation of the task is essential.

- *Reference to company plan:* The general authorization from management to perform this task. The planning task can be cross-referenced to a user plan, general organizational plan, or a management objective directed at data processing.
- *Description of need:* A sufficient narrative description so that the task is comprehensible to both the person submitting it and the managers who will approve it. Note that the administrative group must also understand it in order to organize and present a cohesive plan to management.
- *Success criteria:* The criteria that must be achieved in order to judge the task successfully completed. Note that this may reference another document. The success criteria are the standards against which the task will be measured. For example, the task may be to upgrade disk storage, and a success criterion will be to provide X millions of bytes of on-line storage.
- *Date needed:* The date on which the success criteria must be accomplished (this is discussed further in Chapter 6).
- *Priority:* The importance of this task in relation to other tasks. (Note: Prioritization systems are discussed in Chapter 6.)
- *Constraints:* Any criterion or obstacle that needs to be considered in determining whether the task should be included within the final plan, or scheduling considerations, such as if a software system is not installed by X date, it will be of no value.
- *Effect on people:* Any considerations involving the people who will develop, maintain, or implement the task.
- *Effect on systems:* Any considerations involving how this task will cause application systems to be modified or altered in any manner.
- *Effect on cost:* The cost/benefits associated with implementing this task. Ideally, a return on investment would be presented to management as a result of implementing this task.
- *To be completed by DP administration:* The individuals within data processing responsible for implementing this task should provide the following information:

> *Estimate to implement:* The DP estimate to implement, which should be included on the effect on cost, but if the user provides the cost, DP may propose alternative costs.
>
> *DP responsibility area:* The area within DP responsible for implementing the task.
>
> *Dates:* Suggested start and stop dates for implementing the task.

The planning requirements example illustrated in Figure 25 is for the acquisition of an estimating software package. The example assumes that estimating is now performed manually, but that after the acquisition it will be standardized using a software package. This is a continuation of the needs defined in Figures 16, 18, and 19.

One of these forms should be completed for each task included within the plan. Many organizations number these tasks so that they can easily be turned into assignments, and controlled during implementation. It is also desirable to reference the tasks to accounting codes if such codes are used for budgetary and cost recording purposes.

Target dates should be established for the completion of the forms. It is advisable for administration to contact all groups a few days prior to the submission date, reminding them of the need to comply with the target dates. Although it is desirable from an administration perspective to state that the planning information received after the target date will not be considered, from a business perspective this is not practical. Unfortunately, the administrators may have to be baby-sitters in assuring that all of the planning information is collected.

A good method for ensuring that all planning information is collected is to prepare a checklist of all persons who should submit planning information. As the data are received this is noted on the checklist. The administration group then follows up with those groups that have not submitted the needed information within the appropriate time span. Where necessary, data processing management should be asked to apply appropriate pressure to assure that the appropriate information is submitted.

Some suggestions that help obtain good planning data on a timely basis are:

1. *Involve senior DP management.* The request should come from the boss.
2. *Circulate lists of completed status reports.* Send out lists of those who have completed the planning reports, and when. This is circulated to all managers *without* interpretation. (Note: This is an example of management by embarrassment.)
3. *Follow up.* Personally contact each involved person to determine if he or she has questions or problems.
4. *Develop a staff-designed planning process.* Ask the staff to design the process for collecting planning information (helps get support for use of the process).

Step 3. Definition of Constraints

Constraints are those obstacles that stand in the way of completing the task successfully. If the constraints are not properly identified, management may not be able to assess adequately the probability of achieving the task. For example, if it is not known that the success of the plan hinges on acquiring a data base management system, the acquisition of the data base management system may be deleted but the task approved.

It may be feasible to list categories of constraints in the planning procedure, and then just use a code which can be explained if necessary. The categories of constraints that should be considered include:

- *Skill levels:* Special skills are required by the implementers of this task.
- *Hardware/software:* Some special feature, capacity, or operating software package is needed to be implemented prior to the implementation of this task.
- *Cost:* If the cost to implement the task exceeds X dollars, the task should not be completed.
- *Date:* If the task cannot be implemented by a specific date, the task should not be completed.
- *Legislative requirements:* The task must be implemented by a specific date to satisfy a regulatory agency requirement or law.
- *Intersystem:* This task must be completed before another task can be implemented.
- *Compliance to standards/policy:* This task is necessary in order to comply with a current or proposed standard or policy within the industry, data processing, and/or professional societies, such as a general accounting procedure.

Step 4. *Estimation of Tasks*

The resources required to accomplish a task must be estimated. From a data processing perspective, these are the data processing resources. On the other hand, the requester of the task should estimate all of the resources, not just the data processing resources. The data processing resources should be estimated by a data processing staff member, or agreed to by a data processing staff member.

Step 5. *Prioritization of Tasks*

Prioritization of tasks is needed to determine the sequence of implementation, and perhaps whether the task will be implemented at all. The prioritization should be made by the person requesting the task.

There are two general approaches to establishing priorities. First, priorities can be established within areas. For example, the accounting department can establish the priorities within the accounting department. Second, priorities can be established within the total organization. Obviously, this is more difficult, but has significant advantages over local prioritization.

Data processing is a corporate resource. If one area consumes too much of those resources, too little will be available for another area. Obviously, if there are as many or more resources than work available, this is no problem. However, in most organizations the backlog of requested data processing work far exceeds the available resources.

The administrative function should establish a prioritization method. This method should be consistent with the desires of data processing management and senior management of the organization. Suggested prioritization systems are discussed in Chapter 6.

There are many methods used in developing planning estimates. Obviously, the resources expended on estimating should not exceed the benefits derived from the estimates. In other words, a highly precise estimate may not be warranted. It may be sufficient for the estimate to be accurate within plus or minus 25 percent, or even plus or minus 50 percent.

It is important in estimating that all groups use the same estimating procedure. For example, if the cost of a systems analyst is estimated to be $40 per hour, everyone should use the $40 per hour estimate. In general, consistency may be more important than accuracy.

The administration function is responsible for developing a standardized estimating method. Note that the method used in estimating for planning purposes may be different from the one used in obtaining project approval throughout the work year. It is recommended that only one estimating system be used, but if different precisions are required for planning versus specific approval, two estimating methods can be used.

In an approval process there is both general and specific authorization. General authorization provides the authority to do work but not the ability to do a task. Specific authorization will be needed for that purpose. Planning is a general authorization process and thus tasks included within an approved plan do not provide the authority to do that task. Specific authorization is needed, and some DP management may want more accurate estimates for specific authorization than they do for general planning purposes.

Developing methods for estimating is a responsibility of administration. A discussion of the more common estimating alternatives is included in Chapter 5.

Step 6.   Scheduling of Accomplishable Work Load

The available resources must be matched against the work load in a manner that best accomplishes the organization's mission. This may not mean that all high-priority jobs are completed by the data processing department. Data processing must develop a realistic work plan based on its resources. To accept work for which it has a low probability of success, because of lack of appropriate skills, machine capacities, and so on, would be a mistake. Other options are available to data processing, such as delaying projects and contracting outside.

The sequencing of work must take into account the priority of the work, the sequence in which it must be performed, and the availability of the resources needed to accomplish the work. This involves some technically complex scheduling in order to maximize the use of resources. Staffing size, the time frame of the project, and the skill level of personnel all affect the amount of resources required to do a job. The administrative function is responsible for developing the process that will produce the most effective plan. Chapter 6 proposes solutions to this scheduling dilemma.

Step 7.   Test Plan

Prior to testing, a draft data processing plan must be developed. The plan cannot be tested in pieces, but should be tested as a complete plan. Testing is designed to determine that the plan provides a high probability of success for the data processing department to accomplish its mission.

An example of a planning document is illustrated in Figure 26. This shows the type of information that is desirable to include in a planning document, and includes:

- *Task Number:* A unique identifier for each task.
- *Task:* A brief but complete definition of each task.
- *Success criteria:* The basis on which the successful completion of the task will be evaluated.
- *Area of responsibility:* The individual, project, or section responsible for completing the task.
- *Budget:* The amount of dollars and/or other resources, such as machine time, allocated for completion of the task.
- *Staffing:* The number of people and/or person-months allocated to completing the project. (Note: If special skills or people are required, they would be indicated within the staffing column.)
- *Schedule:* The dates on which the project is to begin and end.

Figure 26 includes an example of one task. This illustrates the need to expand the billing system by adding a new product line. Although the actual document may expand on the information contained on this form, the addition of extra data is optional. The underlying theme of this book is to err on the side of too little administration, and then expand it as necessary, rather than overadministrate and control.

EDP ADMINISTRATIVE GUIDELINE 17

It is best to begin with too little administration and control, and then expand as necessary—but only a little at a time.

The testing of a data processing plan should fall into the following three categories:

Task Number	Task	Success Criteria	Area of Responsibility	Budget	Staffing	Schedule
12345	Incorporate product line X into the billing systems	All product line X products on the master files Product line X billing in compliance with pricing schedule Completed by June 1	Revenue system	$75,000	30 person-months	Begin Jan. 1, end June 1

Figure 26 *Data Processing Plan for the Year 19XX*

1. Reasonableness of accomplishing the plan
2. Compliance of company plan
3. Avoidance of duplication

It is easier to develop a plan than to accomplish it. Data processing peo-ple, by nature, tend to be optimistic. This optimism has affected the credibility of the data processing function. Many senior managers have little faith that the data processing professional can deliver the product stated, on the scheduled date, with the resources available. The plan needs to be tested to determine if it appears reasonable.

The reasonableness of the plan can be tested in any one or all of the following ways:

1. Evaluate the approximate amount of work to be accomplished this year versus last year. Adjust for staffing, and if this year's work appears larger or more complex than last year's work for the same staff, it probably cannot be accomplished.
2. Assess the difficulty and technical complexity of accomplishing the work in this year's plan versus the preceding year's plan. If the difficulty and technical complexity is greater in this year's plan than for that accom-plished with equivalent resources in previous years, the plan probably is not achievable.
3. Determine that the plan has left resources available for some undefined requirements. If the plan does not provide for undefined or unknown requirements that will have to be implemented, the probability of the plan being accomplished is minimal.
4. Prove the mathematics. The staffing person-months should not exceed the available personnel, work should not be scheduled so that it cannot be completed with the available staff on schedule, and the individual budget items should not exceed the total budget.

The plan should be tested for compliance with the company's plan. Items within the data processing plan should be a subset of the overall company plan. Compliance to the company plan can be tested by:

1. *Cross-referencing the data processing plan to the company plan:* If items within the data processing plan cannot be cross-referenced to needs in other areas, either directly or indirectly, they probably do not belong in the plan.
2. *Challenging both the letter and intent of both plans:* It is possible that the plans will appear consistent, but that when the intent is known, will vary.
3. *Reviewing the data processing plan with a member of senior manage-ment planning:* Normally, a quick review by someone knowledgeable

regarding the company plan can comment on the consistency of the data processing plan with the intent and objectives of the company plan.

The last test is to ensure that there is no duplication within the data processing plan. This requires that the reviewer fully understand the individual tasks. What the test is designed to accomplish is to identify tasks which are similar in nature, for further investigation. The type of tests that can be conducted here are:

1. *Key word searches:* If the same general words appear in different tasks, they can be investigated. For example, if job control language and JCL both appear in multiple tasks regarding improving the process, one might suspect duplication.
2. *Sorting by subject:* The tasks can be coded by key words indicating the subject and then sorted by those words. The administrative staff does the coding and the sorting. When apparent duplicates appear, they can be investigated.

Step 8.   Approval and Modification

At the completion of the planning process, plans must be approved by various levels of management. At a minimum, this normally involves data processing management and at least one member of senior management. Until approved, the plan is a proposal. After approval, it is an action document that serves as a basis for implementation.

If management rejects part of the plan, or adds or deletes tasks, the plan must be modified. If one believes in a planning life cycle, any change causes the plan to go back to the start of the life cycle and be rethought. In the steps proposed in this chapter, a change by management restarts planning back at the data-gathering process and then requires stepping through the process back to the approval step. Indiscriminately adding, changing, or deleting a task without reflecting the impact on the entire plan may cause implementation problems. On the other hand, it is not nearly as time consuming to repeat the steps a second time as it is to do them the first time.

AN ADMINISTRATIVE PLANNING CHECKLIST

Planning is a complex and tedious process. It is easy to overlook items that should be performed during the process. The planning checklist shown in Figure 27 is designed for two purposes. The first is to help develop a program for planning. The checklist indicates the types of items that should be included within a planning program. The checklist can also be used as a

Item	Response			
	Yes	No	N/A	Comments
1. Has the administration function established a planning process for the data processing department?				
2. Does data processing management concur with the planning process?				
3. Does the planning process include procedures to alert the persons involved sufficiently ahead of the planning process so that they can prepare properly for the process?				
4. Is data processing management supportive of the planning process?				
5. Is planning for the data processing function a subset of, or coordinated with, the overall organizational plan?				
6. Are continuing data processing requirements reevaluated during the planning process (e.g., is a zero-based budgeting concept used)?				
7. Are users requested to submit new requirements during the planning process?				
8. Are users requested to indicate services/systems/reports that they no longer will require in the next planning period?				
9. Are data processing personnel requested to supply input to the planning process?				
10. Does the department use the statistics gathered by the department to analyze work load and provide input into the planning process?				
11. Is the current charter (mission) of the data processing department one of the planning constraints?				
12. Are the resources available to accomplish the plan one of the planning constraints?				
13. Are constraints that will affect implementation of the individual tasks in the plan identified and associated with the plan?				
14. Are planning tasks prioritized in order of importance to the project?				
15. Are planning tasks prioritized in order of importance to the organization?				
16. Have the resources required to implement each task been identified?				
17. Has the cost of implementing each task been estimated?				

Figure 27   *Planning Checklist*   (continued)

Item	Response			
	Yes	No	N/A	Comments
18. Has a schedule been established to accomplish each item in the plan?				
19. Has the person/group/function responsible for each task been identified?				
20. Does the person accountable for each task know that he or she is responsible for implementing the task?				
21. Is the test plan reviewed for reasonableness?				
22. Is the test plan reviewed to ensure that it complies with the company test plan?				
23. Does the test plan contain any duplicate items?				
24. Has the test plan been approved?				
25. Does the planning process require that modifications to the plan go through the entire planning process to ensure that they do not negatively affect tasks in the plan?				

Figure 27 (continued)

self-assessment document to evaluate the completeness of the planning process at its completion. This checklist is designed for administrative personnel to use to assess the adequacy of the administration and control of the planning process. In using the checklist, a "yes" is indicative of a desirable answer, and a "no" indicates a potential weakness in the planning process.

EDP ADMINISTRATIVE GUIDELINE 18
Developing a plan means signing an undated resignation. Failure to accomplish a plan may mean your job.

Chapter

5

Estimating
and Budgeting

Estimating is the process of calculating the amount of resources needed to complete a task. The estimate is used by both the data processing department and the user department. The accuracy of the estimate depends on the need for which the estimate will be used. The estimate is the basic building block for the budget.

This chapter explains the administrative role in estimating. This role involves establishing the estimating process and overseeing the effectiveness of that process. Even though the administrative group may never make or evaluate the estimates, they should attempt to measure the reliability of the estimates produced by their estimating process and then adjust the process as necessary.

COMPUTER ESTIMATING—STILL A BLACK ART

It is said that any sufficiently advanced technology is indistinguishable from magic. To many, the computer qualifies as technological magic. Unfortunately, the magicians have had great difficulty in providing senior management and users of computer services with realistic estimates for their services. Many managers still joke about whether you should multiply the data processing estimate by 2, 3, 4, or 5 to approximate what the actual costs will be. This is no joke for the DP manager because it affects his or her credibility.

Estimating, in most data processing organizations, is still an art rather than a science. In many organizations each systems analyst estimates the cost of modifying the system, or the cost of building a new system using his or her own estimating system. Little guidance as to how to estimate is given to these persons because it appears that most people believe that computer systems personnel are born with the ability to estimate the cost of accomplishing a computer task. Even in many organizations that recognize that their estimates are poor, little is done to provide people with the tools needed to produce realistic estimates.

One data processing manager has a dartboard with different cost figures on it. When a user wants an estimate, the manager picks up a dart, throws it at the board, and says that whatever number it hits is the cost to do the job. Although this may seem funny at the time, poor estimating is representative of a poorly run data processing organization.

If you are unhappy with your organization's data processing estimates, ask yourself the following questions:

1. To what courses or seminars do we send our staff so that they can learn how to estimate? (If you do not, where did they learn how to estimate?)
2. Do you provide your people with feedback on the accuracy of their estimates? (If not, how do they know whether or not they are doing a good job of estimating?)
3. Are *all* DP estimates prepared using exactly the same method? (If not, how can you depend on consistency in estimating?)
4. If estimates are wrong, is an investigation undertaken to find out why? (If not, how do you expect to improve the process?)

Estimating should be viewed as a project within data processing. Estimating is a system whose requirements must be defined, a process implemented, and then adjusted as necessary based on the reliability of the estimates produced by the system. The development of this process is the responsibility of the administration function.

Developing a good estimating process means answering the following questions:

*   What is the purpose of creating an estimate?
*   What type of precision is required in the estimate?
*   Who should make the estimate?
*   What method should be used for creating the estimate?

CREATING AN ESTIMATING POLICY

Data processing management should develop an estimating policy. Without such a policy, it is difficult to develop procedures, standards, and guidelines that are supportive of the intent of management. With a policy, all of the methodology can be tied directly to that policy.

In developing the policy, management must consider whether estimating should be:

- Centralized versus decentralized
- Standardized versus customized
- Designed for a single purpose or multiple purposes, and if so, for which purpose(s)

Let us look at these managerial decisions individually.

Centralized versus Decentralized Estimating

Centralized estimating means that all estimates are processed through a single person or group. Decentralized estimating means that estimates are prepared by the person who will perform, or is responsible for, implementing the task. The centralized versus decentralized question is one of the key issues in most data processing policy decisions.

Estimating traditionally is decentralized. When work is required, the person responsible for implementing that work develops the estimate. In most instances, this is the project leader.

The purpose for decentralized estimating is twofold: first, to have the estimate developed by the person most knowledgeable on the project; second, to hold the estimator responsible for accomplishing the job within the estimate. This process works well as long as the estimator is effective in making the estimates. People who make bad estimates not only hurt the department but hurt themselves.

Centralized estimating is a newer concept and offers some advantages over decentralized estimating. It is consistent with the specialization concept that is used in many other aspects of data processing. The professional estimator, through experience and practice, should be able to provide more consistency than a wide variety of persons who make only periodic estimates. Note that once centralized, it can be automated.

The centralized estimator is equivalent to a service manager in a new car agency service department. When you drive your car into the service area of a new-car dealership, you are met by a service manager dressed in white. This person with a clipboard determines what is wrong with each car and then develops an estimate for repairing the car. The estimates are based on standardized charges for performing different services. If the problem is new and unique, and there are no standardized charges, the service manager must develop what he or she believes to be the best estimate.

If you accept the estimate from the service manager, the repair process begins. The estimate is given to the mechanic and the mechanic is paid based on how well he or she performs compared to the standardized estimate. If the mechanic can repair the car in less time than the estimate, he or she earns more money, whereas if the mechanic takes longer than allowed for in the estimate, his or her hourly wage drops. Although this concept works well in new-car agencies, it has some drawbacks in a data processing department. Notably, there are fewer standardized jobs in a data processing department than there are in a new-car dealership.

In centralized estimating, the estimator normally solicits the agreement of the project manager that the estimate is fair. If the project manager accepts the estimate, the work is to be done utilizing the resources determined in the estimate. On the other hand, if the project manager believes that the estimate is too low, the estimate is disputed. If the estimator and project leader can agree on an acceptable estimate, and the user still accepts that estimate, the work proceeds. On the other hand, if there is a dispute between the estimator and the project manager, a higher-level manager must decide what estimate will be used.

The estimating policy should state whether estimates are to be performed in a centralized or decentralized manner. If a centralized estimating function is used, that function should be part of the administrative group. The function is normally staffed with one of the more senior systems analysts, and that person normally uses informal procedures to estimate, because it is unnecessary to spend large resources formalizing a process that only one or two people may use. In smaller shops this can be a part-time function.

If estimating is decentralized, the administrative group should define the estimating methodology for the project people. The procedures should indicate what tools and techniques are to be used by the project personnel in developing estimates. The administration group should also help project people in developing estimates in the event that they have problems understanding or using the estimating process.

Standardized versus Customized Estimates

Many professions develop standards for use in their estimating process. In our previous example of the new-car dealership, a predetermined schedule of prices had been prepared for such services as tune-ups, new brakes, painting the car, and so on. Building trades develop estimates that include such concepts as the dollar per square foot cost for constructing a building.

Experience has shown that in most cases standardized estimates are as good or better than customized estimates. It also takes considerably less time to use a standard than to determine a customized estimate. Also, the standardized estimate can be used by people with minimal experience.

Customized estimates are those uniquely developed for each task. The estimator takes into account all of the variables and then tries to develop an estimate for accomplishing the job. In many instances, the estimator does not even need a worksheet or checklist to ensure that all the variables have been considered.

The argument in data processing for the customized estimate is that no two jobs are alike. It is also argued that there are some unusual variables that can cause a standardized estimate to be off by a factor of 2, 3, or 4. For example, the skill of the person installing the change may have a significant effect on the amount of time required to make the change. In the automotive garage and the building trades, we anticipate that the mechanics will have the necessary skills before they are given the job. In data processing it may take years to acquire the necessary skills.

Options are available to compensate for some of the unusual factors occurring within the data processing profession. For example, the standardized estimate could be multiplied by a factor to compensate for the skill level of the person performing the job. If the person was significantly less experienced than the standard anticipated, the estimate might be increased by 50 percent. This concept has proven effective in practice.

It is important for management to make a policy decision regarding using standardized versus customized estimates. If management does not make a policy, one project area may use customized estimates, and another, standardized estimates. In addition, both groups may do it with very little guidance. When management makes a policy decision, the administration function can develop the necessary procedures to implement that policy.

The Purpose of Estimating

The person making the estimate should clearly understand the purpose of the estimate. The type of estimate developed, the precision of the estimate, and the methods of presenting it will vary depending on the purpose. It is management's prerogative to establish the purpose or purposes for estimating work. Note that many data processing departments do not estimate the cost of doing work for decision-making purposes.

The four main purposes for developing estimates for computerized tasks are:

1. *Decision making:* The cost to do the job will be a factor in determining whether the job should be done, or how it should be done. For example, if it is extremely costly to do task X in the automated part of a system, the user may decide to accomplish the same objective by performing the task manually. Without knowing the cost, the decision as to whether or not to implement the task will be made on factors other than cost. Because this may result in projects that are not cost-effective, the cost of accomplishing work is a valuable input into the decision-making process.

2. *Planning:* The data processing function is given a variety of tasks to accomplish and resources with which to accomplish those tasks. Without knowing the amount of resources required to accomplish each task, the

manager of the data processing function will have problems managing. Without estimates, a manager will not know when to plan on the job being completed, so that those persons can be considered for additional tasks. Estimates are needed to develop both short- and long-range plans in order to have realistic scheduling.

3. *Performance measurement:* Estimates for computer tasks can be used to measure the performance of the person implementing those tasks. The estimate becomes the standard against which the person's performance is measured. Thus the standard becomes the objective in the management by objective philosophy. However, unless the quality of the work can be controlled closely, meeting the estimate may become the overriding objective, while the results produced by the task are ranked second to that of completing the project on time and within budget.

4. *Charging customers:* The estimate can form the basis for charging customers for work performed by the data processing department. In some organizations, the estimate may become a contract and the actual charge. In other instances, the EDP department guarantees that the charge will not exceed the estimate. In most organizations, the estimate is a planning figure and the charges made to the user are the actual resources expended. Because estimates can be dissatisfiers in the instances where actual charges far exceed estimates, they should be used with extreme caution when the customer's charge and the estimate may be two significantly different amounts.

One only has to put oneself in the place of a customer having a television set repaired for which the estimate is $100 and the actual charge is $275. The customer may be enraged, but if the estimate had been $300 and the actual charge $275, the same level of dissatisfaction would not have occurred.

Estimates can be used for any or all of the purposes noted above. It is important to the administrative function in developing the estimating methods to know management's intention for using the estimate. There are different approaches that can be used when the estimate is used for decision-making purposes than when used for chargeout purposes.

An Estimating Policy Statement

A sample policy for estimating is shown in Figure 28. This is a suggested policy for adoption by data processing management. Note that the policy should be adjusted based on management decisions in the three areas noted above. The recommended policy is that of the author, not that of any specific organization. In fact, very few data processing managers ever develop a policy on estimating, yet their subordinates develop procedures for implementing that policy without knowing what the policy is.

All tasks performed by the data processing department must be estimated before implementation. The purpose of the estimate is to provide the requester with sufficient financial information to make a decision regarding the cost/benefit of implementing the task requested. The estimate will also be used as a means of measuring data processing performance in completing the tasks.

Estimates are to be centrally developed using a standardized method for developing the estimate. The estimating process should be monitored and adjusted to ensure the continued reasonableness of the estimating process. It is the intent of the estimating process to provide estimates with sufficient precision to enable good business decisions to be made.

Figure 28 *Recommended Estimating Policy*

METHODS FOR ESTIMATING DATA PROCESSING TASKS

No one method for estimating data processing tasks has proved significantly more reliable than any other method. This is attributable to the following:

1. *Lack of management direction:* A clear policy and purpose for estimating has not been stated.
2. *Unskilled estimators:* Rarely does the data processing department train its personnel in how to develop highly precise estimates.
3. *Lack of a good method:* Few data processing departments have developed detailed methodologies for their people to use in creating the estimates.

FACTORS IN ESTIMATING

Many approaches are used in estimating. All of these methods utilize a common set of factors, although each method does not use all of the factors. In addition, the factors are used in different ways. One method may attempt to cost the factor, whereas another uses the factor subjectively.

One existing software package (ESTIMACS) has identified, through research, a number of factors that are believed to affect estimates for developing and maintaining application systems. We will examine these factors and show how they are related to an estimate for the development of a computer system.[1]

The basic premise in building an estimate is that gross business specifications (called project factors) are determinants of the estimate dimensions.

[1]"Interactive Macro-Estimation of Software Life Cycle Parameters," Howard A. Rubin, PhD., Management and Computer Services, Inc., 1982.

This can be visualized as:

PROJECT FACTORS--------->ESTIMATES

A tool constructed from this premise can yield some results that are even *more* important than the estimate. If capabilities for sensitivity analysis and feedback are incorporated in the implementation of the model, the estimate can be explored and understood. The consequence of this is better customer/developer communication and early exploration of alternatives.

This model structure can then be mapped into submodels for each estimating dimension. In each case, project factors are defined as being aspects of the business functionality of the target system that are well defined early-on, in a business sense, and are strongly linked to the estimate dimension.

The first step in building the submodel structure is to identify the key project factor determinants of each estimation dimension. A number of major works in the area of estimation were examined for common determinant threads. Most notably Barry Boehm has summarized the characteristics of the most "popular" estimation approaches. As described below, many universal factors were found and integrated into the model architecture. Using this research, coupled with recent productivity and maintenance studies as a base, the following submodel structures were developed:

Estimation Dimension	Project Factors
Effort hours	Customer complexity
	Customer geography
	Developer familiarity
	Business function size
	Target system sophistication
	Target system complexity
Staff/cost	Effort hours
	Staff productivity
	Skill level deployment
	Rate at each skill level
Hardware	System category (e.g. Batch)
	Generic system type (e.g. IMS)
	Operating window
	Transaction volume
Risk	System size
	Project structure
	Target technology
Portfolio	Resource needs of concurrent projects
	Relative project risks

These submodel structures and the aforementioned estimation path were originally implemented as the QUEST (QUick ESTimation system). Data was drawn from published studies as a foundation for the necessary statistical analysis. Early users of the system also cooperated in the validation of the models. Because of the interest in the system and the strong positive reaction of the initial users, it has been renamed ESTIMACS and integrated into the MACS line of productivity tools. (MACS is Management and Computer Services of Valley Forge, Pa., (215-648-0730).

ESTIMACS DESIGN PHILOSOPHY   *Read*

There are two purposes for using ESTIMACS. One is, of course, to generate reliable estimates in accordance with the definition of macro-estimation. The second is to decrease the level of uncertainty about system specifications through heightened customer/developer interaction.

In this second category ESTIMACS imposes a discipline for initiating projects in which a series of consistent questions are always asked. In responding to the questions, customers and developers may resort to three other techniques indicated by Davis for deriving requirements—deriving, synthesis, and discovery. The questions cover the following areas:

Effort Estimation

why are these used?

    Number of organizational units participating
    Number of geographic locations participating
    Mass of the units
    Experience of the customer
    Experience of the developer
    ○Level of customer management concurrence on system objectives ○←
    Quality of customer developer relationship
    Possible team structure
    Possible team geographic deployment
    System size—number of business functions, number of business inputs, outputs, data bases, files
    Familiarity with business functions and their current degree of automation
    Envisioned operational environment
    Type of system
    Criticality of the system

Back-up and recovery criteria
Specific load and/or performance criteria
Logical business complexity
Expected rate of business adaptation
Longevity of the business application

Staff/Cost

Projected effort to develop/maintain system (derived from effort estimator)
Work hour availability of different skill levels
Application of skill levels to project work
Cost for each skill level
Charges for computer resources

Hardware

Operational window of the system
Loads imposed by existing systems that may run concurrently
Business transaction volume
Operating characteristics of existing or planned hardware
Generic system type
Number of terminals to be used

Risk

(Virtually all of the information collected in the three aforementioned models is passed on with the following supplemental information requested)
Degree of change required to implement the system procedures or hardware
Flexibility
Level of confidence in responses to other model questions
Management commitment

Portfolio

Anticipated start times for all new work
Current background workload
Level of risk of all work
Staff deployment for each project (derived from the other models

In order to enable participatory development, macro-estimation must be viewed as more than a process by which values are input to a model and the resultant outputs are observed. It is a process of interaction, exploration, and understanding. In fact, macro-estimation itself is a design tool by which implementation tradeoffs can be explored in all of the critical dimensions to increase the level of customer/developer awareness of their linkages.

The implementation of the ESTIMACS submodels uses the form of a highly graphic programmed instructional exercise. A personal computer was chosen as the vehicle because of its ability to be "embraced" by its user. This is meant in the sense of operational complexity and familiarity. Additionally, the graphic features available on personal computers can only be duplicated at high cost on mainframe systems. The objectives of an ESTIMACS session are to generate a meaningful estimate AND to understand it. To this end, there are four discrete states that the user passes through during estimate formulation:

1. Data input/Estimate evolution—in which data is supplied to the model and during which the estimate continually evolves. In this way an initial sense of cause and effect relationships is conveyed to the user.
2. Estimate summarization—in which all aspects of the completed estimate are displayed.
3. Macro-sensitivity analysis—in which major project factors are related to their contribution to the total estimate.
4. Micro-sensitivity analysis (not possible in all the submodels)—in which individual inputs are related back to the total estimate and ranked in importance.
5. Revision—in which any input may selectively be modified and the entire estimate is recomputed. The user is returned to the Data input/Estimate evolution mode.

All work performed during a session is saved for later alternatives analysis and printing.

THE ESTIMACS MODELS

All models have been implemented on the Apple II + and IBM personal computers.

ESTIMACS SYSTEM DEVELOPMENT EFFORT ESTIMATOR

This module is used for the estimation of software development effort in terms of total effort hours.

Critical project factors include information relating to the developer's knowledge of the application area, the complexity of the customer organization and its geographic dispersion, and the size, sophistication, and complexity of the target system as expressed in business terms. Information is entered in two major question sets which relate to the "soft" (organizational) and "hard" (system description) project factors. The first set requires the user to answer eight questions, the second, 17. The model utilizes a data base of life cycle phases and relative work distribution. This data base is customizable in both terminology and quantitative content. Output includes project work effort in hours by project phase displayed both in graphic and tabular form. An estimation bandwidth is produced which varies along a scale of relative business complexity of the system. This aspect of the estimate is derived from function point based research. Projected function point values are also displayed as a basis for comparing the relative size of systems. The primary focus of this model is exploration and understanding of the elements of total project work effort.

ESTIMACS STAFFING AND COST ESTIMATOR

Utilizing the result of an effort hour calculation developed from the previous model, this module estimates staff needs at each development life cycle phase and related personnel costs.

Additional inputs include employee productivity, and salary for each skill level. Again, a customizable life cycle data base is used to provide work distribution and deployment information. Outputs include team size by phase, distribution of staff, cost by phase, and cumulative cost. Peak resource load values are displayed along with peak costs. Experimentation with all input parameters and computed parameters, such as elapsed time, is possible.

The primary focus of this model is the exploration and understanding of the relationship between team size, cost, and project duration.

ESTIMACS HARDWARE CONFIGURATION ESTIMATOR

This model is used to size the operational resource requirements of the target system.

The model can accommodate both batch and online work loads. Input parameters include operating window for the application, total expected transaction volume, and generic application type. If the target system does not match one of the pre-defined categories, capacity planning data may be entered. The model output is a time of day graph showing required processor power by hour along with peak channel and secondary storage requirements to ensure adequate service times. The data base of processors and device characteristics is customizable.

The primary focus of this model is analyzing the impact of adding the target system to the organization's operating portfolio.

ESTIMACS RISK ESTIMATOR

This model is used to approximate the level of risk associated with successfully implementing the proposed system.

The model is based largely on the Dallas Tire Case and takes input in the form of answers to approximately 60 questions covering the project factors of size, structure, and technology. Answers to about 30 of these questions are generated by use of the other ESTIMACS modules. Outputs include both graphical and tabular display of the elements of project risk along with a sensitivity analysis identifying the major contributing responses. A portfolio of multiple projects can be created for planning analysis purposes.

The focus of this model is an understanding of the major contributing factors to the risk of the project. In this way tradeoffs which minimize risk can be formulated and evaluated.

ESTIMACS PORTFOLIO ANALYZER

This model allows the concurrent effects of up to 20 projects covering 10 years of work to be viewed.

Input to this module comes from both the *Staff/Cost Estimator* and the *Risk Estimator*. Projects can dynamically be scheduled on a Gantt chart. Displays of total staffing by skill level, cumulative cost, monthly cash flow, and relative risk are available. Comparisons of alternative portfolios and their implications can be displayed.

The primary focus of the module is the understanding of the resource demands of concurrent projects and the peak loads generated by them.

USER EXPERIENCE

A large number of major organizations ranging from consulting firms to financial institutions to manufacturers have been using ESTIMACS for the past 18 months. It has had a broader impact on the systems development process than anticipated. Basically, five major impacts have been noted.

First, the estimates have been shown to be reliable. Estimate uncertainty is at its highest level early in the life cycle. ESTIMACS forces both the developer and customer to focus clearly on the major determinants and define them accurately early in the project. This greatly decreases the uncertainty of the macro-estimate and has brought it into the range of 15%.

Second, ESTIMACS has brought the developer and customer together by having them share in the estimation process. This once "black magic" technique has new visibility and credibility.

Third, long-range planning can be performed with more credibility and a greater number of alternatives can be tried and analyzed. ESTIMACS enables portfolio planning.

Fourth, productivity metrics which have been hard to impose on the systems community have become accepted. In many instances, developers have rejected function point and software science metric data collection as being an added burden to their work without any payoff. ESTIMACS collects such information as an added value to the estimation process and has made such efforts possible.

Fifth, ESTIMACS increases application development productivity particularly along the customer/developer interface. It has fostered the participatory design process. Interestingly enough, most users of the system have identified the improvement in the customer development relationship as the greatest benefit of the system. The generation of reliable estimates is viewed as a secondary effect.

Conclusion

A feeling expressed universally by developers is that they must get the customer more involved in the system development process. The concept of participatory design has evolved from this need. As is the case in psychological therapy, third party intervention is often necessary as a catalyst for communication. Interactive macro-estimation via personal computer is a third party focal point for broadening the bandwidth of customer/developer communication, clarifying the communication, and increasing the certainty of the estimation process.

ESTIMATION METHODS

The administration function responsibility is to provide, maintain, and teach an effective estimating method. The methods most frequently used in data processing are:

- Judgment
- Historical
- Breadboarding
- Component
- Risk

Each of these methods will now be discussed.

JUDGMENT METHOD

Judgment relies on the skill of the estimator to develop a realistic estimate. In most instances, the people using this method are those who are, first, knowledgeable in the area where the task will be implemented, and second, normally responsible for implementing the task. The prime advantage of this method is that the person estimating is most knowledgeable in the project, but one disadvantage is that because that person will be held accountable for the estimate, there is a possibility that the person will estimate high.

Judgmental estimating generally can be improved if the estimators are required to document those estimates. A sample judgmental estimate documentation form is shown in Figure 29. The objective of this form is to require the estimator to document those criteria upon which the estimate is based. The purpose of the form is to force the estimator to think through the proper criteria rather than to develop estimation documentation. On the other hand, the documentation can be used for experience in developing a better estimate or estimating procedure.

The information requested on the judgment estimating worksheet is:

- *Need:* The description of the task being estimated.
- *Skill level:* The types of persons required to accomplish this task successfully.
- *Constraints:* Any limitations that will be placed on people in implementing this task.
- *Affected areas (programs):* All of the software, programs, job control language, operating systems, hardware, training, documentation, and so on, that will be involved within the implementation of this task.
- *Estimating factors:* The criteria considered by the estimator in completing the estimate. For example, these might be number of records changed, types of documentation to be completed, and so on.
- *Estimate:* The people, machine, and other resources needed to implement the task.
- *Staffing levels:* The number of people that can be assigned at any one time to the task.
- *Estimated precision:* The precision for which the estimate was calculated. For example, the estimator believes that the estimate is accurate within plus or minus 25 percent.

The sample estimation documentation included in Figure 29 is for a maintenance change to the payroll system to add a dental health insurance plan. Judgment was used by the payroll project leader to develop the estimate.

Need: Add a dental health insurance plan to the payroll system.	
Skill Level: System analyst and programmer with minimum of two years' experience with payroll system.	
Constraints: Must be completed by 10/1/XX.	

Programs: Affected Areas
Programs: 1313A (data validation)
              1313B (update)
              1313C (ins. calculation)
              1313D (report writer)	

Estimating Factors: Four programs to be one-third rewritten and/or extended.	
Estimate: 400 hours	
Staffing Levels: • 1 system analyst—200 hours • 1 programmer—200 hours	
Estimated Precision: ±20%	
Comments: Must start by 3/1/XX to finish on time.	
Prepared by: M. Murphy, Payroll Project Leader	**Date:** 2/1/XX

Figure 29   *Judgment Estimating Worksheet*

HISTORICAL METHOD

The historical method utilizes the past experience of the project or organization in developing an estimate. It is similar to judgmental, but uses the quantitative experience of the area. In the simplest format, the experience could price the average cost of a change and then use that standardized price for future estimates. This is similar to a restaurant charging one price for all dinners, or a fixed price for a smorgasbord. In more sophisticated uses the experiences are categorized to provide guidance in making future estimates. In our previous example, we might know that in this system it requires 100 hours to make a major modification to a program or that a previous change, such as a tuition aid benefit, had taken 400 hours.

BREADBOARDING METHOD

Estimates are just what they claim to be—estimates. Except from the perspective that they may affect a decision to implement or nonimplement, the quality of the product is not affected by the estimate. The estimate is merely information provided to people to help them to plan, decide, or manage the project. The end result may be the same whether or not the effort required was estimated.

One must then ask: What is the purpose of estimating? If it is to provide general guidance, a general estimate will suffice. Breadboarding is a method designed to accomplish just that.

The breadboarding method attempts to decide the approximate size of the task to be accomplished. Once the size has been estimated, the estimator goes to a table and selects an estimate. It must be recognized that the precision of this estimate may not be great, but it may be precise enough to satisfy the purpose of the estimate.

Breadboarding is then a two-step process, as follows:

1. *Determine the size of the task*. This is normally done by an experienced person who categorizes the effort into one of several classifications. The one being suggested in this chapter has 12 categories, which are lettered A through L. A is the smallest task that will carry an estimate, and L the largest. The estimator begins by determining if the task is a type A, B, C, and so on.

2. *Select the estimate from a breadboarding table*. The method proposed in this book uses estimates from 50 through 10,000 hours. In a series of 12 categories, the estimator selects an estimate within that range. Those organizations using this concept state that the actual effort comes within a reasonable tolerance of the breadboarding estimate. The suggested breadboarding estimates for ·his method are:

A = 50 hours	G = 1500 hours
B = 100 hours	H = 2000 hours
C = 200 hours	I = 3000 hours
D = 400 hours	J = 5000 hours
E = 750 hours	K = 7500 hours
F = 1000 hours	L = 10,000 hours

The advantage of breadboarding is that it is quick and reasonably accurate. The disadvantage is that it forces all estimates into categories, which in the larger categories may be several thousand hours apart. If the precision within breadboarding becomes too exact, the benefits of breadboarding are lost. For example, if 30 to 40 categories are used, the estimator almost has to go through customized estimating before he or she can pick one of the breadboard categories. As long as there is a reasonable span between the categories, estimators can, with reasonable accuracy, choose the category that normally approximates the actual hours. For example, they might pick 3000 hours and the actual estimate would be 3750 hours, but in many instances that is close enough to fulfill the purpose of estimating.

COMPONENT METHOD

In the fields that perform estimating, component estimating is one of the most common methods. In this method, the estimator works from a list of the charges to implement an individual component. In calculating an estimate, the estimator identifies all of the components and then accumulates the cost for implementing each individual component. The total cost is the estimate.

The component method provides for high precision with little effort expended during the estimating process. On the other hand, an extensive amount of time may be required to develop the table of estimates for individual components. Thus, although the method is easy to use, the process may be costly to develop.

The key to successful component estimating is the identification of the components. If the actual effort required to implement components can be measured, the estimates for those components can easily be developed. If components are selected for which it is very difficult to determine the amount of resources required to implement the component, the creation of good estimates is difficult.

The administration function is the group that should identify the components and develop the charges for implementing each component. A suggested method of components, with suggested hours, is illustrated in Figure 30. The components are not meant to be exhaustive, but rather, the more common components used in systems development and maintenance. The hours selected are generalized but are meant to approximate the values that could be used in estimating. An organization may want to experiment with some of these values for a grouping of recently completed tasks. If the estimates produced by this table closely approximate the actual expenditure of resources, the table can be used as is. If the actual estimates vary significantly, the values in the tables should be changed.

In using the component method, a worksheet should be provided to the estimator. The worksheet would be very similar to the table provided in Figure 30. Two more columns would be added, one for number of components used in this task and the one for total hours. At the bottom of the total hours column would be a grand total, which would be the estimate.

The component method is designed primarily for the project leader to

Name of the Component	Hours to Implement Component
Change/replace data element	10
Add data element	20
Compilation	
Easy	5
Average	10
Complex	20
Data edit	15
Record search/match	10
Update one to three data elements	10
Update more than three data elements	15
Change one report variable	5
Add report variable	10
Add/change report variable requiring computation	10
Add/change system of controls	20
Complete one-page narrative documentation	5
Update one to three documentation forms	5
Change operating software parameter (e.g., JCL)	5
Create one to three pages of preprinted form documentation	5
Conference with user	5

Figure 30   *Component Estimating Table*

use. It has the advantage of centralized estimating in a decentralized manner. The administration function determines the method and basis for estimating, and the project leader implements that method.

RISK METHOD

Risk estimating is one of the newer methods for estimating. It is normally used in conjunction with one of the other methods. The objective of the risk estimate is to identify the degree of risk so that the other estimate can be modified accordingly. The assumption is that high-risk projects will take longer to complete than low-risk projects.

The concept of risk is one evolved from the insurance industry. A risk is a condition that may result in a loss. If these conditions (i.e., risks) can be defined, the probability of a task not being implemented successfully can be determined. Insurance industry uses this to determine whether a person is insurable. The risk conditions for people are high blood pressure, history of medical problems, overweight, old age, and so on. The more of these conditions or risks that a person possesses, the less insurable they become.

The insurance concept can be applied to data processing. We determine what criteria cause data processing systems to fail. These become our risk conditions. If a proposed task possesses a large number of these conditions, the probability of being successfully implemented is low if a normal estimate is given. If the risk is taken into consideration in developing the risk, we increase the probability of successful implementation.

Let us look at an example. Suppose that a small subsystem is estimated to take 1000 hours to complete. An analysis of this subsystem shows that the project personnel lack some needed skills, and the subsystem aggressively pushes technology and has very complex logic. Intuitively, we know that this may be a difficult system for the team to implement. If we can identify the risk and then upgrade the estimate to, say, 1500 hours, the probability of it being successfully installed within the estimate increases significantly.

A risk estimating worksheet is provided in Figure 31. This worksheet identifies 17 risks associated with computer systems. The more of these conditions that are present in any task, the higher the risk.

For each of the 17 risks, 3 risk points are allocated. Three points are given in the highest risk condition, 2 points for an average risk condition, and 1 or no points for low or nonexistent risk conditions. Let us look at the first risk indicator. The worksheet indicates that if the value of assets controlled by the task is high, 3 risk points should be allocated, 2 risk points if the value is medium, and 1 if the value is low.

The risk estimating worksheet uses generalized terms to define the degree of risk. In actual practice, these generalized terms should be converted to specifics. For example, in discussing the value of assets controlled by the EDP system, high may be over $1 million, 40 percent of the budget, and so on. However, experience in the organization must be used to determine the values assigned to high, medium, and low. For example, $1 million in assets may be very high for a small corporation, but very low for a large corporation. Even the values for items such as number 5, user involvement, should be converted to such things as percent of time expended in developing the task, number of hours, or some other meaningful value. As much judgment should be removed from the checklist and replaced with factual conditions as possible.

The estimator using this concept would pick out one of the other estimating methods, such as component estimating, and develop an estimate using that method. The estimate should be developed for a task of average risk. The risk is then adjusted according to the number of risk points.

Risk Criteria	Risk Points
1. Value of assets controlled by task	
High 3 points	3
Medium 2	
Low 1	
2. Probability of fraud (assets controlled by system)	
Cash 3 points	3
Merchandise 2	
Large assets 1	
None 0	
3. Regulatory agencies receiving reports from system	
Over two 3 points	2
Two 2	
One 1	
None 0	
4. Senior management commitment to task	
High 1 point	1
Average 2	
Low 3	
5. User involvement	
More than average 1 point	2
Average 2	
Low 3	
6. Auditor involvement	
More than average 0 points	2
Average 1	
Low 2	
None 3	
7. Size of system staff	
Large 2 points	2
Medium 1	
8. Size of project	
Large 3 points	2
Medium 2	
Small 1	
9. Use of technology	
Pushes technology 3 points	3
Old technology 2	
State of the art 1	
10. Skill level of EDP project team	
Highly skilled 1 point	1
Average skills 2	
Low skills 3	
11. Turnover of EDP staff	
High 3 points	1
Average 2	
Low 1	

Figure 31 *Risk Estimating Worksheet*   *(Continued)*

Risk Criteria		Risk Points
12. Security/privacy level needed		3
Tight security	3 points	
Average security	2	
Low security	1	
13. Complexity of logic		2
Very complex	3 points	
Average complexity	2	
Low complexity	1	
14. Time span to install		2
Tight	3 points	
Average	2	
Easy	1	
15. Skill level of user in EDP		1
High	1 point	
Medium	2	
Low	3	
16. Skill level of EDP personnel in user area		1
High	1 point	
Medium	2	
Low	3	
17. Adequacy of controls		2
More than adequate	1 point	
Adequate	2	
Less than adequate	3	
Total Risk Points		38

Figure 31 (continued)

A project of average risk should score 25 points. For each point above or below 25, the estimate should be adjusted by plus or minus 4 percent. For example, a task scoring 26 points would receive 104 percent of the calculated estimate developed by using any of the previous methods, and a task scoring 24 risk points would receive 96 percent of the estimate calculated previously.

The risk estimating worksheet (Figure 31) has been completed for a demand deposit banking system for a commercial bank using teller terminals with online updating. The system is a replacement for a batch system. Note that it received 38 risk points, so the estimate calculated should be increased by 42 percent (i.e., 13 risk points over 25 times 4 percent per point, or 42 percent) over the estimate developed for an average system of this scope.

Estimating Precision

The precision produced by the estimate should be consistent with the use of the estimate. The more management and users rely on the estimate, the greater the precision required. For example, if staffing will be obtained based on the estimating process, the staff acquisition may be off by several people if the estimates are off. On the other hand, if the estimate is used only for planning purposes or decision purposes, high precision may not be required.

Some organizations work at different levels of precision, depending on the time in the task development life cycle or the type of precision needed in using the estimate.

One organization uses the following precision throughout their system development life cycle:

- *Requirements phase:* Estimate should be accurate within plus or minus 50 percent.
- *Design phase:* Estimate should be accurate within plus or minus 25 percent.
- *Programming phase:* Estimate should be accurate within plus or minus 10 percent.

Managers requesting estimates should be asked the precision required of that estimate. They may be given options as follows:

- Precision plus or minus 100 percent
- Precision plus or minus 50 percent
- Precision plus or minus 25 percent
- Precision plus or minus 10 percent

Depending on the desired precision, the method for estimating can be selected. For example, if the estimate is required only within plus or minus 100 percent, judgment may suffice. On the other hand, when very high precision is required, the estimate may be prepared using one or two of the methods above to determine that the same estimate is obtained by different methods. If not, additional investigation will be undertaken to determine the variance between the different methods.

Selecting an Estimating Method

The method selected for estimating should be consistent with the purpose of the estimate. This principle has been reiterated throughout the chapter. A matrix cross-referencing the estimating purpose with the five estimating

Method	Purpose			
	Decision Making	Planning	Performance Measurement	Charging Customers
Judgment	✔			
Historical		✔	✔	✔
Breadboarding	✔			
Component			✔	✔
Risk	✔	✔		

Figure 32 *Estimating Method/Purpose Matrix*

methods is illustrated in Figure 32. This is intended as a guide for the administrative manager in making decisions about which estimating method to select based on the purpose of estimating as outlined in the data processing estimating policy.

ESTIMATING METHODOLOGY

A six-step process is recommended for estimators to follow in developing an estimate. This methodology assumes that the administration function has developed methods for estimating and has trained the estimator in the use of these methods. The six-step process is as follows:

1. Define required precision.
2. Define requirements.

3. Define estimating factors.
4. Develop estimate.
5. Challenge estimate.
6. Document estimate.

Step 1. Define Required Precision

The desired precision should be determined before any estimating work is undertaken. In some instances, a user may only need to know if the task is going to cost a thousand dollars or a hundred thousand dollars. Many users of data processing services have no idea what something may cost. What they perceive to be complex is cheap to install, and what they perceive as easy to install is very costly. Having clearly established the desired precision, a logical estimating process can continue.

Step 2. Define Requirements

The key to the estimating process is a good definition of the task being estimated. Too frequently, the estimator has only an approximate idea of what is wanted. This may be satisfactory if the desired precision is low.

The types of requirements will vary by the estimating method. For example, if the component method is used, sufficient detail must be obtained to describe the component. Other methods require slightly different requirements. It is recommended that organizations use the same form and process to define requirements for estimating as they do in accepting a job for implementation.

Step 3. Define Estimating Factors

There are many factors that should be considered in developing an estimate. The risk estimating method has described 17 criteria that can affect the reliability of the estimate. These are fine for a worksheet to develop a risk score, but it is far too complex a process for people to consider intellectually.

The organizations that have studied estimating in depth have identified 25 factors that should be considered by every estimator. Among these, the more important factors are:

- *Time span:* The length of time allocated to implement the task. For example, very short time spans may put undue pressure on the project team.
- *Skill level of implementation team:* If known, the skill level can significantly affect the ability to install the task within the estimated resources.

Low skills should be allocated more time than that allocated to teams that are highly skilled.

- *Structure:* The complexity of the structure affects the amount of time needed to install it. The more complex the structure, the longer it normally takes to install a task.

- *Technology:* The more aggressively technology is used, the more difficult it is to install a system. Using technology aggressively can be measured in two ways: first, it can be aggressive for the skill level of the people; and second, it can be aggressive for the state of the art of the technology. For example, immediately after a new technological advance is released, the use of that feature requires the implementers first to learn it and then frequently to debug it for the vendor.

- *Size of task:* Large tasks are proportionately more complex than small tasks. The extra complexity is partially due to communication between the people involved in implementing the task, and partially to defining and maintaining the interaction between the variables within the task.

The risk estimating method takes these factors into account. However, if risk estimating is not used in conjunction with one of the other methods, the estimator should take these factors into account. If the factors indicate that it will be more difficult than normal to implement the task, additional resources should be estimated; on the other hand, if the task appears easier than normal, fewer resources should be allocated.

Step 4.   Develop Estimate

The estimator should select the appropriate method and develop the estimate. This would be performed in accordance with the methods described previously. Sometimes it may be advantageous to estimate two ways to ensure that all probabilities have been considered.

Step 5.   Challenge Estimate

Estimates should be developed by one person and challenged by another. If centralized estimating is used, the person responsible for implementing the task should be the challenger. If the implementer of the task is also the estimator, it may be good to have the estimator's supervisor challenge the estimate.

The estimate should be challenged in the following ways:

1.   Challenge for reasonableness.
2.   Challenge regarding the inclusion of the appropriate risk factors.
3.   Challenge based on previous experiences of the implementing team.

Step 6.   *Document the Estimate*

Laws in a number of states require that estimates to customers by public businesses be in writing. This is a good practice for all estimates. Verbal estimates can easily be forgotten and later challenged. Written estimates cannot. Normally, the estimates are documented on the worksheet, and the requester is given a copy of the worksheet, or a memo stating the estimate if the calculations would not be of value to the requester.

USING ESTIMATES FOR CHARGEOUT PURPOSES

It is considered a good control to charge users for their services. This makes the user accountable for the resources they consume; whether the user is charged is a management decision. It is important to keep in mind that low estimates are dissatisfiers. To offset this, many data processing organizations guarantee that the actual cost will not exceed the estimate. Other professions also use this concept. The author believes that it is a good one. One data processing department artificially increases all estimates by 10 percent and then guarantees that the estimate will not exceed the amount of the estimate, and in fact may be less.

It is recommended that if the data processing department is unwilling to guarantee that the costs will not exceed the estimate, a precision figure be included on the estimate. For example, the user would be guaranteed that the actual charges will not exceed 120 percent of the estimate. A variation of this concept is to require that user approval be obtained if the actual costs will be greater than 20 percent above estimate. Whatever method is selected is not as important as the fact that a method *is* selected.

EDP ADMINISTRATIVE GUIDELINE 19

Estimates are only as good as the credibility of the estimator. The only method to improve the credibility of the estimator is to make good estimates.

ESTIMATING CHECKLIST

As administrative groups develop estimates for budgetary, planning, and decision-making purposes, they should be continually assessing the process. The checklist shown in Figure 33 is provided for administrative managers, to help them assess the adequacy of their estimating process. A "yes" answer is indicative of a good estimating practice, and a "no" indicates that a potential estimating weakness exists and should be investigated.

Item	Response			
	Yes	No	N/A	Comments
1. Has data processing management created an estimating policy?				
2. Are all estimating procedures tied to the estimating policy?				
3. Have the data processing staff, or central estimator, been trained in estimating?				
4. Have one or more methods for estimating been adopted?				
5. Have worksheets, training sessions, and manuals been prepared on how to use those estimating methods?				
6. Has the purpose for estimating been determined?				
7. Are the actual costs compared to the estimates to determine the reliability of the estimates?				
8. Is the estimating process changed if the reliability of estimates is considered inadequate?				
9. Do estimates take into account the various risk factors, such as skill of project team, structure of system, use of technology, etc.?				
10. Do requesters of estimates indicate the precision required for each estimate?				
11. Are estimates documented and given to the requester?				
12. Does someone in a responsible position challenge each estimate before it is used?				
13. Can requesters of tasks rely on the fact that actual costs will not vary significantly from the estimates?				
14. Are the estimators satisfied with the estimating process?				
15. Are the requesters satisfied with the estimating process?				

Figure 33 *Estimating Checklist*

Chapter

6

Scheduling and Status Reporting

Data processing is a production process. The computer center produces processing results while the systems development and maintenance areas produce systems. The data processing department normally operates as a production job shop.

Scheduling systems vary in complexity from simple Gantt charts to the complex mathematics of critical path scheduling. The simpler methods can be performed manually, whereas the more complex methods are best performed by computer. Generally, the small organization can survive with manual scheduling, but the larger data processing organizations should acquire a scheduling software package.

The objective of this chapter is to discuss the policies, strategies, prioritization methods, and criteria for scheduling. The mathematics of the more advanced scheduling systems are complex and will not be discussed in this book. In this chapter the criteria of a good scheduling system are discussed—those that should be considered when acquiring a scheduling software package.

SCHEDULING POLICY

The key to effective scheduling begins with a data processing management policy on scheduling. This policy should define management's intent. Without this definition, scheduling may be inconsistently applied, and management may not support the work schedule.

A suggested scheduling policy is illustrated in Figure 34. This policy is designed to serve as a basis of discussion in developing a specific scheduling policy. Obviously, the policy must be consistent with other management policies, especially the estimating policy.

The objective of the data processing department is to satisfy user requirements. To help accomplish this objective, a scheduling system shall be used to schedule and track jobs. The method of scheduling should minimize the resources allocated to complete a task unless the project's target date precludes that option. Those tools necessary to facilitate scheduling should be acquired and used.

A scheduling system will be implemented with the objective of improving the productivity of the work flow. All tasks implemented by the data processing department are to be included within the scheduling system. However, the schedule as prepared should allow for sufficient slack time in order to handle a reasonable number of emergency and unplanned tasks.

Figure 34 *Suggested Scheduling Policy*

THE SCHEDULING CYCLE

Scheduling is a continuous function within the data processing department. Schedules are prepared in support of the annual plan and budget, but those schedules need to be modified and updated as requirements change.

Schedules are normally updated in accordance with management scheduling periods. In some organizations, detailed scheduling is done monthly, in others, quarterly, and in still other departments, weekly. Although this may seem unorderly, there is a scheduling cycle which is the basis for planning and developing schedules.

The scheduling cycle as illustrated in Figure 35 is comprised of four phases.

1. *Identify scheduling attributes.* The tasks from the planning process become input into the scheduling cycle. The types of information that must be gathered for an effective scheduling system include the resources, relationships, size, and prioritization of tasks. These attributes are discussed later in this chapter.

2. *Prepare acceptable schedule.* The tasks must be matched with the resources in accordance with the scheduling attributes. It is unusual when there is only one best schedule. Normally, there are many schedules that will accomplish the desired tasks with the resources available. What must be done during this phase is to develop schedules and then apply judgment to determine which appears to be best. Note that in automated scheduling systems, most tasks can be accomplished by the computer.

3. *Report on status of schedule.* Workload status must be reported on a regular basis. Ideally, this status comes out of either the staff or job accounting system. The results of this phase will be reports indicating whether the tasks are ahead of schedule, on schedule, or behind schedule. The concepts of status reporting are discussed in a later section.

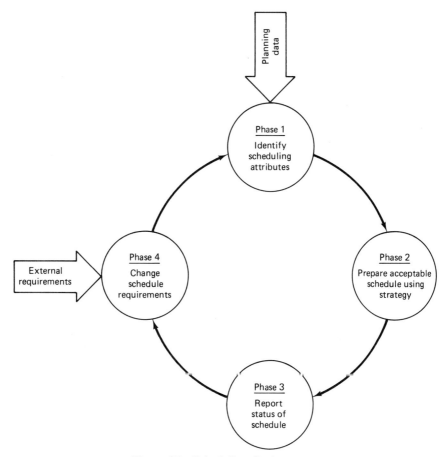

Figure 35 *Scheduling Cycle*

4. *Change schedule requirements.* An analysis of the status reports, plus new external requirements, will result in changes to the requirements going into the scheduling system. The external requirements will be initiated by users of the computer resources, and changes due to the status of work to date will be developed from analysis of the status reports. Normally, these changes are developed in conjunction with user personnel.

The new changes are then fed into phase 1 of the scheduling system so that the attributes of those changes can be determined. For example, tasks behind schedule may require changes in priorities to ensure that the schedule date is not missed. When the attributes have been identified, a new schedule is prepared and implemented. Status reports are now made from that new schedule, which will result in more changes, and the cycle continues.

PHASE 1: IDENTIFY SCHEDULING ATTRIBUTES

The approved tasks from the planning phase become input to the scheduling phase. Associated with these tasks are several attributes. These attributes are used to develop the schedule. Any scheduling system must consider these attributes while developing a schedule.

These six scheduling attributes, together with suggestions on how to define them, are as follows:

1. Type of task
2. Date required
3. Size of project
4. Priority of project
5. Skills/resources needed
6. Relationship to other projects

These attributes are described briefly with examples in Figure 36.

Type of Task

The scheduling system should be provided information on the categories of tasks to be scheduled. This is important because the types of resources needed to accomplish a task can be categorized in the same manner. These categories should coincide with the type of work performed by the data processing department.

A sample list of categories, together with codes that can be used to define each category, follows:

A = hardware selection/upgrade

B = operating software selection/upgrade

C = interface between hardware/operating software and application systems

D = application systems (note that a separate category should exist for each application system—in addition, the maintenance aspect of an application system might be separated from the developmental efforts)

E = administrative/planning tasks

F = outside consulting services

G = training

Attribute to Be Considered	Description	Example
1. Type of task	Area for which the task will be performed	Computer operations XYZ application system
2. Date required	Date on which task should be completed	February 22, 19xx 3 months after task B
3. Size of project	Magnitude as expressed in dollars, hours, and/or processing load	$40,000 650 hours 85,000 records to process weekly
4. Priority of project	Importance this project gets in relation to other projects	Number 1 priority Prerequisite to installing New operating system version
5. Skills/resources needed	Type and/or quantity of resources/ skills needed to complete the task	Data base skills Statistical sampling utility program
6. Relationship to other projects	Description of the sequence in which events must occur (if applicable)	Task B must be completed prior to this task Hardware device x needed 3 months prior to the completion of this task

Figure 36 *Attributes of a Good Scheduling System*

H = technical support services (e.g., develop standards)

I = other (specify)

Date Required

The scheduling system works from the dates supplied the system. In the simpler system, only start and stop dates are required. In the more advanced scheduling systems, checkpoint dates are added.

It is important that the dates supplied to the scheduling system be realistic. If groups begin asking for tasks prior to when they need them, just so that they get done, the scheduling system may not maximize the use of data processing resources.

Although it is a difficult task to police dates, it is an important task in ensuring that the scheduling system fulfills its intended mission. The administrative function should spot check the reasonableness of the dates supplied by users. This does not mean that administration should second-guess when a user says that he or she needs a project but rather, determine if the projects are used on the dates supplied. Users who continually ask for a task to be completed weeks or even months before they are needed should be reminded of how their requests affect the needs and requirements of other users.

Size of Project

The magnitude of the task or project to be performed must be indicated. The variables that can be input to the scheduling system are specified by automated systems and dictated in the procedures for manual systems.

The size of the project can be measured by any or all of the following dimensions:

- Number of people to be allocated and the time frame for which they will be allocated
- Amount of dollars
- Number of hours to complete the task
- Volume of records
- Amount of computer time
- Amount of storage space required
- Capacity required
- Type of people required, such as one project leader, two analysts, four programmers, and so on
- Technical support services
- Administrative/clerical support services

One scheduling system may not be able to encompass all facets of a task. For example, if the task requires clerical support, computer time, and user personnel, it may require several scheduling systems or a master scheduling system to accomplish the needed scheduling task.

Priority of Project

Priority systems have traditionally meant "doing what I want when I want." Unfortunately, what is best for an individual user may not be best for the organization. Priority systems limited to single projects or users should be reconsidered when there is a move in the organization toward integrated systems or data base technology.

One study by a large public accounting firm showed that in the United States there were over 50,000 different payroll systems. The conclusion was that a common application such as payroll did not appear to warrant 50,000 versions. Unfortunately, there are probably as many or more versions of priority algorithms.

Priority methods can be categorized into five general categories. These are listed below, shown with their advantages and disadvantages in Figure 37, and then described.

1. Customized by project
2. First in–first out
3. Ranking
4. Classified by group
5. Classified by business concern

CUSTOMIZED BY PROJECT

Under this method, the project leader and the user develop a mutually agreeable method for prioritization, and then implement that method. Although the method developed may be one of the other four described methods, the method will not be used consistently throughout the data processing depart-

Method	Advantage	Disadvantage

Customized by project	No restrictions
	Adaptable to project
	   needs
		Inconsistent
		Does not consider
		   organizational need

First in–first out	Treats everyone fairly
	Priority does not change
		May not let important
		   jobs be finished first
		Does not consider
		   organizational need

Ranking	Lists projects in
	   order of importance
	Meets user's current
	   needs
		Each new task requires
		   ranking all incomplete
		   projects
		Does not consider
		   organizational need

Classified by group	Easy to apply
	Common priority system
	   for all projects
		Does not prioritize
		   within group
		Does not consider
		   organizational need
		Easy to abuse

Classified by business
   concern
	Takes business priorities
	   into consideration
	Common priority system
	   for all projects
		Does not prioritize within
		   group
		Requires knowledge of
		   business

Figure 37 *Advantages and Disadvantages of Priority Methods*

ment. In a company there are no restrictions on how priorities are established. Any project can adapt any priority system acceptable to their user needs. The priorities developed this way will be inconsistent when viewed from other projects, and this may make it difficult to differentiate which task has the higher priority when comparing several project areas.

FIRST IN–FIRST OUT

This method takes whatever tasks are received first and implements them first. The method can be applied department-wide or by individual projects. It normally means that each task is dated or sequentially numbered so that its spot in a queue is ensured. The method has the advantage that it treats everyone fairly because the priorities do not change. On the other hand, a more important job received after a low-importance job would have to wait until the job of lesser importance was completed. If management overrode the process frequently, the advantages of the first in–first out method would disappear.

RANKING

The ranking method requires that all uncompleted tasks be ranked 1 through n. One is the most important task, which will be completed first; n is the least important task and it will be completed last. When a new task is entered into the queue, all of the tasks are ranked again. Note that there is probably little reranking within the group, but the new task or tasks may be interspersed among the current ranking. This method offers the advantages that it lists the important tasks first, and that the prioritization method meets users' current needs because of the continual reranking. The disadvantages are that the reranking process may have to be performed almost daily and like the other methods previously discussed, may not permit the comparison of the importance of tasks within different projects unless all users use the ranking criteria equally.

CLASSIFIED BY GROUP

This is one of the more common priority methods. It is used by IBM in their operating software. A prioritization scheme is developed showing different classes of priorities. These priorities may be given letters, such as A, B, C, D, or names, such as urgent, very important, important, and average.

   In this method, a new task is merely given the appropriate classification. It is then put into the system in line with other tasks of that same priority. For example, if a new task was determined to be a class A priority, it would be put ahead of all of the B, C, and D priorities. The advantage of this method is that it is easy to apply and it uses a common system for all projects. The disadvantages are that it does not prioritize within the individual classifications. For example, there is no way of telling which class A priority should be implemented first. The normal method is to use the first in–first out concept within a classification. The other disadvantage is that the system is easy to abuse. For example, normally all class A tasks are completed before all class C. Thus, if I wanted to get my work ahead of another user, I would use the highest possible classification. If many users begin this practice, the process disintegrates.

CLASSIFIED BY BUSINESS CONCERN

This is one of the newer methods of prioritization. It uses the classification concept, but rather than classify by importance, it classifies by business concern. The organization attempts to rank these business concerns in the order of their importance to the business.

A prioritization system using business concerns to classify tasks follows:

- *Gain competitive advantage.* The task requested will provide the organization with an advantage in the marketplace over their competitors.
- *Increase revenue/decrease expense.* The purpose of this task is to perform work in a more economical way. The results will either be more sales and thus greater revenue, or reduced cost and thus greater profit.
- *Improve management decision information.* Managers use computer-produced information to make decisions. The more reliable that information, the better decisions a manager can make.
- *Reduce fraud.* The change will reduce the opportunity for people to defraud the system, or reduce the maximum amount that can be defrauded.
- *Correct record keeping.* Remove inaccuracies that are occurring in the record-keeping system.
- *Comply with legislation.* Conform to new regulations, or correct misinterpretations of existing regulations.
- *Comply with company policies, procedures, and/or standards.* Conform to new policies, procedures, and guidelines or correct misunderstandings of existing policies, procedures, and standards.
- *Comply with generally accepted accounting procedures.* Present accounting information in accordance with the standards of the accounting profession.
- *Avoid/reduce business interruption.* Take those steps necessary that will reduce the probability of business interruption.
- *Prevent/reduce loss of assets.* Take those steps necessary to reduce the probability of assets being lost.
- *Improve effectiveness/satisfaction.* Perform those tasks that will enable work to be performed more effectively and/or more to the liking of the user.

Each user requesting a change under the priority classified by business concern must list which of the categories above is addressed by the task. This has the advantages that it takes business priorities into consideration and establishes a common priority system across different projects. The disadvantage is that the system does not prioritize within the group or classification, and it requires a knowledge of the business to establish the appropriate priority.

This prioritization method has two significant advantages over all other methods. First, it turns data processing priorities into business priorities. Without this type of concept, what is desperately needed to assist the business in the marketplace may receive a lower priority than complying to a data processing standard because of the way people prioritize them using one of the other methods. Second, this method permits easy analysis of the priorities within a variety of systems. Thus, if one system had a group of priorities relating to increasing revenue and was short of people, while another project was only attempting to improve the effectiveness of its system, resources could be shifted to handle the major business needs first.

Each organization views priorities slightly differently. Therefore, a business priority setting worksheet is provided in Figure 38. This is to permit each organization to rank the 11 business priorities in the order in which they believe they should be ranked. For example, if they believe that compliance with

Business Priority	Priority Ranking
1. Gain competitive advantage	
2. Increase revenue/decrease expense	
3. Improve management decision information	
4. Reduce fraud	
5. Correct record keeping	
6. Comply with legislation	
7. Comply with company policies, procedures, and/or standards	
8. Comply with generally accepted accounting procedures	
9. Avoid/reduce business interruption	
10. Prevent/reduce loss of assets	
11. Improve effectiveness/satisfaction	

Figure 38   *Business Priority-Setting Worksheet*

legislation should exceed gaining a competitive advantage in the marketplace, they would rank complying to legislation as 1 and gaining competitive advantage as 2.

Using this system, status reports could be put out showing the amount of backlog of work and the business purpose for which that backlog exists. This should be much more meaningful to management than merely stating that there is a 12-month backlog of work, or an 18-month backlog, and so on.

EDP ADMINISTRATIVE GUIDELINE 20

Using a priority system for data processing that is consistent with the mission of the organization puts data processing in step with senior management.

Skills/Resources Needed

One of the prime objectives of the scheduling system is to match needs against resources. To do this, the resource must be defined. The simpler the definition of resources in the scheduling system, the less effort that has to be put into defining this attribute.

The resources of the data processing department should be inventoried. This is not a physical inventory of hardware but rather, an inventory of resources. Among the items that should be inventoried are:

- Processing capacity
- Data storage capacity
- Skills availability (number of staff members by category, together with their skill level)
- Technical support resources
- Administrative/clerical resources, including training

If the tasks define the resources/skills needed, there should be a corresponding inventory of available resources to satisfy those tasks. As the resources keep changing, so must the inventory, and thus the input into the scheduling system.

One of the challenges that has faced data processing departments is how to identify the skill level of the professional staff. Obviously, skills can be segregated by functions such as systems analysts, application programmer, system programmer, and so on. It is beyond that level where it becomes more difficult. Pay grade and years of service are two criteria that can be used. Unfortunately, some older systems analysts have allowed their skills to get "rusty" and although they have the pay grade and the years of service, they are not technologically proficient with the new hardware and software. Some say that a 10-year employee can have one year's experience 10 times.

One administrative group developed a solution to that problem. They created a skill score, just like the risk score that was described earlier for estimating purposes. The skill score took into account the following bits of information:

- Educational achievements
- Certifications acquired
- On-the-job experience
- Professional development training
- Individual self-study

The points attributed to these skills are totaled to find the skill level of the person, recognizing, however, that if a person does nothing, his/her skills will deteriorate. Therefore, each year a predetermined number of points are subtracted from the skill score which, if replaced, maintains the same skill level; if surpassed, increases the skill level; if the person does nothing, the skill level will drop.

A listing of the specific criteria and suggested skill points is included in Figure 39. These need to be adopted for specialized types of training, such as video courses, computer-aided instruction, and so on. The scores allocated in Figure 39 should provide guidance as to how to determine ratings for other types of educational and job experiences.

Each year a person should be evaluated on his or her performance for the year. The total award at the end of one year becomes the beginning number of skill points at the start of the next year. The calculation would be as follows:

Previous year skill score	XXX
Plus points awarded during the year	+ XX
Less technical obsolescence of existing skills	− 4
Total skill points at the end of the year	XXX

Some managers use this to demonstrate the changing skill level of their data processing department. It is like accumulating the dollar value of your assets. When the skill points are accumulated for all of the personnel and departments, a movement from year to year is quite obvious. For example, it might show with the same staff a 5 percent increase in skill, or 7 percent, and so on. This is useful to show senior management how the skill level of their data processing resource is changing. If that skill level should drop, it should be of concern to management and perhaps corrective action would be needed.

Skill/Experience/Education	Skill Points	Criteria to Earn Skill Points
College education, full-time work, all levels	4	Awarded for each full year of schooling
Individual college courses taken during the work year (must be job related)	1	Awarded for each college course
Continuing professional educaton	1	Awarded for one full week (40 contact hours) of continuing professional education or equivalent
Professional certification, such as CDP (certified data processor)	4	Awarded for each certificate
Seminar/conference speaker/ leader	1	Awarded for each full day of instruction or presentation
Joining/attending professional association meetings (local)	1	Attending a minimum of 75% of the meetings during a year
Read a current technical book	1/4	Awarded for each book read, up to a maximum of 1 point
Review periodicals regularly	1/4	Awarded for each periodical read regularly, assuming a minimum of 12 issues per year, up to a maximum of 1 point
Develop administrative pro- cedures/standards/technical guidelines for the entire department	1	Maximum per year for this effort
Participate in an EDP quality circle	1	Attend 75% of all quality circle meetings for a year
On-the-job experience in data processing	2	Awarded for each full year of data processing experience
Technical obsolescence award: Due to the rapid growth of data processing, skill points are removed from each individual each year	− 4	One point for each quarter of the year worked is removed from the total individual skill score due to the technical obsolescence of previous knowledge

Figure 39   *Data Processing Skill Points*

> ### *EDP ADMINISTRATIVE GUIDELINE 21*
>
> You cannot manage what you cannot measure. By measuring the skill level, departmental managers can manage the skill levels of their staff.

Let us look at how we calculate a skill score:

Joe has a college education (4 points), is a CDP (4 points), and has worked in DP for five years ($5 \times 2 = 10$ points). Joe has a total skill score of 18 points.

This year Joe worked all year in DP (2 points), went to one week of training (1 point), read four technical journals ($\frac{1}{4} \times 4 = 1$ point), and wrote a DP standard (1 point), for a total of 5 skill points during the year.

Joe's new skill score is calculated as follows:

Skill score at the start of the year	18
Plus points awarded during the year	+ 5
Less technical obsolescence of existing skills	− 4
Skill score at the end of the year	19

Relationship to Other Projects

Tasks in data processing are frequently related to other tasks. The sequence in which they are performed is important. In addition, having sufficient time to accomplish all of the tasks that must be performed in sequence may affect the ending date of the project. For example, if six one-week projects must be performed in sequence, in other words, project 2 cannot start until project 1 completes, then even by assigning extra people the project could not be completed in less than six weeks.

Most priority software requires only that each task indicate which other task or tasks must be completed before this task can be started. Normally, it is only one task, unless the tasks are in unrelated projects.

This information will be used to build the critical path through the project system. This is the path that establishes the minimum time in which the project can be done. These critical tasks should be scheduled first to ensure that the project will be done within the minimum or prescribed time frame.

PHASE 2: PREPARE ACCEPTABLE SCHEDULE

Numerous options are available for scheduling. These options are built around management scheduling strategies. Using these strategies, the scheduling program attempts to balance work load with resources. The actual process can be manual or automated.

Scheduling Strategies

A variety of options are open to data processing management for scheduling work. These strategies should be studied and a scheduling policy adopted to select the strategies desired by management. Unless a positive policy statement is made by management, strategies will be selected by default. It is even possible that different strategies will be used by different groups within the data processing function for the same purpose. However, one strategy might be used for systems development and another for computer operations.

The four basic strategies that management should consider are as follows:

1. Full scheduling versus built-in slack time
2. People versus job scheduling
3. Block versus variable scheduling
4. Simple versus complex scheduling

FULL SCHEDULING VERSUS BUILT-IN SLACK TIME

Data processing management must determine what percent of the DP resources they desire to schedule. It is extremely rare for data processing departments to schedule at 100 percent capacity. The real question is not whether slack time will be included in the schedule, but how much and for what purposes.

In determining slack time, management must consider what would be considered, first, full capacity for:

- People
- Computer
- Schedule

and second, what percent of each of those variables they want to schedule.

People capacity is normally measured in terms of hours per year. In a 52-week work year, a person has 2080 hours available. However, it is unrealistic to assume that they will work 2080 hours. Management must then subtract nonproductive time. This includes holidays, vacation, sick time, training, administrative work, and so on. For planning purposes, many organizations have adopted 1600 hours as a reasonable work year per person.

Computers can operate 24 hours a day, seven days a week. Again, it is unrealistic to assume that all of these hours would be productive. The computer will be nonproductive when being maintained, when hardware fails, when shut down for holidays, internal housekeeping, and so on. Many organizations have picked 16 hours per day as the maximum productive time for hardware.

Once these decisions are made, management must then decide what percent of the remaining capacity will be scheduled and what will be left for contingencies. It may be realistic to further reduce the workload by 10 percent to account for these unaccountable factors. Depending on the volatility of the organization, data processing departments allot anywhere from 10 to 33 ⅓ percent of the capacity for unplanned work.

EDP ADMINISTRATIVE GUIDELINE 22
Planning for unplanned work is a good plan.

PEOPLE VERSUS JOB SCHEDULING

The scheduling process must schedule either jobs or people. Obviously, both are included in the schedule. The question is: Which is the primary basis for scheduling? The strategy selected will be dependent on data processing management's perspective of what they want to control.

Professional firms, such as certified public accountants and lawyers, are concerned primarily with scheduling people. They view their resources as people, and thus attempt to maximize the use of their people. This establishes a scheduling objective as full scheduling of people.

Other production environments, such as automotive service centers, schedule jobs. This sets the objective of controlling jobs as they move through the organization. Obviously, both are important, but it is difficult to control both at the same intensity.

The advantage of controlling people is that they may possess different skills and capabilities, and through controlling people we can maximize the use of resources. On the other hand, the data processing function is a service function and should be concerned about completing jobs. Most data processing departments put their primary emphasis on jobs, which poses a potential vulnerability for the ineffective utilization of people. When people are emphasized, it is important to know their skills, future workloads, and so on.

BLOCK VERSUS VARIABLE SCHEDULING

Block scheduling schedules a "block of resources" to accomplish a task. Variable scheduling identifies the optimum staffing level and schedules people according to that level. Again, rarely does an organization use pure block scheduling, but on the other hand rarely do they use effective variable levels of staffing.

Block scheduling is the easier of the two methods. The method recognizes that there will be different levels of staffing during the project, but does not attempt to be too specific in exact staffing levels. For example, three people might be allocated for requirements, five for design, and eight for programming and testing. As the time approaches for the task to be completed, personnel will be assigned in accordance with the block estimate as they become available.

Variable estimating, on the other hand, attempts to optimize the productivity of the project through staffing. Staffing levels are selected based on productivity analysis. The variables that need to be considered in staffing for productivity include:

- System development life-cycle phase
- Relationship between work load and time span to complete work load

These concepts and the differences between block and variable scheduling can be explained by looking at different staffing curves. Figure 40a shows a block estimating curve. This shows that for each phase of the life cycle X number of people are assigned to complete that phase. It is recognized that all of the staff may not be assigned all of the time, but for scheduling purposes staff is allocated to the project. Note that during this phase some of the phase may be completing a previous project, and after the phase is completed, those staff members may still have odds and ends to do to complete the project.

Figure 40b shows variable scheduling. Five different curves are shown for a project, although many more curves exist. The curves represent the time span to complete with various staffing levels. Curve A results in the project being completed first, but may not be the most cost-effective way to complete the project. For example, curve E may use fewer resources to complete the project than curve A, but take longer to do it.

The mathematics of variable scheduling can be complex. One large bank has borrowed the Rayleigh curve concept from industrial engineering. The objective of this curve is to determine the type of staffing that is required to complete a project within different time spans, as well as determining the optimum staffing level to complete the project with minimal resources. Readers interested in this type of scheduling should study and use the industrial engineering Rayleigh curve concept.

Figure 40c represents the relationship between systems development and maintenance staffing. The curve assumes that these are distinct projects. In other words, one team develops the project, and the second team completes the project. In this concept there is a turnover period which is represented on the curve. The developmental project completes the project and stays with it until shortly after it goes into production to finalize loose ends. However, prior to implementation the maintenance team begins to learn and take over the project. The curve shows the scheduling of the two groups and the overlap between the groups, which results in the project being relatively constant throughout development and maintenance.

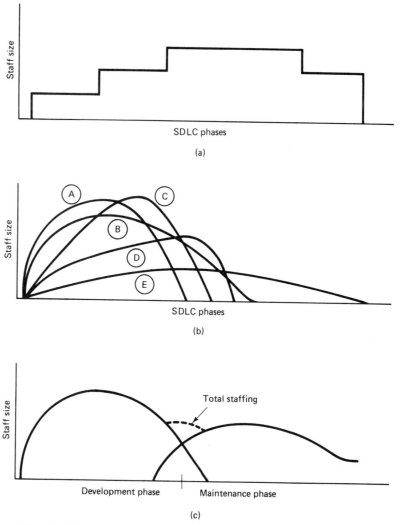

Figure 40 *Staff Scheduling Curves: (a) Block; (b) Variable; (c) System Development/Maintenance*

SIMPLE VERSUS COMPLEX SCHEDULING

Small data processing organizations should use simple scheduling methods, whereas larger functions may need complex methods to ensure the effective utilization of resources. Data processing organizations of fewer than 25 people can normally schedule their work manually. Although a computer scheduling package may be helpful, it is rarely necessary. On the other hand, as the size of the organization begins to exceed 25, the need for an automated package becomes more apparent.

The complexity of scheduling is also dependent on the type of work and the managerial style of the function director. If the staff is committed to a few large projects, meaning that assignments are long in duration, staffing becomes easier. On the other hand, as the number of tasks increases, so does the need for an effective scheduling system. Note that as the data processing function matures, the number of maintenance tasks increases, which complicates the scheduling of jobs. Criteria for selecting scheduling software are discussed later in the chapter.

Scheduling to Balance the Data Processing Risk

Data processing traditionally has had problems meeting schedules. This has undermined the credibility of the department in the eyes of senior management and users. Although the reasons for the missed schedules are understandable, they are frequently not excusable in the eyes of management—not excusable from the perspective that data processing failed to recognize and plan for these contingencies within their scheduled work plan.

A new philosophy is developing in scheduling, called the "balanced risk portfolio." The objective of this concept is to balance the risk of the scheduled tasks against the skill levels of the people assigned to implement them. The process is first done in general terms for annual planning, and then is done in assigning staff to specific projects. Those organizations that have balanced their risk have found that they are doing a better job at scheduling their work and improving their own credibility.

The concept is simple in theory and is not difficult in practice if the appropriate scheduling attributes have been identified. The two primary attributes needed for the balanced risk portfolio approach are:

- Skill scores of professional staff (see Figure 39)
- Project/task risk score (see Figure 31)

The objective of the process is to balance the risk score against the skill score of the staff. Those projects that are of high risk should be performed by staff with high skills; medium-risk tasks, by staff with medium skills; and low-risk tasks, by staff with low skills.

Interpreting the risk score and skill scores into high, medium, and low, we can easily perform this match. The breakdown of the skill scores and risk scores using the method outlined in this book is illustrated in Figure 41. If the number of tasks and staff is relatively low, this match can be performed manually.

It must be recognized that risk balancing is a planning tool. It is not meant to be highly precise. Judgment should be used by the persons balancing the risks so that a reasonable work portfolio is prepared. The guidelines presented in Figure 41 should serve for preliminary planning purposes.

Level of Risk/Skill	Applicaton Risk Score	Individual Skill Score
High	34–50 points	40–up points
Medium	18–33 points	21–39 points
Low	0–17 points	0–20 points

Figure 41 *Balanced Risk Portfolio Score Categories*

An annual balanced risk portfolio plan can be developed using the worksheet illustrated in Figure 42. All of the applications/tasks requiring data processing staff should be listed on this worksheet in the appropriate section. In other words, all high-risk applications/tasks are in the high-risk part of the worksheet. The person-months of effort for each application staff that will be expended during the planning years should be listed. Next, all of the staff members with high skills are listed in the high-risk part of the worksheet. These can be listed individually or in total. The worksheet is then completed for medium and low tasks and for staff with medium and low skills.

The person-months of work are now totaled in the three categories, as is the available staff resources in each category. Then the assessment begins.

The assessment starts with the high-risk category. If the available staff

Risk	Application/Task	Person-Months	Staff	Disposition
High	1215	8	A	Second half
	1617	10	B	First half
	1814	7	C	Second half
	1913	23	D	First half
	2314	9	Not enough staff	Delay
Medium	4320	16	E	First half
	1699	11	F	First half
	1733	9	G	Second half
	1255	4	H	First half
	1943	13	I	Second half
Low	1173	8	J	Second half
	1249	17	K	First half
	1533	8	L	First half
	1817	12	M	Second half
	1955	6	Not enough staff	Delay

Figure 42 *Annual Balanced Risk Portfolio Planning Worksheet*

equals or exceeds the person-months needed, the portfolio in the high-risk category is assumed to be balanced. If the available staff with the needed skills is less than required, management must make one of the following three decisions:

1. Delay the project until the appropriate skills become available.
2. Add members to the staff with the appropriate skill level.
3. Contract the project to an outside contractor.

The exercise continues downward to the medium- and low-risk projects. The objective of the exercise is to avoid data processing management accepting projects of a level of risk (i.e., complexity) when they do not have the staff to complete that project successfully. This is what many people believe has caused a loss of credibility of the data processing function.

The same concept can be used in developing quarterly, monthly, or plans for a specific task or project. The risk of the project is stated and then staffed accordingly. Note that every staff member assigned to a high-risk project does not have to be a highly-skilled person. What we are really looking for in this exercise are the key personnel who are going to make the project work and can adequately supervise staff members with lower skills.

A simplified example of the balanced risk portfolio is illustrated in Figure 42. This assumes that person can do 12 person-months of work per year. In the example, there are not enough highly skilled personnel to do the high-risk applications. Therefore, application 2314 is delayed while the other high-risk applications are scheduled for either the first or second half of the year. Enough adequately skilled staff is available to do all of the medium-risk applications, with some time left over. This time can be directed either downward, which should ensure a good job, or upward, with the associated risk of being unable to do the work satisfactorily. In this example, the downward path was chosen. Since there was more work than staff, application 1955 also had to be delayed.

Selecting Automated Scheduling Software

Numerous software packages are available for scheduling. In addition, many organizations develop their own scheduling package, although this factor should be discouraged. The characteristics that an organization should look for in this software in addition to running on the organization's hardware and being reasonably priced are:

• Inclusion of the scheduling attributes described previously
• Easy-to-use forms
• Predesigned collection system for status information
• Simple training materials

- Critical path scheduling
- Simple straightforward input
- Scheduling of iterations that show relationships between time frame and staff size
- Algorithms that consider cost-effectiveness in developing a schedule

Several data processing organizations are acquiring microcomputers for scheduling purposes. These micros can be purchased by the administrative function and run by them. Many of the micros have scheduling software and except for very large and complex organizations, this may be a very cost-effective way to schedule. It permits administrative personnel to experiment with different mixes of work to develop the most effective schedule for the department. An added advantage is that the administrative group has continual access to scheduling information.

PHASE 3: REPORTING SCHEDULING STATUS

A major error made in most status systems is that the information reported is used for evaluating performance. This places people in a position of personal conflict. If they report status information accurately, and it may have a negative impact on their performance, they may be reluctant to report that status information accurately. On the other hand, if the status information is not used for performance evaluation, the probability of getting good information increases.

The following three strategies are recommended for developing a meaningful status reporting system:

1. *Report on status of work—not hours.* Knowing hours expended is of some value, but not much value, in evaluating status. Work should be divided so that there are checkpoints or deliverables to be produced during the execution of the task. Status should be reported against completing these deliverables or arriving at checkpoints. It may not even be necessary to report hours or days worked. This is important only when those hours are used to charge users or to evaluate where the system or estimate may have fallen short, and this frequently can be accomplished by a separate accounting system.
2. *Report status on a timely basis.* People may forget to report certain types of accomplishments if an extended period occurs between when the event happens and when it is reported. The method selected to report status should enable the staff to report status in some manner as soon as a noteworthy event has occurred to report.
3. *Implement status as a by-product of the development system.* The best reporting system is one in which the system itself reports status. If through

some system action, the status of work is recorded, that information should be captured for the scheduling status reporting system. In addition, if data are reported into other systems, such as accounting or time-keeping systems, data should be captured in those systems for status reporting purposes wherever practical. The less people have to do, the more accurate the status information should be.

Attributes of a Good Status Report

Most status reports are dull. They are difficult to read, crammed with both valuable and meaningless information, and are often presented in formats that are difficult to understand. Status information should be management information and not accounting information.

A good status report on the data processing workload should possess the following attributes:

- Graphs, charts, pie diagrams, and other pictorial representations of status are used.
- The reader's eye is directed toward problem areas.
- Detailed information is omitted from the main status reports (detailed information can be placed in appendices).
- It is short in length.
- It is sent to the person who is responsible for the status.
- It is delivered to the person responsible for taking action in the event that the status is not on target.

PHASE 4: CHANGE SCHEDULE REQUIREMENTS

The schedule should be revised periodically throughout the year. Many DP organizations do this quarterly unless the process is automated, in which case the revision is done monthly.

The quarterly or monthly schedule interprets the annual plan into a detailed work program. The annual plan must be modified to take into account changes in workload, new requirements, and changes in staff and technology.

It is recommended that one person be made responsible and accountable for scheduling throughout the year. This responsibility should include:

1.   Obtaining new requirements
2.   Monitoring work status to determine what jobs are ahead or behind schedule and by how much
3.   Updating people and technology resources
4.   Updating job priorities

Item	Response			
	Yes	No	N/A	Comments
1. Has the data processing department established a scheduling policy?				
2. Does the schedule provide sufficient capacity to handle expected contingencies?				
3. Is the scheduling system divorced from a performance appraisal system?				
4. Is a scheduling system divorced from a time-reporting system?				
5. Does the scheduling system report status of measurable work?				
6. Does the priority system take into account business needs?				
7. Is the priority system such that it is difficult to abuse?				
8. Can the priorities in one area be equated to the same priority category in another area?				
9. Does the scheduling system take into account the risk of the project?				
10. Does the scheduling system take into account the skill level of the staff?				
11. Does the scheduling system attempt, at least annually, to balance the risk of the projects against the skills of members of the staff performing those projects?				
12. Is most of the scheduling information produced as a by-product of the production systems?				
13. Do all members of the data processing department use the same priority and scheduling system?				
14. Are regular reports produced on the status of the schedule (e.g., monthly)?				
15. Is the schedule adjusted to reflect new requirements from users?				
16. Is the schedule adjusted to reflect differences between the actual status and the scheduled status of work?				
17. Can the data processing department measure the changing skill level of the staff?				
18. If the professional staff numbers more than 25, has an automated scheduling system been evaluated?				
19. If an automated scheduling system exists, does it possess the following attributes? a. Type of task b. Date required c. Size of project d. Priority of project e. Skills/resources needed f. Relationship to other projects				

Figure 43 *Scheduling Checklist*

5. Updating job risks
6. Updating the balanced risk portfolio
7. Developing detailed work schedules as frequently as appropriate
8. Acquiring and managing scheduling software and status reporting system

A SCHEDULING SELF-ASSESSMENT CHECKLIST

The checklist shown in Figure 43 is provided for the administrative manager to assess the scheduling and status systems. The self-assessment checklist is structured so that "yes" answers represent good scheduling practices, and "no" answers represent areas for investigation and potential improvement. It is recommended that this checklist be used periodically so that the program is assessed on a regular basis.

Chapter

7

People Management

Professional real estate sales people say that the three most important things in selling a home are location, location, and location. It could be restated to say that the three most important things about managing the people in a data processing department are communication, communication, and communication. In general, data processing professionals are poor communicators.

Managers who are good communicators run good departments. Managers who are poor communicators continually have people problems. In the experience of most people, it is not the personnel policies and procedures that count but rather, the ability of data processing management to communicate with and motivate the data processing staff.

This chapter analyzes the data processing environment and categorizes it into areas of communication. Guidelines are provided on how to improve communications in those areas. The basics are also covered, such as personnel policies, but they are discussed in a supportive role, as the basis by which people are managed.

THE CHALLENGE—COMMUNICATION; THE REWARD— IMPROVED PRODUCTIVITY

The telltale signs of poor people management are easy to detect. Some of the more common signs of demotivation and people turnoff are:

- High turnover rate (even if salary is cited as the reason)
- High absenteeism; late arrivals and early departures
- Excessive errors and omissions
- Disputes with users and within the staff
- Excessive use of punishments and reprimands

Many data processing professionals who are good technically are promoted into managerial positions. However, many like the technical part more than the managerial part. Sometimes this philosophy emulates from the manager and a philosophy of working supervisors is developed. This philosophy can lead to no supervision, which is symptomatic of the breakdown in communications.

W. Edward Deming, the person recognized for the turnaround in the Japanese economy through quality concepts, states that one of the key elements in a quality environment is well-trained and active supervisors. However, Deming goes on to explain that this is a role of a counselor and communicator and not a role of heavy work direction and measurement. Once these concepts are in place, Deming states, productivity increases rapidly.

The Administration Role in People Management

EDP administration has two major roles in personnel management. First is the pure administrative role of record keeping, policy development, and communicating information to the data processing staff. The second role, and one that is extremely important, is that of a public relations department for the data processing function.

A public relations firm is involved in two activities. The first is a data-gathering activity regarding potential problems and their solutions; and the second is to present their client in the best possible light. Administration must keep its hand on the pulse of the data processing department to identify problems. It is also the responsibility of the administrative manager to look for ways to improve communication, staff comradery, and the image of the data processing department in the eyes of the staff and outside parties.

It is important that the administrative personnel be good communicators in order to fulfill this mission. The administrative personnel should also assess the supervisors' ability to communicate effectively with the staff and among themselves. When weaknesses are perceived, the administration group should take corrective action to improve communications.

ELEMENTS OF GOOD AND BAD COMMUNICATION

Communication is an art that takes time to master. It also takes time to conduct effective communication. Unfortunately, too many data processing personnel do not want to take the time to communicate. And when they do communicate, it is usually in a staff meeting talking about projects or problems as a group, which frequently results in one part of the group taking sides against the other—poor, poor communication.

There are books written on how to communicate and not communicate. Most of these are applicable to the data processing profession. However, some are more applicable than others to the data processing profession. Let us look at the elements of good and bad communication.

How to Stifle Communications

Data processing management did not invent ways to stifle communication, but many have perfected the technique. Some of the anticommunication methods in use are:

- *We did it before and it didn't work:* Rather than listening to determine whether a new wrinkle or concept has been added to an old idea, which may be the key to why it did not work in the past, the supervisor flatly rejects the idea as one tried and proven false.
- *Martyrdom statements:* Supervision has untold problems and must work day, night, and weekends to get them accomplished. Such phrases as "I worked on them last night" or "I'll do it this weekend" tell people that basically their problem is that they do not work enough hours.
- *The sterile environment:* Many managers act like people didn't exist. Everything is related to the machine. Even *Time* magazine named the personal computer the man of the year in 1982. Equating people to machines does not provide the type of empathy and interface needed to conduct a good conversation.
- *Comparisons:* The manager compares what is being done to what has been done somewhere else. It is frequently a way of belittling the individual in that they either fail to equal the performance of someone in another company or within their own company. Experience, work conditions, and so on, are all ignored and just flat comparisons made.
- *Prophecy:* The DP manager frequently tells you what is going to happen in a degrading manner. Such comments as "You'll shut down the computer" or "It will never work" do not form the basis for a good discussion when someone is looking for help.
- *Lecturing:* The senior technician talks to the junior technician from a vast background of experience. When a simple question evokes a college lecture, it is a one-way conversation to which the staff person may turn off.
- *Attacking with a barrage of questions:* The systems analyst is trained to inquire, so that in many supervisory subordinate conversations the supervisor treats it more as an interrogation than as a conversation.
- *Interrupting or changing the topic:* Many DP managers attempt to hurry the conversation and put words into the subordinate's mouth, change the topic, or interrupt the subordinate's train of thought to get a fact that is important to the supervisor.

Elements of Good Communications

We said that the attributes of a good home are location, location, and location. The attributes of a good conversation are listen, listen, and listen. If the two parties do not listen and understand what the other party is saying, the communication will soon break down. In addition to good listening practices, which is the number one practice, suggestions to improve communications include:

- *Describe what is wanted.* Many conversations begin with a negative tone, such as "You haven't tested that program adequately." It would be much better to state that the program needs more testing and then communicate on how to accomplish that objective. It will be obvious to the subordinate that not enough testing has occurred.
- *Provide information.* Communicators should not try to conceal information from one another. Playing games to lead someone to a solution may work once in a while, but for a long-term relationship both parties must be open and above-board. Neither parties should make the other guess what the other wants or is trying to accomplish.
- *Describe what is expected.* Too frequently, people undertake a task without knowing what management expects from them. If the goals are not known, let that be known, but if management knows what they want, state precisely what is expected from people so that they will know on what they will be measured. It is also a major productivity tool.
- *Criticize the product, not the person.* The objective of communication is to improve the workplace and the products produced in that workplace. Berating people is not conducive to improvement. Both parties want the best possible product, but when the conversation degrades to a person's character, defenses are raised.
- *Describe feelings when unhappiness exists.* There is nothing wrong with a manager saying that an act committed by a subordinate bothered him, or put him in a difficult position with management. This discusses someone's behavior, and not the person as a person. Behavior is correctable—most traits are not.
- *Put yourself in the other person's shoes.* The manager must, during communication, attempt to understand how the other person feels. Without this knowledge, it is difficult to be sympathetic toward the person's position and help the person accomplish his or her goals.

THE COMMUNICATORS IN DATA PROCESSING

There are four distinct groups in data processing requiring good communication between and among themselves. These are:

1. *Staff:* The application programmers, system programmers, computer operators, clerical people, and other support personnel responsible for the day-to-day work of the department.
2. *Peer groups:* Persons within the same pay grade and level of responsibilities communicating about their working conditions, processes, and status of work.
3. *Supervision:* The first-line supervisors up through the data processing manager. These are the people responsible for accomplishing the data processing mission.
4. *Administration:* The people or group responsible for administration in the data processing function.

AREAS OF COMMUNICATION

Communication is a continual process within the data processing department. In an effort to provide guidance on methods for improvement, the types of communication are categorized as follows (communication with users and vendors is covered in later chapters):

- Recruiting
- Work assignment
- Performance appraisal
- Salary administration
- Professional opportunities/benefits
- Department news
- Staff suggestions
- Career development
- Guidelines
- Administration

The person or group who normally initiates each of these conversations is indicated in Figure 44. This data processing communication matrix shows which of the people involved in communication is the primary initiator (indicated with a P) and the other member of the communication process is indicated as a secondary initiator (indicated with an S).

Each of these areas is discussed individually. The discussion is aimed at two persons. First, the primary initiator, because that person has responsibility for people management in that area. Second is the administrator who has a responsibility in the department to help improve communications within the staff and between the staff and supervision.

Areas of Communication Need	Normal Initiator of Communication[a]			
	Staff	Peer	Supervisor	Administrator
Recruiting	S		P	
Work assignment	S		P	
Performance appraisal	S		P	S
Salary administration	S		P	S
Professional opportunities/benefits	S		S	P
Department news	S		S	P
Staff suggestions	P	S	S	
Career development	S		P	S
Guidelines	S	P	S	
Administration	S		S	P

[a]P, primary initiator; S, secondary initiator.

Figure 44   *Data Processing Communication Matrix*

Personnel Policies

Each area of importance in data processing should be defined by a managerial policy. This policy should define the intent of management, which would then be supported by individual personnel policies. However, much of the personnel policy will be dictated by the overall organizational policy.

Such items that need to be addressed in the personnel policy are:

- Hiring from within the organization versus hiring outside
- Hiring at the lowest level in the organization as opposed to hiring managers
- Pay policy in regard to the general data processing rate scale for industry (e.g., pay equal to or better than the prevailing wage in the community)
- Career development
- Performance measurement and salary administration
- Travel and training
- Lines of communication (e.g., open door policy to data processing management)

Each of these policy areas should be supported by one or more procedures explaining how the policy is to be implemented. Standards should then be developed explaining specifically what is expected of each area. All members of the data processing department should be given or have access to the policies, procedures, and standards.

Building an Effective Data Processing Staff: The Basics

The basics around which all relationships between supervision and staff will revolve are:

- *Data processing charter:* The mission of the data processing department
- *Data processing personnel policy:* The general rules of governing people's work, performance, and evaluation
- *Organizational chart:* An explanation of how the people in a department interrelate organizationally
- *Job descriptions:* An explanation of what is expected of each person, and how the person's performance in accomplishing those expectations will be measured
- *Career development program:* An interrelated program of supervisory counseling, training programs, performance evaluation, and a known method for gaining more responsibility and advancing within the department

These basic items define the environment in which communication exists. Without them, there can be misinterpretation about what is expected, how it will be measured, and the specific intent of management. With these items, communication can be positive and direct.

IMPROVING COMMUNICATION AREA BY AREA

After the basics are established, the management and the staff of the department meet to work at communication. The initiation to improve communication must come from management and be supported by its staff. It is unusual when a sincere desire to improve communication on the part of management is rebuked by the staff.

There is no single method or technique that will guarantee good communication. On the other hand, there are a lot of practices and techniques used in various data processing departments that have proved effective in helping communications. These methods and techniques are discussed in each of the 10 areas of communication discussed previously (see Figure 45 for a synopsis of the tools and techniques in each of the 10 areas).

Area of Communications	Communication Improvement Method, Tool, or Technique	Purpose of Communication Method, Tool, or Technique
Recruiting	Recruitee notebook	Show organization of department and refresher for recruitee
	Peer discussions	Tell it like it is
	Meeting senior DP management	Show interest
Work assignment	Establish work objectives	Define tasks to be accomplished
	Written assignment sheet	Put tasks in writing _objectives_
	Train employee in all needed skills and ensure mastery	Give the employee the skills needed to do the job
	Define success criteria	Define how employee will be evaluated and what a successful implementation means
	Define obstacles to success	Tell employee the difficulties he or she will face in achieving task
	Give employee measurement tools	Provide the employee the tools needed to measure his or her own performance
	Staff member responsible for a job must accept it	Employee must agree to do job
	Allow adequate supervisory time	Provide a supervisor with sufficient time to help employee as needed
Performance appraisal	Performance should be evaluated in accordance with job description	Evaluate person on what he or she was hired to do
	Evaluation uses meaningful factors	Evaluation criteria should be valid to the employee
	Supervisor appraisal (written)	Put appraisal in writing (prior to the review)
	Employee appraisal of self (written)	Have employee do a self-appraisal in writing (prior to the review)
	Written comment on formal appraisal form by employee	Employee reaction to review should be in writing
	End result is a plan of action	Performance appraisal should help the employee improve
Salary administration	Raise consistent with performance appraisal	Do not let performance appraisal evaluate at one level and raise pay on another evaluation

(continued)

Figure 45   *Synopsis of Communication Improvement Methods, Tools, and Techniques*

Area of Communications	Communication Improvement Method, Tool, or Technique	Purpose of Communication Method, Tool, or Technique
	Publicly state salary constraints	Let employees know the facts so that they can assess how the supervisor views salary
	Do not promise what you can not deliver	Do not build employee expectations (even a year off) if you can not deliver
Professional opportunities/ benefits	Require all opportunities/benefits to be needed	Avoid the attitude that going to a conference or seminar is a reward
	Document and discuss conference seminar lessons/recommendations	Use what you paid for
	Explain why people are promoted, trained, etc.	Define success criteria
	Promote from within	If a staff member qualifies for an opening, give it to him or her
Department news	Meaningful newsletters *periodic*	Open as many lines of communication as possible if they provide good information
	Terminal message center *mailbox*	Use terminals to store messages
	Daily prelunch briefing	Offer a 5-minute daily briefing on yesterday's happenings to anyone who wants to know
	Letters file *(storage of all past letters)*	Make a copy of all correspondence available for browsing by the staff
Staff suggestions	Open door policy	Boss should be prepared to talk to any subordinate
	Recognition/travel award	Give something special for outstanding work
	Special task force	Assign staff to study groups to broaden their experience
Career development	Career flowchart	Show pictorially how a person can advance
	Skill profile	Keep skill records on each employee and suggest areas to improve
	Department library	Maintain references wanted by staff
	Inventory of professional educational opportunities	Maintain a record of where to acquire needed skills

Figure 45 (continued)

major idews
& suggestions

Area of Communications	Communication Improvement Method, Tool, or Technique	Purpose of Communication Method, Tool, or Technique
	Special assignment allocation	Allot $x\%$ of everyone's time for career development
Guidelines	Quality circles	Peer group studying productivity without management direction
	Peer reviews	Unofficial review of peers' work
Administration	Big brother/sister	A nonsupervisor counselor
	Questionnaires	Survey different opinions
	Give ownership of concepts	Teach concept through experiencing the concept
	Train supervisors to be supervisors	Ensure that all supervisors are proficient in practicing needed supervisor skills

nally

their own idea

Figure 45 *(continued)*

EDP ADMINISTRATIVE GUIDELINE 23

If management treats subordinates as responsible people and works to help them, not criticize them, communications will open up.

Recruiting

The techniques effective in recruiting persons from within and outside the organization for data processing include:

RECRUITEE NOTEBOOK

Data processing personnel are frequently in short supply. Some organizations have even paid bonuses to both data processing personnel and to persons who set up interviews for them. However, it still takes a good impression to hire a professional data processor. One method used is to prepare a notebook to give to each prospective candidate. A well-prepared professional notebook shows a well-structured department, and can present a good story for the candidate to take with him/her and study after the interview is over.

The types of information normally included in a notebook are:

- Data processing organizational chart
- List of equipment/software/special features
- Applicant's potential job description

- Background on company/area/housing (or candidates not currently employees of the organization)
- Sample programming standards
- Data processing plan
- Social/special activities for data processing personnel
- Career development flowchart/career development plan
- Special educational opportunities

PEER DISCUSSIONS

It is generally good practice to let a candidate talk to personnel of the same pay grade that the person is applying for. Obviously, some discretion should be used as to whom you let candidates talk. They should be the more enthusiastic members of the department. On the other hand, it would be poor practice to develop a speech for an employee to use on a candidate. If it is possible to match a candidate with someone from the same school, same general background, and so on, this is recommended.

MEETING SENIOR DP MANAGEMENT

Many candidates feel like just another name on a list when they interview in the data processing department. This can be especially true in larger data processing departments. It is always a good practice to set aside a few minutes for each candidate to talk to a member of senior data processing management. Obviously, it would be advisable to let each person talk to the MIS director, but if there are a large number of candidates, that may not be practical.

The meeting with the senior DP manager should come late in the interview process. Prior to this, the manager should be given a short briefing on the candidate. This should indicate the concerns of the candidate, the potential value of that person to the department, and areas that the DP manager should explore if it would be helpful in a decision regarding hiring the candidate.

Work Assignment

The most important area in which to establish good communications is that regarding people's work assignments. Some of the methods used to improve communication in this area include:

ESTABLISH WORK OBJECTIVES

Work assignments should be very specific as to what an employee is expected to accomplish. If the objectives are well thought through, communication between the employee and the supervisor will be facilitated. It is difficult to hold meaningful discussions unless the objectives are specific. When the objectives are general, the employee must go back and study them, gather information, and attempt to write more specific objectives.

It is recommended that the objectives be measurable. This requires stating objectives such as "increase disk capacity by 30 million bytes" or "add a control to reconcile the balance of accounts receivables per the computer file to the one maintained manually by the accounts receivable department" instead of "add additional disk capacity" or "strengthen the accounts receivable controls."

WRITTEN ASSIGNMENT SHEET

What is written is permanent. What is stated orally is easily misinterpreted and quickly forgotten. Also, oral instructions are subject to two interpretations; whereas written communications, although still not perfect, can be discussed in more detail to ensure a higher probability of mutual understanding.

It is a good business practice to have written assignment sheets. Not only does it facilitate communication, but it establishes a permanent record of the assignment. This record can be used to control the assignment and to perform an analysis at a later time regarding the number of assignments completed, the characteristics of those assignments, and the performance of the person completing the assignments.

TRAIN EMPLOYEES IN ALL NEEDED SKILLS, AND ENSURE MASTERY

One of the quality principles promoted by W. Edward Deming is to provide employees with all of the skills that they need to do their job. Supervision should then take those steps needed to ensure that the employee has mastered those skills. This would be accomplished through a test or on-the-job assessment. Once supervision is assured that the employee has mastered all the necessary skills, the amount of supervision diminishes significantly. The employee is then expected to do the job right the first time. If, after mastering all of the skills, the employee is unable to perform his or her work correctly, the employee should be replaced or transferred. The quality concept says that it is management's responsibility to train employees adequately and ensure that they have mastered those skills. From that point on, it is the employee's responsibility to do a good-quality job. Management should not have to check on their work continuously to ensure that it meets quality standards.

DEFINE SUCCESS CRITERIA

Supervision and the employee should agree on what the employee is to be measured on. Obviously, the work objectives describe the scope of the work.

However, this does not provide the basis for assessing the success of the implementation of the task.

Success criteria are the standards against which the implementation is measured. If the implementation achieves the success criteria, the work is considered successful. For example, if the programmer is to install an on-line inquiry system, the success criterion might be that the proper inquiry would be returned within four seconds. Once this criterion has been established, understood by the employee, and agreed to by the user, all parties know exactly what is expected of the employee. If the employee meets that objective, the person's effort should be considered successful.

DEFINE OBSTACLES TO SUCCESS

When projects are defined, those defining them normally know the reasons why the project might not be successful. Obviously, they believe that these obstacles are not insurmountable. On the other hand, these obstacles are often not defined for the implementers. For example, the requester may know that there is a potential timing problem in acquiring some data, or a potential political problem exists over implementation, or a needed subsystem may be disapproved. Alerting the implementation team to these obstacles provides them with a greater opportunity for success. It also tells the employee that management cares about their success and will tell them both the good and the bad aspects of the assignment.

GIVE EMPLOYEE MEASUREMENT TOOLS

An employee should have adequate tools to measure the success or failure of an assignment. This is another of W. Edward Deming's quality principles. The success of Japanese industry is due partially to the fact they have very few inspectors. Employees are held liable for the quality of their own work, but are given the tools to enable them to measure the quality of their work. Although this may not be practical in every instance in data processing, it is conceptually correct.

We expect data processing professionals to comply with data processing standards. In many organizations, to determine whether or not they complied with these standards, we use quality assurance groups or inspection teams. This team of highly paid professionals must go through the programmer's work line by line to verify compliance to standards. On the other hand, if that employee is given the appropriate checklists and/or other tools, he or she could review his or her own work upon completion to ensure compliance with standards. Not only would this reduce the cost of the product but would be a continual reminder to the employee of what standards have to be complied with. Remember also that prior to this, the employee has been fully trained in standards and evaluated to ensure that the employee understands the proper interpretation of standards.

STAFF MEMBER RESPONSIBLE FOR A JOB MUST ACCEPT IT

Most employees are directed to perform a specific job or assignment. The boss tells them what their mission is and they begin their work. In this type of circumstance it is the boss's assignment given to the employee. The employee does not necessarily accept responsibility for the assignment because it is not the employee's assignment. Until the employee accepts responsibility for the assignment, there is no strong need for intensive communication.

This tool shifts responsibility from the supervisor to the employee. The employee becomes a subcontractor, a small business person. The employee not only accepts the assignment objectives, but also accepts the schedule, time frame, any personnel assigned to the project, and the success criteria. In other words, the employee has bought off completely on the assignment and has full responsibility for it. As such, the employee should be duly rewarded for success, and duly punished for failure.

ALLOW ADEQUATE SUPERVISORY TIME

Working supervisors rarely fulfill their supervisory responsibilities. They are too busy working. In addition, many supervisors are unfamiliar with how to supervise because they have not been adequately trained or given sufficient time to perform their job.

Supervisors should be evaluated on their ability to supervise. A general rule of thumb for supervising states that it takes 1 hour per day to supervise an employee. Thus the maximum a supervisor could handle is eight employees. In that case, a supervisor would not have adequate time for planning or some of the other tasks that supervisors might perform.

Performance Appraisal

Most performance appraisals are poorly handled. Neither the supervisor nor the employee looks forward to them or gains from them. In many instances, the supervisor dreads giving the performance review, and the employee feels that it is a meaningless exercise. Some of the methods that can be incorporated to improve performance appraisals are:

PERFORMANCE SHOULD BE EVALUATED IN ACCORDANCE WITH THE JOB DESCRIPTION

Too frequently, the employee is evaluated against the wrong set of standards. This is particularly true when a person is hired as a programmer and then acts as a temporary project leader. The performance appraisal then evaluates that person as a project leader, which is unfair. The person has received neither the training nor the salary and authority that go with the position. The person is a programmer; they should be evaluated in accordance with the programmer job description.

EVALUATION USES MEANINGFUL FACTORS

Many employees claim that the factors on which they are evaluated are not meaningful in the performance of their job. Performance appraisals are not meant to be popularity contests or beauty contests. Both the employee and the supervisor should agree on the criteria for which the person is being evaluated. If they disagree, one or both are going to be unhappy with the performance appraisal, with a resulting drop-off in communication.

SUPERVISORY APPRAISAL (WRITTEN)

The appraisal that the supervisor makes on the employee should be in writing. The employee should have the right to see the appraisal, either before, during, or after the performance review. If the supervisor is unwilling to show the employee the written appraisal, there is already a communication problem between the two people. Supervisors who are unwilling to work with and help certain employees should attempt to get those persons transferred to another supervisor.

EMPLOYEE APPRAISAL OF SELF (WRITTEN)

Performance appraisals rarely invoke the type of communication that should occur if they are going to be a positive force in improving employee performance. One method that is encouraging communication is to have the employee do a written appraisal of himself or herself prior to the performance appraisal. This does not have to be shared with the supervisor, but it is recommended that it be. When the employee completes this exercise, the employee has a basis to assess the reasonableness of the supervisor's appraisal. If both have the same appraisal, all that is necessary is to develop a mutually agreeable plan of action. On the other hand, if there is a disagreement, the ensuing discussion is normally helpful to both the employee and the supervisor. This concept works only when the employee puts the appraisal in writing. Appraisals in writing tend to be much more specific than some general thoughts an employee might think about himself or herself prior to the performance appraisal.

END RESULT IS A PLAN OF ACTION

The objective of the performance appraisal should be to improve performance. If performance is lacking, behavior changes are needed. These occur only when there is a plan of action. Both the supervisor and the employee should participate in developing this plan of action, and participate in carrying out the plan of action. The supervisor has as much responsibility as the employee does to help improve the employee's performance.

Salary Administration

The company salary administration program dictates heavily what can be done in this area. However, some suggestions that might improve this area are:

RAISE CONSISTENT
WITH PERFORMANCE APPRAISAL

It is devastating to an employee to receive a glowing performance appraisal and a sick raise. Although the two are designed to serve different purposes, no one will ever convince an employee that the two are separate. When they are different, the employee perceives a communication problem, in that the supervisor is normally not giving the employee a fair and open performance appraisal.

PUBLICLY STATE SALARY CONSTRAINTS

The result of a poor raise may be constraints placed on the supervisor. If the maximum raise that a supervisor is allowed to give is 5 percent, and an employee gets a 5 percent raise, the employee should be pleased. On the other hand, the employee might feel that the 5 percent raise is not indicative of a very good performance appraisal unless the employee was apprised of the constraints. This is but another method of how open communication can foster a better supervisory/subordinate relationship, and thus improve productivity.

DO NOT PROMISE WHAT YOU CANNOT
DELIVER

Many supervisors apologize to employees for a poor raise. They lead the employee to believe that this year, or this time, the raise is low but it will be better next time. On the other hand, the supervisor does not know the raise constraints next time, and thus is leading the employee to believe that things will get better when they may not. The supervisor may forget these statements, but the employee will not. Failure to deliver destroys credibility, which destroys communication.

Professional Opportunities/Benefits

Data processing managers can offer their staff a variety of professional opportunities and benefits. Among these are training sessions, participation in professional associations, attendance at conferences and seminars, assignment to special study groups and task forces, and reassignments and promotions. These can be satisfiers or dissatisfiers to the data processing staff, depending on how they are used. For example, if a training session is viewed as a vacation, it undermines the reward that an employee would like to have received for outstanding work. Some of the methods that can be used to improve communication and productivity include:

REQUIRE ALL OPPORTUNITIES/BENEFITS TO BE NEEDED

The concept of giving benefits or opportunities as a reward for service, to fill an unassigned period or other equivalent reason, is a poor concept. Once people believe that data processing professional benefits and opportunities are favors, or a reward, it undermines the professionalism of the opportunity. People should be sent to training for specific purposes and advised of that purpose. People should be assigned to task forces for special purposes and explain why they are being assigned. Unless people are told why things occur, and there are good business reasons for them occurring, miscommunication will occur and may destroy management's credibility, which destroys communications.

DOCUMENT AND DISCUSS CONFERENCE SEMINAR LESSONS/RECOMMENDATIONS

If a person is sent to a seminar, the lessons learned in that seminar should be used in the department. If there is a specific purpose, the person attending should be charged with that purpose. The attendee should document in writing the lessons and recommendations learned from the seminar. These should be discussed with the appropriate people and presentations made to the entire staff if warranted. When this method is used, seminars and conferences take on much greater importance in the eyes of the person attending. That person should also gain more from the seminar under those circumstances.

EXPLAIN WHY PEOPLE ARE PROMOTED, TRAINED, AND SO ON

It is good practice to let people know why others have received a promotion or benefit. This can frequently be done in the notice of promotion or a memo about a person going to a training session. Not only does it squelch rumors about the boss's friends being promoted, but it provides the person getting the promotion with a little more prestige and recognition, which in turn normally pays benefits to the organization. Over time, it also begins to tell the staff what they must do to receive those promotions and benefits.

PROMOTE FROM WITHIN

It is good for the morale of the department to see members of the department promoted either within the department or to good jobs outside the department. In addition, when one person is promoted, it creates more opportunities within the department. If too many outside persons come in and take top jobs, it discourages the staff from working to obtain those jobs.

Department News

Studies show that one of the major sources of information in an organization is the grapevine. This is a poor way for people to learn what their department is doing. Channels should be established to communicate departmental happenings to the staff on a timely basis. Some of the methods used to accomplish this are:

MEANINGFUL NEWSLETTERS

Newsletters are a good way to communicate factual information. They provide a permanent record and yet are unofficial, so they can include material that need not be saved for long periods of time. Obviously, a department cannot afford large sums for professional newsletters, but short, to the point, factual data provide a good information vehicle.

TERMINAL MESSAGE CENTER

If data processing personnel use on-line terminals, a file accessible by that terminal can be used to store newsletter-type information. During slack periods the terminal operator can call up that file and read important items that are happening in the department. Using this concept, it is easy for anyone in a department to insert general pieces of information into the system; for example, if a software bug is found in the operating system, the terminal message center is a way of alerting everyone in the department to that problem.

DAILY PRELUNCH BRIEFINGS

If the departmental supervisors meet daily in the morning to discuss yesterday's results and today's happenings, that information can be given to the employees. If at a predetermined time one member of supervision will give a brief status report of what has happened, any interested staff member can attend that briefing. It is another low-cost opportunity to provide staff members with up-to-date information.

LETTERS FILE

This is an extra copy of all departmental correspondence. It can be stored in a notebook or in a folder by week. The file is made available to any staff member who wants it to peruse to determine what is going on in the department. Obviously, confidential letters would be excluded, but with little effort on anyone's part this is an easy way to transfer information to the staff.

Staff Suggestions

Many good ideas occur to staff members. What is needed is some semiformal method to tap that resource. Practices used by organizations include:

OPEN DOOR POLICY

Employees are given free access to any supervisor to discuss any topic. Thus staff members with good ideas have free and easy access to the decision maker.

RECOGNITION/TRAVEL AWARD

Nothing encourages performance like an extra bonus. Depending on the organization's policy, the bonus can be a gift certificate, an extra day or two off with pay, a trip, the employee's picture on a bulletin board, or any other recognition. The concept works.

What is needed is to predetermine the type of performance that management is looking for: for example, the most improved computer system as represented by a drop in cost to process a transaction. All employees should be alerted to what is wanted and the prize announced.

SPECIAL TASK FORCE

One way to draw out people who may have ideas is to put them in a position of authority. A special task force to work on a departmental problem may serve that purpose. People who have been reluctant to speak up about potential improvements to the department may do so once they perceive that they have a platform from which to speak, and that management is interested in what they have to say. Being appointed by management to a task force fulfills both of these requirements.

Career Development

The employee and employer share a joint responsibility on career development. A supervisor may have great difficulty in making someone improve his or her skills, but on the other hand if someone wants to, supervision should be supportive. Some ideas that help improve skills and provide career planning include:

CAREER FLOWCHART

A career flowchart is a pictorial representation that shows potential promotional paths for employees. The flowchart begins with every entry position into data processing and shows the various career path alternatives that are available. Also, the flowchart either indicates or cross-references to the type of training or skills needed to move to the next step. Thus not only can employees see the most logical career paths, but can embark on a plan of action to acquire the necessary skills to move to the next desired location. It also provides a vehicle for supervisor/subordinate discussions on career planning.

SKILL PROFILE

A skill profile is a listing of all the accomplishments of an employee. It describes all the employee's educational background, job experience, professional development experience, and other noteworthy information. The skill profile can be used by both the employee and the supervisor to assess the current level of skill and to pinpoint areas for improvement. Again, this is a helpful document in a person's career planning.

DEPARTMENT LIBRARY

The department library should be a source of professional information for the staff. It should contain the types of ready references that both the supervisors and staff believe are necessary. At a minimum, the library should include:

- Professional newspapers/periodicals
- Technological books
- Technological updating services
- Books/material on related disciplines

In addition, the library may contain:

- Self-study courses
- Video self-study curriculum
- Telecommunication network tied to data bases and news services

Space should be made available where possible for the staff to spend time in the library to study and read.

INVENTORY OF PROFESSIONAL
EDUCATIONAL OPPORTUNITIES

Data processing departments should maintain records on the professional educational opportunities for the staff. These educational opportunities should include:

- User groups
- Professional seminars/conferences
- University courses
- Video and other self-training materials
- Professional associations

Much of the material comes in the mail and can be stored for future reference. However, prior to going, references about the adequacy of the training session should be acquired. Experiences from persons going to those seminars should be saved for future reference.

SPECIAL ASSIGNMENT ALLOCATION

Professional staff members should be allocated some percent of their time for professional development. Granted that most people will take some time for this purpose, it is a good gesture and one improving credibility and communication when management offers a certain amount of time for professional development. It is a way of management saying: "We care about you keeping up to date technologically," and also saying, "Management considers it an important part of your job." Most organizations allocate about two weeks, or 4 percent of one's time, for professional development activities.

Guidelines

Guidelines are preferred ways of accomplishing tasks. Management prescribes policy, supervision usually develops procedures and standards, but peers develop many of the guidelines. Some of the ways in which management can encourage these productivity-improving guidelines are:

QUALITY CIRCLES

A quality circle is a group of peers allocated time by management to study problems as they perceive them. Quality circles are a Japanese concept that are used primarily as a productivity tool. Quality circles began in the factory and have grown to encompass most positions in an organization. One organization has a quality circle of vice presidents.

The quality circle concept as proposed by the Japanese follows these rules:

- Membership in a quality circle is completely voluntary.
- Quality circles operate as a pure democracy.
- Management authorizes participants in a quality circle to spend one hour per week on quality circle activities.
- Management normally appoints a facilitator to provide guidance to quality circles. Note that the facilitator may not sit in on the quality circle meetings, and if he or she does, may not participate in the discussions. The facilitator is a resource to the quality circle, and a catalyst in getting it started and keeping it going.
- The facilitator explains the concept of quality circles and then invites people to volunteer to be members of a quality circle.
- Quality circles are normally limited to six to nine people.
- Quality circles elect their own leader.
- Quality circles select their own topic. It is normally selected from a brainstorming session to propose topics, and the final topic selected by a democratic vote.
- Quality circles work on one topic at a time.
- The quality circle can select any topic as long as it is not one prohibited by management, such as studying the salary structure.
- Quality circles study only one topic at a time.
- Quality circles can study one topic for as long as it is necessary to arrive at a solution.
- Quality circle recommendations are made to management for them to accept, reject, or modify.
- People can stay on a quality circle as long as they desire, even years.
- Individual members of the quality circle are not to get credit for the work of the circle.
- According to the Japanese, members of the quality circle should not be fired for improving productivity (note that this practice is generally not followed by U.S. industry).

PEER REVIEWS

Peer reviews are analyses made of a systems analyst/programmer's work by other systems analysts/programmers. The results of the review are for the benefit of the person being reviewed, and are not reported to management. Some organizations have adopted a formal method for peer reviews, providing the peers with the methodology to follow. In other instances, it is just one professional reviewing the work of another professional.

Administration

Administrative activities involve many nonproduction activities. As such, administrative personnel interact with all personnel in the data processing department. The following techniques are effective not only in improving communication with administration, but in improving communication in general within the department:

BIG BROTHER/SISTER

A big brother is a counselor to help a less experienced person in the department to do career planning, discuss assignments, and approaches, and to discuss problems that occur in the department that involve the junior person. In some organizations, the big brother/sister is only a short-term proposition, whereas in others everyone except the more senior managers has a big brother/sister for as long as he or she is in the department. Generally, it is helpful to have a senior person other than your supervisor to go to when you wish to discuss problems.

QUESTIONNAIRES

Periodically, administration can develop questionnaires on a variety of topics and send them to people within the department. The questionnaires can be returned signed or unsigned. It is a method to evoke comment and assessment, when that comment and assessment may not be obtained any other way. Frequently, an administration group would use this technique when it perceived some breakdown in communication between the staff and management; or the staff and a specific manager. On the other hand, it may be good occasionally just to get some blind feedback about the status of communication in the data processing department.

GIVE OWNERSHIP OF CONCEPTS

People have trouble accepting concepts until they have experienced them. Once people have experienced something, they "own it." If there are new methods, or controversial concepts, administration should develop methods that help the staff own the new concept. Some organizations use industrial engineers or outside consultants for this purpose. It is proved very helpful in getting the staff to accept ideas that they might not otherwise accept.

TRAIN SUPERVISORS TO BE SUPERVISORS

Few supervisors are born; most are made. Because good supervision is the key to communication, quality, and credibility, the administration function should take it upon itself to develop supervisory training courses. Administration may also want to subscribe to some of the supervisory publications.

```
┌──────────────────────────────────────────────────────────┐
│              EDP ADMINISTRATIVE GUIDELINE 24               │
├──────────────────────────────────────────────────────────┤
│  Good supervisors cause good systems to happen.           │
└──────────────────────────────────────────────────────────┘
```

A PEOPLE MANAGEMENT CHECKLIST

The proper management of people is critical to the success of a data processing department. Many managers fail to recognize that they have problems. The self-assessment questionnaire shown in Figure 46 is designed to point out potential problems for additional investigation. "Yes" answers are indicative of good personnel practices, and "no" answers are the ones that should be subject to further investigation.

Item	Yes	No	N/A	Comments
1. Does the department have a personnel policy?				
2. Are procedures established to implement that policy?				
3. Do the members of the data processing department have access to the policies and procedures?				
4. Is data processing management aware of the practices that encourage communication and the practices that discourage communication?				
5. Does the data processing department have a higher turnover rate than the organizational turnover rate?				
6. Are special steps taken to present the best possible image to a potential candidate for a position in the data processing department, such as providing him/her with a notebook of data processing-related topics and having him/her meet a senior member of DP management?				
7. Are employees given their assignments in writing?				
8. Are employees given the opportunity to reject assignments?				
9. Do assignments include the criteria on which the person responsible for the assignment will be evaluated?				
10. Do employees have the appropriate skills for the assignments they are given?				
11. Do supervisors have adequate time to supervise subordinates?				

Figure 46 *People Management Checklist*

	Response			
Item	**Yes**	**No**	**N/A**	**Comments**
12. Is the employee's performance evaluated in accordance with his or her job as outlined in the job description?				
13. Do the employees agree that their evaluation uses meaningful facts?				
14. Does the supervisor provide employees with a written assessment of their performance?				
15. Do employees make an assessment of their performance (preferably in writing) before they undertake their performance review?				
16. Are employees given the opportunity to comment on their official evaluation form?				
17. Is the objective of the performance review to develop a plan of action to improve an employee's performance?				
18. Are the raises given employees consistent with their performance appraisal?				
19. Do employees know the salary administration policy of the organization, and any salary constraints placed on their department?				
20. Are training sessions, professional benefits, and opportunities given only to employees who earn them?				
21. Do employees going to training sessions and seminars make formal written reports on what they have learned from those seminars and conferences?				
22. Are employees promoted from within wherever possible?				
23. Does the staff know why certain employees are promoted, sent to special training sessions, etc.?				
24. Are there formal means of communicating department news for the staff?				
25. Do data processing managers have an open door policy toward their staff?				
26. Are employees who perform outstanding work given special recognition?				
27. Is a pictorial flowchart prepared showing the different career options to employees?				
28. Is a skill profile prepared on each employee?				
29. Does the department maintain a library of professional material?				

(continued)

Figure 46 *(continued)*

	Response			
Item	**Yes**	**No**	**N/A**	**Comments**
30. Does the department maintain an inventory of good professional educational opportunities?				
31. Do data processing managers believe that a certain percentage of everyone's work time should be allocated toward continuing professional education?				
32. Has the data processing department initiated quality circles?				
33. Has the data processing department initiated peer review?				
34. Are employees assigned a counselor other than their supervisor with whom to discuss departmental problems?				
35. Are employees surveyed periodically to evaluate their attitudes toward the department and management?				
36. When new concepts are introduced into the data processing department, are training sessions developed which give the staff ownership of those concepts?				
37. Is there a formal training process to train supervisors so that they can perform their job well?				

Figure 46 *(continued)*

DIRECTING ADMINISTRATION

There are rarely problems at the conceptual stage of administration. The problems occur in going from a concept to implementation. Proper direction in administering is the key to acceptance, and thus the success, of the administration function.

Chapter

8

Administration of Computer Center Operations

Computer operations is a business within a business. The key to a successful computer center is to run it like a business. Unfortunately, if it is not run like a business, the computer center may be out of business because of the processing alternatives now available. For example, users can now do much of their processing on microcomputers if they so choose.

This chapter describes the business of running a computer center. A successful computer center provides the right service, the right product, and the right cost. Those managers that approach computer operations from the perspective of running a successful business are normally successful.

This chapter explores the business of operating the computer. The chapter explains how to develop and improve the customer base. The criteria for a successful computer operation are described, and the practices that help make the business more successful are explained. A business which feels that it has a monopoly is doomed to failure because alternatives will develop to that monopoly. Only through viewing the computer center as a business can the manager understand the competition and develop the appropriate strategies needed to stay in business.

WHAT IS A COMPUTER CENTER?

A computer center is the part of data processing responsible for the day-to-day processing of business transactions. However, today's computer center is one in transition. During the 1970's the computer center ran a large centralized computer. Even if terminals existed in user areas, processing rules were centrally developed and controlled. Today, organizations have many processing options available and are filling their processing shopping baskets with the available alternatives.

Users began directing computer operations via terminals many years ago. Processing and data are now being distributed to workstations, terminals, microcomputers, and office automation equipment. Data processing is being asked to help other people in their corporation erode their processing workload.

The computer center of today is different from yesterday, and will be far different tomorrow. The common thread through the transition is service. The computer center that will survive the 1980s will be the one centered in service. The key to improving service is to create an environment in which people can identify with the quality of their product. Therefore, this chapter is dedicated to creating an administrative process in the computer center that encourages improved service.

THE BUSINESS OF BEING A COMPUTER OPERATIONS BUSINESS

The computer center is in the business of selling operating capacity. The commodity being sold is a general-purpose commodity. It is available from many resources, including outside service centers, dial-up networks, distributed systems, and in-house computers, including the microcomputers. A computer center is like a service station. All service stations sell gasoline; however, the customer returns to a service station because it either provides better service, better cost, higher-quality service, or all three.

Computer center management can view itself as a cost center or a profit center. As a cost center, the computer center keeps track of its costs and then either includes those in overhead for the organization or distributes those costs to users. If the computer center is a profit center, it returns more to the organization than it receives. Although it is recognized that the computer center does not generate profit in the concepts that a marketing group does, it can generate profits to the extent that it makes money for the corporation on the work under the control of the computer center.

There is a dramatically different perspective within the computer center when the people view themselves as a profit center rather than a cost center. A cost center is concerned about reducing costs but has no real basis for measurement. A profit center will look at every aspect of the computer center to ensure that it operates on a pay-as-you-go basis. Let us look at an example of an off-site backup facility. The cost center perspective says: "How can we provide off-site backup, at the lowest cost?" The profit center says: "Do we need off-site backup, and if so, at what price is it cost-effective to back up processing?" The profit center concept is a much more probing and challenging perspective than the cost center approach.

The data processing manager has two major challenges when viewing the computer operation as a profit center. These are:

1. Purchasing changing technology that provides the lowest possible cost
2. Determining the level of service to provide customers

The computer center manager's role was once described like drawing pictures in the stand at the shoreline. As soon as the manager can draw the picture of technology, the surf washes it out only to be replaced by a new picture. In other words, as soon as the manager selects and adopts technology, a vendor announces something new. The new technology appears cheaper and faster than the older technology, raising the question of why the manager selected the old technology when the new is available. However, the surf again washes out the picture in the sand and a newer technology emerges. It appears that no matter what the computer center manager does, he or she is always behind technologically.

The manager must also decide on the level of service to provide the users. One of the luxuries in life, so say the advertisements, is to own a Cadillac. When you drive the Cadillac to an agency for service, you may be met by someone with coffee. After a pleasant greeting, your problem is discussed, and you may be offered a car to use while your Cadillac is being repaired, or chauffeured to where you want to go. Should you opt to wait for your car to be repaired, you can pass the time in an air-conditioned lounge, equipped with television, coffee, and a wide selection of magazines to read. On the other hand, if you purchased a Chevrolet, you might find yourself waiting in line to get service, and then after a quick notation of your problems, find yourself out on the street trying to find a ride home or to work. Obviously, the Cadillac service costs more than the Chevrolet service. The question the manager of operations must answer is: "Do I want to be a Cadillac computer center or do I want to be a Chevrolet computer center?"

The computer center manager must also address the problem of inferior products. If the computer center manager accepts a defective program, operating software or hardware, the product delivered to the customer may be defective. It would be nice to say that the computer center manager is not at fault in this situation, but the customer will never believe it.

Assume that there is a problem with your car. You take it to the service station to be repaired. When you get the car back, you find that it doesn't work properly. Upon returning to the service station, they tell you that it is not their fault; they got a defective product from the parts supplier. Do you say, "Well, I understand, it's not your fault; the fact that the car broke down on the road and I had to walk a couple of miles is no problem at all; I'll keep bringing my car back to you over and over again no matter how many bad parts you put in it because I recognize that it's not your fault"? That is not the normal reaction. The normal reaction is to hold the service station responsible for the quality of parts they put into your car. Similarly, the user of the computer center holds the computer center manager responsible for the quality of the parts. It doesn't mean that they are happy with the parts supplier, but the computer center manager does not get off the hook for running bad programs.

If programs do not work in the computer center and reports are not delivered on time, or computer capacity is unavailable, the computer center must accept part or all of that responsibility. In a profit center concept the computer center manager does accept that responsibility. The problem is not who is at fault; the problem is how to prevent that defect from recurring.

EDP ADMINISTRATIVE GUIDELINE 25

Customers will flock to the business that provides the best service at the lowest cost (or at a reasonable cost).

The Computer Operations Business

The computer operations business has input, processing, and output. The mission of computer operations is to produce the desired results on a timely basis, utilizing the resources available. The manager who can do that will be successful.

Administration and control are necessary to run an effective business. Without the direction administration can provide, and without the control necessary to produce the best possible product at the lowest cost, the profit center perspective may be unattainable. Operations managers need tools and techniques to manage their business effectively. It takes good planning, good organizational structure, and the proper policies and attitudes to survive in computer operations today.

The business of running a computer center is illustrated in Figure 47. This shows the wide range of inputs that must be managed. The data center manager in building capacity has service agreements, rental agreements, hardware, and operating software. The center has either formal or informal contracts with users to perform work in accordance with the data center management policy. The user work is expressed in terms of data and programs (i.e., processing) which are executed by operations staff using the facilities of the service center. This results in the workload being processed with the available capacity according to the schedules developed. The results of processing are monitored using resource utilization reports. These go to the computer operations manager to evaluate the work of the computer center.

Any business group can be described in terms of the inputs they receive, the processes they perform, and the products they give to their customers. However, it is the analysis or resource utilization reports that differentiate the profit center from the cost center. The cost center may send the results of processing and the cost to the user. The profit center is measuring its cost

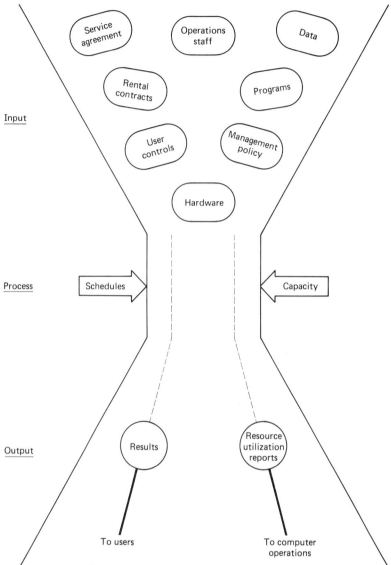

Input

Process

Output

Service agreement

Operations staff

Data

Rental contracts

Programs

User controls

Management policy

Hardware

Schedules

Capacity

Results

Resource utilization reports

To users

To computer operations

Figure 47 *Computer Operations Business*

effectiveness and reducing costs when they do not show the appropriate return on investment.

The Computer Operations Success Triangle

We have defined the obstacles to success in computer center operations as follows.

- The computer center offers a commodity for sale (i.e., computer resources, including people).
- Users of that service have alternative sources of supply available (i.e., service centers, dial-up networks, microcomputers, etc.).
- Today's lowest cost can probably be bettered tomorrow when the next vendor offers a new technological breakthrough.
- The computer center manager may not have a reliable source of supplies (e.g., the manager runs programs that may contain defects).

These obstacles may appear almost unsurmountable. A logical question one may ask is: "Why should anyone want to be a computer operations manager?" The answer to that question is probably no one, unless we can provide that manager with the appropriate administrative and control tools to overcome those obstacles.

The computer operations succes triangle is illustrated in Figure 48. The triangle states that managers must balance the following three operational criteria in order to be successful:

1. Quality of work (delivering to customers the right results)
2. Adequate service level (offering customers on-time performance)
3. Cost-effective processing (charging customers a price they can afford to pay)

The mix of these three items for one customer may be different from the mix of items for another customer. The successful computer center is not a one-price operation. Like the gasoline station, we must offer both regular gas and premium gas. At times we must let the customers work on their own automobiles, whereas at other times we must greet customers with a cup of

Figure 48 *Computer Operations Success Triangle*

coffee, provide a lounge with television, and let customers use our cars while theirs are being fixed.

EDP ADMINISTRATIVE GUIDELINE 26
Everything worth doing is not worth doing well.

Industry makes Chevies and Cadillacs because everyone does not want the same type of automobile. One customer of a computer center has a monthly report reduced for analysis purposes, and is not particularly upset if it is a day or two late. On the other hand, another user needs an instantaneous response in order to close a sale with a customer. A late response may mean a lost sale to that customer. To another, the product is wanted only if it can be produced at a very low cost. The next customer relies heavily on the reliability of information and may not be able to tolerate errors; at the same time another group analyzing sales information for future marketing strategy is not overly concerned about high precision but is concerned about being priced out of a computer-produced report decision.

The manager learns how to balance these three items by continual interaction with the customer. The computer center manager who knows his or her customers can modify the success triangle. The manager who assumes that he or she is in business to stay in business and make a profit will bend as necessary to meet the individual needs of users.

BUILDING GOOD USER RELATIONSHIPS

Users are the customers of the computer center. These may include all of the major areas within the organization: senior management, operational management, and the systems and development section of the data processing department. Under the business concept, it is important to the data center manager that these customers continue to return for services.

Any smart entrepreneur would spend time getting to know his or her customers. One small entrepreneur proudly displays in his shop the sign "The customer is king." Most retail stores instruct their employees that "the customer is never wrong." How many data center managers do you think post the same type of sign in the data center?

In many organizations the computer center is a monopoly, and even if the customers don't like it, they do not have an alternative—now! The logical questions to ask about the computer center is whether they can afford to offer this kind of friendly service, and if so, should they? The answer to this question is "yes." The center manager should take time to learn the following about the customers:

- *Knowledge about future workload:* It is essential to the business of the computer center that personnel have their pulse on the future workload. The more the computer center manager knows about the future workload, the type, mix, and quantity, the better off the computer center manager will be in preparing to satisfy those requirements.
- *Complaints and suggestions:* If the customers of a computer center are unhappy, or have suggestions for improvement, it is far better that they be given to the computer center manager than to the computer center manager's boss. It is only through a close open relationship that complaints and suggestions are passed directly to the computer center manager.
- *Shifting workload:* It may be necessary at times for the computer center manager to speed up or delay jobs. If the computer center manager has a close working relationship with the customers, these problems can be discussed freely, and in many instances the users of the computer center services will agree to shifts in workload. If animosity occurs between the two, this may be difficult or may not happen.
- *The customer's business:* If the computer center manager knows the business of the users, the manager may be able to provide better services. It is difficult to make suggestions about an area for which nothing is known. The close relationship and interest of the computer center manager in the customer should lead to a better understanding of the customer's needs and business.

An interesting thought when the computer center is viewed as a small business is what to do when the customer is dissatisfied with a product. In a small business you would expect the customer to bring the product back and the small business person would refund the customer's money or exchange it for another product. Shouldn't the same policy exist in a computer center? If the services produced do not meet the user's expectation, then shouldn't the computer center manager rerun that system at no cost to the customer, provide another service, or give a rebate if that is feasible? It seems reasonable that the computer center should operate under the policy "full money back guarantee if you are not satisfied."

There are many ways in which the computer center manager can build good customer relations, including:

- *Take a user to lunch.* Periodically, it is advisable for the center manager to meet the major customers on a one-to-one basis. Lunch is a friendly way to do this and it would not be unreasonable for the computer center manager to pay for lunch out of the computer center budget.
- *Show interest in the user's business.* Announcements about some event in the user area warrant a phone call for congratulations or explanation. Showing interest in little things will lead to information about the bigger, more important items.

- *Make formal visits annually.* The computer center management staff should meet annually with all major users to discuss the status of computer center service and areas for potential improvement. This is also a good time to discuss future workloads.
- *Interchange personnel.* It is a good practice to let employees of one area work in another area for short periods of time, or to transfer personnel between areas to improve understanding of each other's area.

The points discussed above represent some general ways to improve relations between the computer center and the customer base. The success triangle stated that the areas that must be addressed in customer relations are service, quality, and cost. These three areas, together with some specific programs to help improve the areas, are discussed below.

SERVICE IMPROVEMENT PRACTICES

Service cannot be defined simply as on-time delivery. It is providing the users with the proper results of processing at the time they want those results. What must be done to accomplish that level of service is a computer center problem, not a user problem.

Providing the appropriate service is primarily a planning function. The computer center must develop plans to acquire the appropriate capacity when needed. This capacity planning or configuration management may be a full-time job for one or more people in a large computer center.

One of the more serious problems faced by computer center management is the long lead time for some computer hardware and software. Needed upgrades in capacity from some vendors may take two years of waiting time. Unless computer center management has a good handle on future workload, they will find themselves with either over- or undercapacity. Both are costly to the business. Some of these capacity problems are cost problems, and others are service problems.

The practices that have helped computer data centers improve service with their customer base are listed in Figure 49 and described below (note that the effectiveness of each of the practices is also listed in Figure 49).

IDENTIFICATION OF THE WORKLOAD

If computer center management truly knows the expected workload, and that equals the actual workload, most of the service-level problems disappear. Unfortunately, few computer centers have a good handle on the expected workload, and then unfortunately find that the actual workload differs from what was expected.

Practice	Description	Effectiveness
Identification of the workload	Estimate workload by week, by day, by hour	High
Monitoring the workload	Maintain continuous analysis of actual versus expected work	High
Production control managers	Persons assigned the responsibility to match workload with capacity	High
War room	Daily analysis and action sessions by operations management	High
Help desk	One telephone to call for any problem	Medium
Keeping supplies near production	Shorten supply lines	Low
Recorded message	Recorded job status, enabling user to call and find current job status	Low

Figure 49   *Service Improvement Practices*

The computer center should attempt to estimate the workload by month, by week, by day, and by hour. They are in a business similiar to that of an electric power company. They must be able to anticipate the demand for power and have that capacity ready at the moment the demand occurs. If the electric power company misses, we may have brownouts or even blackouts. If the computer center misses, production jobs will be late or not run at all.

The expected workload can be obtained from the following two sources:

1. Actual workload history.
2. Expected changes in the workload

One of the best teachers about the future is history. Data centers should keep detailed records on workload over extended periods of time. Peaks and valleys tend to repeat from day to day, week to week, and month to month. However, just keeping total workload figures is not enough. It is important to identify the source and type of workload, such as:

- Which customer submitted work
- Internally generated workload, such as generating new software
- Reruns
- Systems maintenance
- Area of business (or application)

Knowing the types of workload the computer center can then make adjustments based on factors such as:

- Increases in volume in different application areas, such as an increase in the number of invoices which can be translated into future workload
- Changes in percent of time expended on reruns and maintenance
- New lines of business for users, resulting in new applications
- Increase in mix of work between internal data center work, systems and programmer work, and production work

It normally requires a small computer system to record past and anticipated workload information. The computer system can then produce trend graphs and bar charts showing the mix of work by area and the long-term trend of work up, down, or the normal peaks and valleys of workload. This becomes input into the capacity planning process.

MONITORING THE WORKLOAD

The computer center cannot be guaranteed that work will arrive on schedule. Some jobs may be late arriving, others early. In addition, some unanticipated work may come, computer problems may occur, or systems may need to be rerun. All can significantly affect the workload, and all these conditions can occur quickly.

The computer center must continually monitor the workload to ensure its timely processing. As each job arrives, or concludes, that should be related to a monitoring process. The computer center at any moment should know its backlog, which can be combined with anticipated work to show an expected volume the next minute, the next hour, and the next several hours.

It is only by this continual monitoring that the computer center can provide the level of service required. The manager at any moment should be able to determine at any time:

- Workload for the next five minutes
- Workload for the next hour
- Any capacity bind that might occur based on the current workload
- Expected time at which any capacity bind will be relieved

Identifying workload and monitoring workload are two closely interrelated processes. It is best to perform them using a computer system. Some data center operations now use a microcomputer to monitor workload for the computer center. The micro continually monitors, combines actual workload with anticipated workload, and then may present some alternative processing solutions to persons responsible for matching workload with capacity.

PRODUCTION CONTROL MANAGERS

In the factory, the production control manager is responsible for maximizing the work produced by the factory. This may mean making on-the-spot changes to the sequence in which jobs are performed, the workstation at which workers reside, authorizing overtime, sending people home, and so on. This person is a field general directing the production war.

Most computer centers have shift supervisors. These persons act in the capacity of a production control manager, but frequently do not have the authority to go with the position. A true production control manager is in complete charge of the computer center and can marshall whatever resources are available to the computer center in order to meet the current workload.

Any production operation needs a production control manager. You may have experienced being in a restaurant when service is poor, your food is cold when it arrives, and no one seems to care whether or not you are happy. In another restaurant, you may find that the waiters and waitresses are very attentive, they are aware of your needs, your food arrives properly served and warm, and so on. What causes the difference? It is normally a floor manager in a restaurant who is continually watching the customers and the servers. In other words, that floor manager is attempting to match the capacity of the restaurant to serve the customers. When it appears that a customer is not having his or her water glass filled or ashtrays emptied, the floor manager will either personally perform that function or make sure that it occurs. It is not having an extra person in the restaurant, but the person himself or herself that makes good service happen.

WAR ROOM

The computer center is comprised of many subsections. These may include a data library, security function, production coordinators, control clerks, computer operators, and so on. It is the integration and use of all these individual resources that enables the computer center to operate.

The "war room" concept provides a daily strategy session or sessions on how best to handle computer center problems. When the war room concept is used, the section supervisors normally meet at the beginning of each work shift. At this meeting they get status reports on the results of processing from the preceding day, the estimated workload for the day, any potential obstacles for today's work, and the status of projects occurring in the computer center. The problems are dealt with as a group. If changes need to be made, for example, some extra capacity added through changing the workload schedule, a decision can be made through the combined effort of the group, which is agreeable to the entire group.

The war room may be the data center manager's office or a special room set aside for action purposes. If the workload status is on a computer, the war room should have access to the computer. Each manager at the meeting should be provided with status reports and blackboards or the equivalent to list problems for action. The senior member of the computer center runs the meeting, which in many instances may last only a few moments.

If problems occur during the day, the team is again assembled in the war room to take action. One might visualize a battleship with the alert siren shrieking throughout the computer center and the managers running to the war room. Although it may not occur exactly that way in practice, that is the concept. The production control manager handles the minor day-to-day problems, while the war room deals with the larger problems. For example, the war room may decide to subcontract work to a service bureau to alleviate some short-term capacity problems.

HELP DESK

Computer centers serve a wide variety of users. Users experience periods of anxiety when their work is late or appears incorrect. Many users have developed close working relationships with systems analysts/programmers, but may not have that same close working relationship with the computer center manager. For this reason, when problems occur, they may be uncertain as to who is the best person to call. The result may be that they call anybody from a systems analyst, to a programmer, to a computer operator, to a secretary.

The help desk is a concept that centralizes within one desk or person a clearing point for all problem requests directed at the computer center. The types of problems that might be directed to a help desk are:

- Request for status of job
- Query as to why job is late
- Query as to why part of job is missing
- Need to have a job rerun
- Need to clarify a computer center operating procedure
- Unhappiness with a computer center procedure
- Etc.

There are two methods of staffing the help desk. One is to staff it with senior computer operators. This takes some of the most knowledgeable people in the computer center and makes them available on a full-time basis to answer user requests. The second method is to staff the desk with the secretary of the computer center manager. In the opinion of the author, the latter is the preferred staffing method.

The help desk is normally reached by telephone. In organizations that have a four-digit internal phone number, some computer centers arrange the numbers so that it spells "HELP" when they dial the number. This is a gimmick, but it shows some insight and public relations effort going into the help desk concept.

The help desk is normally supplied with a computer terminal. On the terminal is the current status of jobs. The help desk should also have two other resources. One is a list of people in the computer center and their area of responsibility. This is needed so that requests can be directed to the appropriate person. The second list contains the names of key user personnel, and to whom the request should be channeled. For example, if the corporate vice president calls requesting information, that request should probably be directed at the computer center manager. With this second type of listing, the computer center provides for handling requests in a predetermined sequence of importance.

The person at the help desk is responsible for responding to all inquiries. If the help desk attendant can handle that inquiry personally, for example, determining the status of the job on the computer terminal, he or she should do so. If the answer can be gotten quickly, the caller should be asked to hold the line while the help desk attendant gets the appropriate information. This normally means that the attendant has at least two lines, one incoming and one to call for information within the data center. If the attendant is unable to get a quick answer, the caller should be told that the request will be responded to quickly. The attendant should then assign responsibility for the inquiry to the appropriate person and notify the requester who will be responding to them with the information. It is the responsibility of the help desk attendant to ensure that response is made on a timely basis.

KEEPING SUPPLIES NEAR PRODUCTION

Computer operations may be delayed because of the unavailability of supplies. Supplies in a computer center include production files, scratch files, printer paper, and other supplies needed for production purposes. If these supplies are stored away from the production areas, delays ranging from minutes to hours might be incurred before a production need could be satisfied.

RECORDED MESSAGE

Many requests to the computer center are for the status of information. This is the same type of information that is requested from airlines. People are continually calling, wanting to know if flights are on time or if late, how late. Because these calls to the airlines occur in such frequency, the airlines have adopted a system of recording a message giving the status of flights. Anyone calling that number will hear the most up-to-date recording of the status of flights and then be given a number to call if additional information is needed.

The concept of recording the status of computer jobs is being used by many data centers. In the simplest form, it uses a message player on which the status is manually recorded. These devices cost only about $200. In more sophisticated shops, the status is maintained by the computer, and using a voice generator the computer can develop its own recorded message. Thus people call the computer to find the status of jobs. Since most people today are accustomed to recorded telephone messages, they do not object to the concept. At the same time, it frees personnel who otherwise would have to answer the same repetitive requests.

EDP ADMINISTRATIVE GUIDELINE 27

People are upset when their work is late, but the pain of tardiness can be relieved by being informed of the approximate length of the delay sufficiently in advance of the time scheduled.

QUALITY IMPROVEMENT PRACTICES

Everybody knows what constitutes good quality and what constitutes bad quality. The problem is that one person's definition of quality is frequently different from another's. This concept has hurt some data center managers.

Some time ago, I bought a Ford Mustang. On driving the car home and showing it to my family and friends, someone pointed out to me that the car was leaking oil. When I returned the car for service, the service manager looked on the problem as routine. In a few days when the radio stopped working, it was just another problem for the service manager to fix. And again, a week after that, when the car wouldn't start, it was just another everyday problem to the service manager. What the service manager perceived as routine, I perceived as extraordinary and was enraged at the manufacturer.

The difference in quality expectations can lead to the computer center manager being complacent, but the customers being upset. The solution to this dilemma is the mutual agreement between the computer center and the users regarding what quality computer center operations need. For example, if the production of results is received within plus or minus 15 minutes of the expected time, is that acceptable, or will the user be upset when it is one minute late? If the computer center manager believes that 15 minutes is reasonable but the user does not, they have a quality problem.

Some of the practices used by computer centers to improve the actual or perceived quality of their work include (see Figure 50) the following.

QUALITY STANDARDS

Standards are the measure by which quality is assessed. Standards predefine what is expected, and then what occurs is measured against those standards. Differences between actual processing and the standards represent quality problems that need to be addressed.

Practice	Description	Effectiveness
Quality standards	The measures by which a product will be evaluated	High
Quality control	A review process that evaluates the correctness of the products received	High
Output inspectors	People who review the operations process	High
Receiving dock	Centralized receipt of all input to control receipt and condition of product	Medium
SWAT team	An on-site emergency correction team	Medium
Public relations	A formal process directed at improving the image of computer operations	Medium
User group	An informal association of users to discuss and understand computer operations	Medium
Newsletter	Information to users on the status and plans of computer operations	Low

Figure 50   *Quality Improvement Practices*

Among the quality standards that need to be established within a data center operation are:

- Acceptable levels of hardware performance
- Criteria that application programs must meet before they are acceptable to be executed
- Required operations documentation
- Acceptable job-rerun level
- Acceptable operator-error level
- Expected number of jobs to be completed on time
- Expected percent of processing capacity that will be utilized
- Acceptable level of customer complaints

These standards should be developed by the computer center. However, they should be standards that provide the type of performance that is acceptable to the user. A standard acceptable to the computer center which upsets many users is not a good standard.

Without quality standards, there are no goals to achieve or means of measuring performance. If one looks at some level of performance and says, "That's okay," it is just a confirmation that what has happened is all right. It is far better to define expectations and then implement those procedures and practices that make those expectations happen than to just look at what has occurred and state whether or not it is acceptable. Note that to be effective, standards must change over time.

QUALITY CONTROL

Quality control is a formal process that evaluates the quality of a product throughout the production cycle. Quality control can be continuous, or it can measure the product before it is released to the customer. However, it is normally more economical to have quality control checks throughout the production cycle than only at the end of the production cycle.

The quality control function must establish formal quality control procedures. The process of checking quality should not be a judgmental one but rather, a factual one. The process must be supported by any tools or techniques necessary to measure quality.

The quality control function can be performed by an independent quality control group or by members of the computer operations staff. When the staff evaluates quality, each member can evaluate his or her own quality, or quality can be measured by peers or supervisors. Normally, the method of performing the quality control function is less important than the fact that the function is performed.

The results produced by the quality control function are used in two ways. First, if the product is defective, it should be corrected immediately. Second, if the production process in the computer center contributes to creating poor production products, the results of the quality control should be used to change the process.

OUTPUT INSPECTORS

The products delivered to computer center customers should be inspected. The inspection process can be a subset of quality control or processed by itself. The objective is to ensure the accuracy and completeness of information going to user personnel.

The inspection can be performed by computer center and/or user personnel. The process can be performed within the computer center or within the user area. The objective is to review the results, either on paper or terminal, to ensure their reasonableness. This is a people check on automated processing.

The types of conditions that would be the responsibility of an inspector include:

- Output is printed on the right paper.
- Output is printed in the right format.
- New changes are incorporated.
- Reports are complete.
- Messages are directed to the right terminal/location.
- Output device did not fail, such as a malfunction in the printer.
- Negotiable documents are all accounted for.
- Appropriate security procedures are used.

RECEIVING DOCK

In most business organizations, all product received from outside sources goes through a central receiving dock. This serves two purposes. First, it ensures that all ordered products are received; and second, it provides an opportunity to reject an unwanted or poor-quality product.

If products are sent to a variety of people, it is possible that a product would be accepted which was not ordered or which fails to meet quality standards. When the receiving function is formalized, surprises are minimized. The receiving dock formally records all receipts, the condition in which they were received, and then delivers them to the appropriate party.

Computer centers receive two types of products. One is physical, such as hardware, computer media, furniture, and other supplies. The second is logical, such as systems, operating software, and documentation. Generally, it is not necessary to have two receiving functions for these two types of products.

The general procedures followed by the receiving dock are:

1. Obtain notice of expected receipts.
2. Accept all receipts on behalf of the computer center.
3. Reject products that have not been ordered.
4. Count the number of products delivered in conjunction with the shipper to limit the computer center's responsibility to what was actually received.
5. Note any deficiencies in the condition of products received, including software.

SWAT TEAM

A SWAT team is a specialized group organized for the purpose of dealing with problems. A SWAT team would be present in the computer center whenever the center is in operation. Should a problem occur, the SWAT team is dispatched immediately to handle the problem.

The SWAT team is normally comprised of highly skilled operations personnel. These personnel should have a knowledge of applications as well as of operating software. Because it may be an around-the-clock operation, many organizations put SWAT team members on 12-hour shifts, three days a week. This has proved helpful in getting people to volunteer for this elite corps.

The SWAT team normally has the following responsibilities:

1. Visit the source of problems as promptly as possible. Note that operations personnel are usually requested to do nothing until the SWAT team members arrive.

2.   Document the problem and save the necessary evidence (e.g., core dumps).
3.   Take corrrective action if possible, for example, if it is a space management problem, reallocate space.
4.   Call the appropriate party to take action if the SWAT team is unable to correct the problem (this may be systems and programming personnel, vendor personnel, or user personnel).
5.   Monitor the corrective process to ensure that it is done properly.
6.   Periodically summarize the problems encountered and develop recommendations for global solutions, if possible.

PUBLIC RELATIONS

Public relations are formal efforts to improve the image of computer operations. The establishment of a public relations function within the computer center is done to ensure that the functions being performed by the computer center are viewed positively by its customers. Obviously, the computer center cannot afford to expend extensive resources in publications, but it can afford to ask one of its more senior people to look at the activities and ask the questions:

- Does this activity present a positive image to customers?
- Do the employees of the computer center act in a manner that brings credit to the computer center?
- Are there things that the computer center could do which would improve its image within the organization?
- Do the products produced by the computer center convey a professional image?

It is very possible that some computer center activities result in a negative image being portrayed in the organization. Unless someone in the computer center keeps challenging the image, it may never be improved. It is frequently an attitude to detail that for a very small cost can make a very large difference in image.

USER GROUP

Many users have only a minimal understanding of the procedures and problems facing a computer center. On the other hand, many computer centers do not understand the specific needs and requirements of their customers. Forming a user group provides a vehicle for these discussions. Generally, the group is informal, has no authority or power, but becomes a spokesperson for the users. As such, ideas that may not be acceptable to individual users can be implemented through peer pressure. For example, many computer centers have a problem getting changes to systems installed in releases instead of on a change-by-change basis. Once the user groups understand the value, the group itself may lobby for it, even though the concept might be unacceptable if imposed on users by the data center.

In organizations having user groups, the groups frequently meet twice a year. Meetings rarely last longer than a day. The typical agenda would be for the computer center manager to present plans and problems of the computer center. Through informal discussions with the users, the computer center manager would then arrange for workshops and discussion groups. These groups would report back to the full body of users, who might then through democratic action adopt recommendations to the computer center for changes that would benefit all users.

NEWSLETTER

Newsletters are a means of communicating factual information to users. It is a way of telling users that the computer center cares enough about them to tell them about things that are happening in the data center. Items that can be included in a data center newsletter include:

- New equipment on order
- New equipment being installed
- Capacity and speed of equipment
- Scheduling information
- Factual information on amount and type of material
- Information explaining the computer center's ability to meet its quality standards (e.g., the hardware is operational 99.5 percent of the time, etc.)

Newsletters should be issued on a regular basis. Depending on the size of the computer center, the newsletters might be issued quarterly or monthly.

EDP ADMINISTRATIVE GUIDELINE 28

The bitterness of poor quality remains long after the sweetness of meeting the schedule has been forgotten.

COST-EFFECTIVENESS IMPROVEMENT PRACTICES

As the cost of computer processing drops, more user activities become economical to automate. The computer center manager has many options available to reduce the cost of computer processing. The manager should take these options, because if costs are not controlled, users may seek alternative methods of processing. Some of the practices that the data center can use to control and reduce costs include the following (see Figure 51).

COST ACCOUNTING SYSTEM

What the computer center manager cannot measure, the manager cannot control. If the computer center manager does not know where the computer center funds are being expended, it is difficult to identify the high-cost areas for potential reduction. Cost accounting systems are a method of identifying and associating the cost to develop or produce a product.

A prerequisite to installing a cost accounting system is to identify the areas of cost. Next, a method must be installed to collect those costs. Finally, the cost accounting system accumulates cost by product. Having this detailed information, the computer center manager can search out for further study individual costs that appear out of line and hopefully, change procedures or seek alternative methods to reduce those costs. Unless the manager can identify where costs go, the probability of cost reduction is minimal.

UNBUNDLING COMPUTER CENTER COSTS

The normal method for developing computer center costs is to accumulate all of the funds expended and then allocate those funds among jobs run on the computer. The accumulated costs include the data library, disaster plans,

Practice	Description	Effectiveness
Cost accounting system	Method of identifying and associating cost within a product	High
Unbundling computer center costs	Charge customers only for the services they use	High
Profit center	Divide computer operations into individual profit centers	High
Charging price, not cost	Provide funds to upgrade technologically as needed	High
Variable rates	Charge different rates for services as needed to smooth work flow	Medium
Financial analysis	Perform cost analyses	Medium
Using outside services for overload	Have peak volume work performed outside	Medium
Supply management	Minimize on-hand supplies	Low

Figure 51   *Cost-Effectiveness Improvement Practices*

security procedures, control groups, and so on. The question becomes: Is this the fair way to charge users for services?

The computer center has three options on charging users. First, the method described above can be continued. Second, the computer center can unbundle so that users are charged only for the services they require. For example, if certain users do not require off-site storage, they are neither provided with or charged for it. Third, the computer center can continue to charge each user for all the services, but explain precisely what is being paid for.

If the full chargeout method is used, users may look at alternating pricing when services are not equal. For example, many of the services included in an in-house computer center may not be offered by an outside service bureau. Yet a user may move to the outside service bureau because of a belief that the costs of computing are cheaper. Unbundling explains to users the true cost of each service.

PROFIT CENTER

The profit center concept divides the computer center into several operating units. Each unit is considered a profit center. This means that the unit must demonstrate that it can generate a return on investment for its services. This forces each unit to consider its costs carefully.

The profit centers generate revenue by charging for their services. For example, the projects may pay a fee to store their tapes in the data library, or a fee for security services. The charging of a fee provides the following advantages to controlling costs:

- The cost of each service is known.
- The change in cost of each service will be known.
- Ineffective management for the service encourages users to seek alternatives, which in turn applies pressures to keep costs low.
- Supervisors of an area have their job enriched because they operate as small entrepreneurs, and thus have the incentive to manage a business.
- Supervisors are trained to be managers.

CHARGING PRICE, NOT COST

The typical computer center chargeout method accumulates all costs and transfers those costs to user areas as chargeout rates. The objective of the system is for the computer center to break even at the end of the year. Unfortunately, this concept can lead to the obsolescence of application systems and computer resources.

The computer center manager has an obligation to maintain the technical proficiency of the computer center. To do this, the computer center manager must have discretionary funds to make technological changes as necessary. If the chargeout rate is cost, the discretion to use that money may reside in the hands of the users of the computer center. In other words, they may arbitrarily decide that they do not want to increase the cost and thus veto the recommended technological changes.

On the other hand, if the computer center manager charges a "price" for services, that price can include sufficient funds to maintain the technological currentness of the computer center. When price is charged, the decision over the use of funds to improve the computer center is moved from the user of the data center to the manager of the data center. Thus the manager has the option to act as a small businessperson but at the same time will be held responsible if the technological moves do not result in lower costs over the long term.

VARIABLE RATES

Many organizations, such as the telephone company, charge different rates for services during different hours of the day. The objective of charging variable rates is to smooth the workload during the day, which in turn makes more effective use of the computer center resources.

Computer operations have peak workloads at certain times of the day, certain days of the week, and certain weeks of the month. If these peak times can be plotted, the rates charged for services at those times can be increased to discourage casual users from using those peak times. Users who need the service during those times will have no problem paying the higher fees, whereas users who have discretion over when they use the computer, such as computer programmers or users developing routine reports, can opt to use the resources when the costs are lower. Note that in many instances, when there is idle time during the day or week, charging lower rates for that idle time will encourage people to perform activities they may not have attempted at the higher rates. Thus the variable-rate changes may, in effect, reduce all of the rates for computer services.

FINANCIAL ANALYSIS

Financial analysis is an accounting tool used to evaluate performance. In its simplest format, the analysis will show:

- Comparison of this year to last year
- Year-to-date totals
- Increases or decreases in cost or revenue from last month or last year
- Trend analysis of costs over time
- Bar chart comparing performance of various profit centers

Financial analysis can also calculate numerous ratios and relationships to help the data center manager evaluate performance. Some analysis of this type includes:

- Return on investment
- Supplies turnover per year
- Potential areas of waste, identified by abnormal increases in cost areas

If accountants with financial analyst skills are not available in the computer center, the computer center manager may wish to get assistance from the organization's accounting department. This assistance can suggest what analyses would be helpful and how to perform them; in some instances the accounting department may, in fact, perform them.

USING OUTSIDE SERVICES FOR OVERLOAD

One of the challenges that faces data processing departments is acquiring sufficient capacity for peak loads. Peak periods are normally hectic times for the computer center because it is operating at full capacity and may have a production backlog. Not only does this put undue pressure on the computer center personnel, but it can cause dissatisfaction among users as they wait for desperately needed reports.

An available alternative, which is used in many other industries, is to contract out excessive work at peak times. Within the office additional clerical personnel can be hired from secretarial services organizations. The same concept can be applied to computer center processing.

The data center manager can contract with service centers, other organizations, or hardware vendors to use their equipment on a part-time basis. Obviously, the cost of processing will be higher per unit of work, but the net cost to the organization should be less than if additional resources are acquired and left idle most of the year. The same analogy holds true for the secretarial services assistance. The hourly rate is significantly higher than that paid employees for the same work, but when the peak load work is finished, the temporary personnel are dismissed.

SUPPLY MANAGEMENT

Excessive supplies on hand increase the cost of the supplies. In addition, those extra supplies may never be used, as business conditions may change or new equipment may be acquired. The computer center management should consult with the inventory management experts in the organization. These people could provide the data center manager with guidelines or economic order quantities and other concepts, such as partial shipments. The savings involved

	Response			
Item	Yes	No	N/A	Comments
1. Has the data center established service standards?				
2. Has the data center established quality standards?				
3. Does the data center maintain detailed accounting records on cost?				
4. Is the data center considered a profit center in the organization?				
5. Does the data center maintain records on current and future workload?				
6. Does the data center have a long-range plan defining expected capacity and methods of achieving that capacity?				
7. Does the data center manager take an interest in the business of the users?				
8. Does the data center manager meet regularly with each major user?				
9. Does the data center monitor workload on an hour-by-hour basis?				
10. Is there one person on each shift in the data center with the authority to make the necessary changes to match workload with capacity?				
11. Does the data center have a help desk?				
12. Does data center management meet regularly to discuss workload and operational problems so that immediate corrective action can be undertaken?				
13. Is there a quality control function within the data center?				
14. Are the outputs from the data center reviewed before delivery to the users?				
15. Does the data center have procedures to record problems and take quick action on problems?				
16. Is there an informal association of data center users who meet periodically to discuss data center problems and solutions to those problems?				
17. Does the data center provide a newsletter of factual information to data center users?				
18. Is there a cost accounting system in place in the data center?				
19. Does the data center know what each item in the computer center costs the users?				
20. Are subsections of the data center considered to be profit centers?				
21. Does the data center charge price and not cost for its services?				
22. Does the data center charge variable rates to smooth the workload?				
23. Are financial analysis techniques used to provide the data center manager with information to help in controlling costs?				
24. Are outside services used to handle peak workloads rather than building the necessary internal capacity?				
25. Has the cost of services provided by the data center been decreasing continually over the past several years?				
26. Are data center users beginning to utilize alternative sources for computing?				

Figure 52   *Computer Operations Checklist*

can be in space freed for other purposes, immediate budget reduction by not having to purchase supplies for some period of time, and reduction in the carrying cost of money to buy the extra supplies.

EDP ADMINISTRATIVE GUIDELINE 29
Accounting training for the data center management will not only result in lower data center costs, but will teach that manager the language of management—which is accounting.

A COMPUTER OPERATIONS SELF-ASSESSMENT CHECKLIST

It is healthy for any organization to undergo periodic assessments. The objective of the checklist for computer operations shown in Figure 52 is to assist the administrative manager in reviewing the administrative practices of the data center. ''Yes'' answers to these questions are indicative of good data center administrative practices, while ''no'' answers indicate areas that should be investigated for potential improvements in service.

Chapter

9

Systems Administration

Project Management (handwritten)

Directing a computer project is an administrative and technical challenge. The project leader who emphasizes the technical part of project management to the exclusion of administration will continually be fighting an uphill battle. Administration is the process of ensuring the effective utilization of resources. It has been said that if the South had better administrative procedures at Gettysburg, they would have won the war. Unfortunately, the South's system did not permit the effective movement of information so that the forces could be redirected at the appropriate time.

The effective project leader understands the supervisory, procedural, and administrative responsibilities of the function. When these forces are in harmony, projects tend to go smoothly. This chapter provides project administrative guidance aimed at optimizing scarce data processing resources. The chapter explores each aspect of running a systems development and/or maintenance project and then proposes how to coordinate all of the project tasks through effective administrative and control procedures.

WHAT SYSTEMS NEED ADMINISTERING?

Data processing has a broad range of system responsibilities, including administrative responsibility for:

- In-house developed systems
- Purchased applications
- Service bureau processing
- Time-sharing services
- Distributed systems
- User-operated systems (microcomputers, etc.)
- Office automation systems (which interface with information systems)

The administrative role and responsibility will vary depending on:

1. Amount of user control over processing
2. Origination of software (in-house versus purchased)
3. Location of processing

Generally, data processing will have either a direct or an indirect responsibility for any automated application within the organization. To let users flounder is not fulfilling DP's information processing responsibilities. DP should establish a method of administering *all* corporate information-processing systems.

What Is Systems Administration?

In a single word, systems administration means "managing" a systems project. It is the totality of the nontechnical tasks that need to be performed to ensure that the project is successful. The tasks to be performed will vary according to the specific role DP has for the system. For example, with an in-house DP-developed application, DP will have an extensive administrative role, while the administrative role normally will be only oversight and counsel on a user-purchased and operated application.

THE PROJECT MANAGER'S ADMINISTRATIVE ROLE

The data processing mission in most organizations is to develop, acquire, and implement systems to satisfy the operating requirements of the organization. The project manager is the person assigned responsibility for one of those operating systems, for example, payroll. The project manager is the field general entrusted with the responsibility to plan, organize, direct, and control the development, implementation, and maintenance of an application system.

Few project managers are trained for this role. The normal progression in most organizations is to begin as a computer programmer, advance to become a systems analyst, and then finally be appointed to a project manager position. In this process, the person is normally well trained to be a computer programmer. However, the systems analysis skills are acquired primarily on the job by observing others—good or bad. The elevation to project manager may be as much attributable to time in grade or good programming and system skills as to managerial skills. However, the project manager is a manager and requires new skills to be successful in that role. One of the needed skills is project administration.

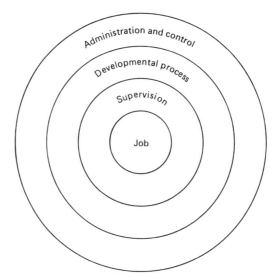

Figure 53   *Project Manager's Role*

The breadth of the project manager's role is illustrated in Figure 53. At the center of the role is the job assigned to the project manager. This is normally paramount in the thinking of data processing management, to the exclusion of other project manager responsibilities.

The project manager has supervisory responsibilities over the staff assigned to the project. One might speculate that much of the high turnover in data processing is attributable directly to poor first-line supervision. Project managers tend to be technicians, most of whom prefer the technical part of the job, as opposed to being supervisors. In discussing morale in many data processing departments, it is very obvious where the interests of the project managers lie.

The data processing department provides a process for the project manager to use in accomplishing the assigned job. These processes are frequently referred to as system development life-cycle methodologies. However, like many aspects of the data processing department, the project leader may not be highly skilled in this process, and in addition may not have to follow it precisely. In many data processing departments the project leaders have a great leeway in determining which parts, if any, of the developmental process they care to use in accomplishing their job. When first-line supervision ignores departmental policy, it induces a negative attitude on the part of their staff regarding the need to follow any direction given from data processing management. Thus few systems analysts and programmers follow departmental standards.

The last part of the project manager's role is the administration and control of the project. This encompasses record keeping of resources consumed, authorized, and needed; deliverables produced by the project; and the project status. Much of the administrative function is ensuring that the project development is adequately controlled, control being the vehicle to ensure the effective use of resources and the timely completion of project objectives.

The role of the project manager is to determine project control and administration. The administration and control procedures must be consistent with departmental policy and applied effectively during project implementation. Unfortunately, many have fallen short on the administrative roles and thus, although the project may produce the results specified by the project, the wounded at the end of the project include:

- Disillusioned systems analysts/programmers
- Missed schedules and cost overruns
- Users frustrated over their ability to interact effectively with the project

The systems development battleground is frequently strewn with the wounded. In reviewing systems after implementation, the auditors have been accused of entering the battlefield after the battle and shooting the wounded. However, good administrative and control procedures will leave a healthy and enthusiastic army to move on to another project battlefield.

ORGANIZING A SYSTEMS PROJECT TO WIN

All systems projects are comprised of four criteria: scope, schedule, resources, and administration. Most projects are organized in a manner that optimizes the technological aspects of a project while minimizing the administrative and control aspects. The reason for this is that technology is considered the primary mission, and administration a secondary or "as time is available" responsibility. In addition, it may be assumed that the project leader will do all of the administration, and the other people assigned to the project will perform only technical tasks.

The traditional project management organization is illustrated in Figure 54. This shows the project manager in charge of the project with systems analysts reporting directly to him. The programmers report to the systems analysts. In this organizational structure, the project is broken up technically into pieces, and technicians assigned responsibility for implementing those individual technical pieces. The size of the staff and division of the workload, will depend on the size of the project.

A suggested organizational structure for a computer project is illustrated in Figure 55. This structure is not meant to represent bodies but rather, to represent functional project responsibilities. Note that these coincide closely with the four project criteria discussed earlier (i.e., scope, schedule, resources, and administration). Let us look briefly at each area:

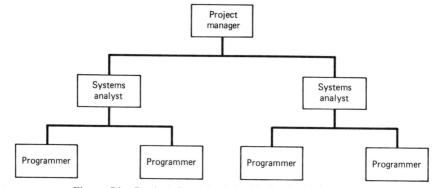

Figure 54 *Project Organized for Technological Emphasis*

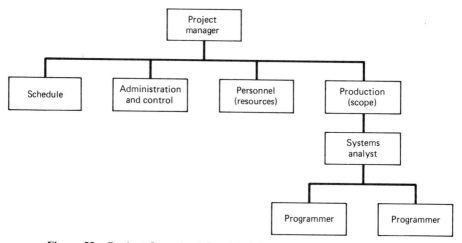

Figure 55 *Project Organized for Administrative and Control Emphasis*

- *Schedule:* Those aspects of project planning that determine the sequence in which events will be performed and the resources to be allocated to those events.
- *Administration and control:* The planning and record-keeping functions of the project. Responsibilities include such things as documentation control, compliance to standards, maintaining an inventory of deliverables, and so on.
- *Personnel:* Acquiring, assigning, and evaluating personnel performance. Activities include working out for the interest of personnel assigned to the project, ensuring that they are adequately trained, and attempting to improve morale and productivity.
- *Production:* Those tasks involved in accomplishing the project requirements.

Under this organizational structure, each of the functions necessary to the success of the project will receive appropriate attention. In very small projects the project leader will still assume most of the responsibility for these functions. As the projects become larger, it is best to delegate the various responsibilities to different people. Note that in some departments a formal administrative function may work with project personnel to accomplish some of these tasks. The key to a successful project is not who performs the function, but that the project is appropriately identified and executed. The remainder of this chapter describes techniques and practices helpful in fulfilling the administrative and control responsibilities of a project manager.

ADMINISTERING THE COMPUTER SYSTEMS PROJECT

One of the old cliches of data processing is: "We never have time to do it right the first time, but always have time to correct it." Much of the not doing it right is attributable to insufficient administration and control. Because we cannot see administration and control in the final product, it is frequently felt to be unnecessary.

The driver takes off in an auto for a new destination. She or he has vague directions on how to get to that location. On the way, it becomes apparent that the directions are incomplete. However, knowing what some of the landmarks should be, the driver continues on and hopes to find one of the landmarks. Not finding them, the driver, on impulse, takes another road, and then another road. After some ranting and raving about the poor directions and retracing the route many times, the driver finds the desired location. It is obvious to anyone observing this situation that the driver should have stopped and asked directions (i.e., administered and controlled the trip). Unfortunately, in many instances the driver is too proud, does not want to ask for help, or for a myriad of other reasons fails to do the obvious. We see the same situation repeated over and over in the implementation of a computer project. Those few seconds expended to stop and ask directions can return a big investment in increased productivity and decreased frustration.

The administrative process in a computer project is comprised of the following three areas (again note that the type of administration will vary based on the project and DP involvement in the project):

1. *Interface to other areas:* The project is not an island. It is connected and interfaces with many other parts of the data processing and user department(s). Ensuring the effective interface is an essential part of project administration.
2. *Control:* Project control comprises all of the methods and measures used within the project to safeguard its assets, check the accuracy and reliability

of project information, promote operational efficiency, and encourage adherence to data processing policies, procedures, and standards.

3. *Record keeping:* Project managers are normally charged with the responsibility to maintain records on the project status, for the use of resources, and for the significant project actions and decisions.

Each of these three parts of administration are comprised of a series of tasks. The project leader in organizing the project should ensure that the appropriate tasks are included in the project plan, assigned to personnel, and performed throughout the life of the project. The individual tasks and suggestions on implementing them are discussed next.

EDP ADMINISTRATIVE GUIDELINE 30

You cannot manage what you do not know—project administration tells you what you need to know in order to manage properly.

ADMINISTERING PROJECT INTERFACES

The complexity of today's technology requires a team of multidisciplined experts working together to manage a system project. In the early days of computing, a single person could develop and operate a system without outside assistance. As technology expanded, the physical movement of data, administration of data, data validation, report writing, and interface to the operating system moved under the auspices of systems programmers and other specialists, and in some cases to outside vendors and service bureaus.

The project manager can be viewed as a general contractor on a project. Much of the work will be allocated to subcontractors to perform. It is the responsibility of the project manager to select these subcontractors, negotiate a price for the service, and monitor the work of the subcontractor. Although the overall responsibility for the project remains with the project manager, much of the work does not.

The eight areas with which many projects interface are illustrated in Figure 56 and explained below.

REVIEWS

Most new design methodologies call for review groups to evaluate the project at predetermined checkpoints. These reviews can be conducted by professional EDP quality assurance personnel, peer groups, users, or a combination of any of these groups. The administrative responsibilities in conjunction with the review include:

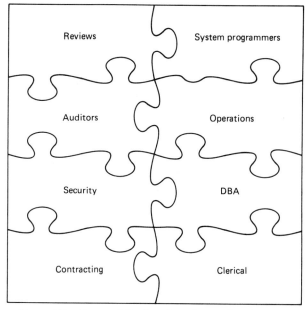

Reviews	System programmers
Auditors	Operations
Security	DBA
Contracting	Clerical

Figure 56 *Parts of Project Interface Administration*

- Scheduling the review
- Providing the review group with project material prior to the review (the review group will usually request what they want)
- Ensuring that the project has performed those tasks that the review group will be evaluating
- Allocating project personnel time to be present during the review
- Concurring with or refuting review findings, and making any necessary changes accordingly

AUDITORS

Internal auditors are responsible to assess the adequacy of controls in computer systems. Auditing literature recommends that this review occur during the developmental process. In some organizations auditors participate on a general review board, whereas in other organizations they conduct independent reviews themselves. The review begins by identifying risks and then determining if controls are adequate to reduce those risks to a reasonable level. If not, the auditors document these vulnerabilities and recommend that additional controls be added.

The primary interface with the auditor involves control documentation. The most commonly requested control documentation by auditors are control flowcharting and transaction flow analysis. Control flowcharting indicates the points of control in a computer system and the specific controls installed

at that point. Transaction flow analysis shows the flow of individual transactions through a computer system, indicating the controls in place throughout the processing cycle.

The audit interface will be lessened significantly if control documentation exists. If the design methodology does not call for this, the auditor may
need to sit down with project personnel and document the system's controls.
Auditor-detected vulnerabilities will be presented in the form of recommendations requiring time to accept or reject the recommendations and make
control changes accordingly.

SECURITY

The project may become involved with the data processing security function
in two ways. First, authorization may need to be obtained to enter and access
programs into the operating environment. Data used by those programs may
also have to be authorized. Second, the application itself may need to be protected by a security system. In the latter instance, the project manager must
specify security requirements for installation by the security function.

The type of administrative interface needed may include:

- Identification of programs/data to be entered into the operating
  environment
- Project team members having authorization to use the programs and/or
  data
- Project-developed resources that require protection
- Level of production
- Individuals/programs authorized to have access to the new resources

The project manager should also be concerned about the security of project documentation and information. If this is a concern, the project manager
should consult with the organization's security officer regarding appropriate
security measures to take. It may be desirable to acquire locked file cabinets
to store the documentation, and/or store the documentation in centralized
storage locations.

CONTRACTING

Some of the services required in implementing the project may be acquired
from outside sources. For example, special hardware or software may be needed, the use of consultants, special training services, and so on. These may
result in the project leader contracting for outside services.

Most organizations have formalized methods for acquiring outside services. The project leader must then interface with that purchasing function
first, and the service to be contracted with second. Depending on the organiza-

tion, the process may be quite complex if competitive bidding is required and/or formal documentation of specifications prior to the bidding process.

Once a contract is approved, the project manager is responsible for monitoring the implementation of the contract. This will involve working with the contractor, and reviewing the work of the contractor to ensure that the contractual specifications are complied with. It is also desirable at the end of the contract to record the type and quality of service received so that good contractors will be reused, and poor contractors prohibited from bidding on future contracts.

The interface between the project and the contractor will include:

- Preparing contract specifications
- Recommending contractors to bid on the job
- Selecting a contractor
- Providing clarification and guidance on the work
- Reviewing contractor deliverables
- Approving contractor deliverables
- Requesting changes in contractor deliverables and/or specifications
- Enforcing the contract
- Evaluating the contractor
- Acquiring needed maintenance
- Advising third parties on the merits of bidding specifications, a contract, a contractor, or accepting and working with a contractor

SYSTEM PROGRAMMERS

The system programmers' function is to provide the project with technical assistance in using software packages. The application programs must pass parameters back and forth to various operating software systems. The system programmers normally write the instructions that permit this interface to occur.

The operational efficiency of the application system can be improved by the work of the system programmer. The interface between the project and the system programmer is involved in determining what operating software facilities will be used by the program, in what order, and the method of interfacing. Because of the effect that this interface can have on the operating efficiency of the application system, the project manager should be convinced that the system programmer has optimized for the application system the use of hardware and operating software.

The interface between the project and the system programmer will include:

- Identification of files, data bases, terminals, and so on, involved in processing data to and from the application system
- Size and usage of data files/data bases
- Audit trail information that should be retained by the various operating logs

- Special operating features that the system programmer needs to prepare, such as routines using the operating system user exit options
- Utility programs that will be incorporated into the application, such as sorts
- Retention periods of data files

OPERATIONS

Application systems must be tested and then placed into a production environment. The interface with computer operations for these purposes should begin early in the project life. It is desirable as soon as the project knows the general operating characteristics that they begin discussions with computer operations regarding the availability of the needed hardware, software, and capacity.

The larger the processing capacity needed, the more important it becomes to interface early with computer operations. In some instances it can take two years to acquire the needed hardware. Interfacing late in the project may mean that operations is squeezed for capacity and may have to pay premiums to acquire the hardware needed.

The type of interface with operations will change as the project moves through the life cycle. During requirements and design, the interface is one of planning. During implementation, capacity may be needed for tests and/or the acquisition of special facilities for the project. As the project gets closer to going into production, files will need to be established, production programs recorded, libraries and operators given the necessary instructions, and the production jobs scheduled. During operations, the task is one of day-to-day coordination on volumes, changes, and special needs.

Computer operations may be heavily involved in testing. It is desirable to have operations run the test without any coaching from the project team. In addition, computer operations may require that the project meet certain standards before it can be placed into production. If so, computer operations will be performing an acceptance test on the implemented system to ensure that it meets their operating standards.

The types of interfaces that are common with operations are:

- Advising operations on anticipated workload
- Reviewing projects from an operations perspective
- Preparing operations instructions
- Preparing restart/recovery instructions
- Identifying backup data requirements
- Updating operations requirements, volumes, instructions, and documentation as the project changes
- Specifying status reports
- Complying with operations standards

DATA BASE ADMINISTRATOR

As organizations begin to administer data, the design process will change. Applications will need to interface into existing data structures. This will mean early and perhaps long consultations with the data base administrator (DBA).

In an advanced data base environment, the addition of new data elements, or modification of existing data elements, is done only with the approval of the data base administrator. Applications do not have the freedom to add data, change files, and so on, as they are but one of many users of the organization's data.

The types of interfaces that are common with the data base administrator include:

- Requests for listings from the data dictionary
- Early consultation on the current structure of the data base and changes that could be made to assist in the development of the project in question
- Requests to use data in the data base, which may involve changing some data base authorization codes to permit use of the data
- Training sessions on developing applications in a data base environment
- Requests for formalizing project subschemas
- Adding/deleting/changing data definitions and/or data structure
- Reviews of the use of data by the data base administrator
- Requests for special analyses of data base
- Requests for establishment of special data bases for test purposes

CLERICAL SUPPORT

The project may have its own clerical support or may use that of the department's administrative function. The types of clerical support that may be needed by the project include:

- Typing letters
- Key-entering data
- Ordering supplies
- Telephone answering services
- General typing/filing/assembling documentation
- Cataloging/indexing documentation
- Other jobs that can be performed more economically by clerical people than by professional people

One of the mistakes that many project managers make is to have many of the clerical functions performed by professional personnel. Although this may appear to be the simpler solution, it is normally a costlier solution. Project managers should identify and plan for the use of clerical personnel as they do any of the other resources they call upon during the development of a project.

EDP ADMINISTRATIVE GUIDELINE 31
Do not assume that the other person will do his or her job—if you want to be sure it is done, check on it!

ADMINISTERING PROJECT CONTROL

Projects can fail to achieve their stated objectives due to unanticipated or unexpected problems. The objective of control is to reduce problems associated with the threats to a successful project. Properly designed controls should improve the quality and productivity of the project. Controls should be used to reduce the cost of the project.

The areas requiring control in most computer projects are listed in Figure 57 and described below.

DOCUMENTATION

Documentation is required to maintain the system and to explain how processing occurs. The objective of controlling documentation is twofold: first, to ensure that it is complete; and second, to ensure that it is in conformance with the intent of the documentation procedures.

The steps that should be used in controlling documentation are:

1. Identify each piece of information that is to be prepared.
2. Make one project member accountable for preparing that documentation.
3. Develop a schedule of when the documentation should be prepared and verify that it was, in fact, prepared.
4. Have the documentation reviewed by an independent source to ensure that it meets the intent of management's documentation standards.
5. Store the documentation in a centralized documentation library (this can be within the project or centralized within the department).

RESOURCE UTILIZATION

Without proper planning and direction, the resources assigned to the project may be misused. People will be available before assignments are fully established, or work on poorly defined requirements and have to do the work over. The proper control over resources is a key to improving productivity.

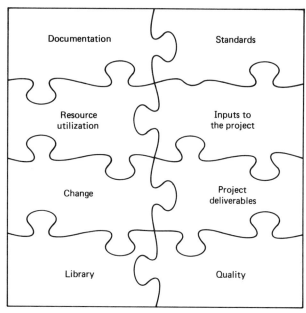

Figure 57 *Parts of Project Control Administration*

The steps that should be taken in a project to control the utilization of resources are:

1. Identify resources.
2. Define tasks in measurable terms so that progress can be measured.
3. Schedule each person for at least two tasks, so that if progress is temporarily halted on one task the person can proceed on the other.
4. Review status of each person's work frequently, and change workload as appropriate.
5. Establish milestones for each person and measure progress against those milestones.

CHANGE

The only thing constant in the project is change. It is of little value to attempt to reduce change, but of much value to control it. All changes should be funneled through a central point, in order to control change.

The steps that have proved effective in controlling change are:

1. Record and number all changes (this assumes that they are approved; if not, they should be evaluated and approved before being entered into the control system).
2. Determine if they are a structural or a nonstructural change. A struc-

tural change is a change to the requirements, whereas a nonstructural change is an isolated change, such as changing the name of a report.

3. Schedule nonstructural changes for implementation.
4. Enter structural changes as a requirement to design through programming.
5. Install changes in batches or releases at prescheduled times, such as monthly or quarterly. People cannot assimilate change more frequently—except under emergency conditions.
6. Do not install any changes, except emergency changes, during the month prior to installing a system into a production environment.

LIBRARY

At a minimum, projects use a source and an object code library. In some organizations, additional libraries may exist. Programs and other project specifications and interfaces are recorded on the libraries; updated; moved from library to library; and deleted. Controls ensure that the right program or data is on the right library at the right time.

Library controls should follow the following steps:

1. Develop a numbering system that takes into account multiple versions of the same program.
2. Date all programs on the libraries to indicate their starting date and the date on which they are to be removed from active status.
3. Maintain a project log indicating what programs or data are on what library.
4. Delete unneeded programs and data as soon as possible.

STANDARDS

Standards are the means by which performance is measured. For this reason, projects should follow standards to ensure that they are in compliance with the intent of data processing management. However, in many organizations there are numerous standards, and continuous changes to the standards. This poses a dilemma to the project regarding how to ensure compliance.

Controls that the project manager should install to ensure that the project is in compliance with the department's standards are:

1. Maintain one up-to-date set of standards in the project area. Ensure that project personnel are familiar with the standards relating to their work.
2. Notify all project personnel that they are expected to comply with the departmental standards.

3. Develop self-assessment checklists for the standards by type of standard, such as programming standard, system design standard, and so on.
4. Request for every project task that the self-assessment be performed by the person responsible for the task, to identify those standards which have and have not been complied with.
5. Request that the person responsible for the standards sign the self-assessment document as a correct statement of compliance to the standards.

INPUTS TO THE PROJECT

Requirements and other project data are delivered to the project continually. To lose or mislay that information can be both embarrassing to the project manager and harmful to the project. Establishing a point of control over data going to the project provides greater assurance that the information will be received and acted on.

The suggested controls over input documentation to the project are:

1. Establish a central receiving point for all project input.
2. Create an input log and record all inputs in that log.
3. Deliver the input to the appropriate person for action.
4. Record on the log who received the input.
5. Appoint someone to follow up periodically to ensure that all appropriate action has been taken.

PROJECT DELIVERABLES

Project methodologies specify the deliverables to be produced at each system checkpoint. These deliverables will be needed for maintenance. It is important to know that they are complete and where they are stored.

The controls over project deliverables should include:

1. Log of expected deliverables
2. Person responsible for the preparation of each deliverable
3. Date on which deliverable was complete
4. Disposition and/or storage of deliverable (note that all this information should be recorded on the deliverable log)

QUALITY

Quality in an application system is achieving user expectations. To control quality, those expectations must be defined. The areas of quality expectation as developed through research for the U.S. Department of Defense are illustrated in Figure 58.

Factor	Definition
Correctness	Extent to which a program satisfies its specifications and fulfills the user's mission objectives
Reliability	Extent to which a program can be expected to perform its intended function with required precision
Efficiency	The amount of computing resources and code required by a program to perform a function
Integrity	Extent to which access to software or data by unauthorized persons can be controlled
Usability	Effort required to learn, operate, prepare input, and interpret output of a program
Maintainability	Effort required to locate and fix an error in an operational program
Testability	Effort required to test a program to ensure that it performs its intended function
Flexibility	Effort required to modify an operational program
Portability	Effort required to transfer a program from one hardware configuration and/or software system environment to another
Reusability	Extent to which a program can be used in other applications—related to the packaging and scope of the functions that the programs perform
Interoperability	Effort required to couple one system with another

Figure 58   *Quality Factors*

Each project perceives quality in a different way. These varying expectations can be controlled through the use of the quality factors as follows:

1. In the beginning of the project, have the users rank the factors defined in Figure 58 in importance to them. Unimportant factors should be deleted from the list.
2. For each of the factors, define the criteria that must be achieved to satisfy the user's expectation for that factor. The factor then becomes a success criterion.
3. Include those success criteria as project requirements.
4. Measure to ensure that those requirements are implemented.
5. Request user to test system to verify that quality requirements have been achieved.

EDP ADMINISTRATIVE GUIDELINE 32

If it is worth doing, it is worth controlling.

ADMINISTERING RECORD-KEEPING CONTROL

It is important in a well-run computer project to keep score. The project manager must know whether he or she is winning or losing at the project game. Some of the record keeping will be required by the department, whereas other record keeping is desirable for the project.

The record keeping should be centrally administered. Ideally, the project would like to have a project comptroller to oversee the project record keeping. In reality, the project manager, or assistant project manager, will have the record-keeping responsibilities.

Wherever practical, record keeping should be automated. Note that in many companies some of these record-keeping functions are centralized. Many project managers maintain their records on minicomputers or through small computer files. The objective should be to maintain the best possible records at the minimal cost.

The areas requiring record-keeping control for system projects are illustrated in Figure 59 and explained below.

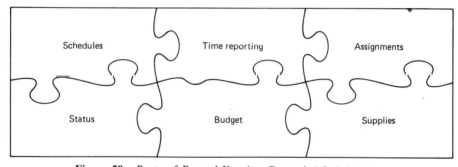

Figure 59   *Parts of Record-Keeping Control Administration*

SCHEDULES

A schedule is the detailed plan for completing the project. Ideally, the schedule should be automated and tied into the developmental methodology. A good schedule is tied to distinct measurable tasks and holds specific persons accountable for the completion of that task. Unless there is a method to substantiate that a task is complete, schedules usually do little more than account for people's time.

The element of a good schedule includes:

- Distinct measurable tasks
- Identification of the sequence in which tasks must be performed
- Identification of desirable start and stop dates

- Identification of amount of resources assigned to the task
- Identification of specific personnel assigned to the task
- Identification of person accountable to complete the task

STATUS

Project status indicates the percent of the project completed at a specific point in time. Status, like schedule, is meaningless unless it can be tied to specific measurable tasks. Knowing that 75 percent of the assigned resources have been consumed tells little about the project. An old data processing axiom says that projects never get behind schedule until they are 90 percent complete.

The attributes of a good status system are:

- Identification of specific measurable tasks
- Identification of percent of total project effort that each task represents
- Identification of completed and partially completed tasks
- Identification of project status from the perspective of both tasks completed and potential critical path scheduling problems

TIME REPORTING

Most data processing groups intermix status reporting and time reporting. This generally results in poor status reporting. It is a much better practice to have two distinct reporting systems for data processing staff. Time reporting is in hours of staff work, whereas status reporting should be in terms of completed tasks.

The elements of good time reporting include:

- There is a simplistic system to follow.
- Daily reporting is used to increase accuracy.
- Reported information is of value to the project and/or data processing management.

BUDGET

It is recommended that project costs be collected regardless of whether users are charged for the services. It is important for data processing management to know where their resources are being consumed. These data are essential if managers are going to develop realistic data processing plans.

Budgetary data should be collected by work category needed for planning purposes. The elements of a good budgetary record-keeping system include:

- Data are accumulated as by-products of other systems (e.g., people's time recorded through the time-reporting system).
- Data are reported by category meaningful for planning purposes.
- Causes of significant overages or underages are identified.

ASSIGNMENTS

Records must be maintained on the specific tasks assigned project members. This information becomes input to the scheduling system. However, from a record-keeping system it is important to know relationships between assignments and the skill levels of personnel assigned. As discussed in Chapter 5, people lacking the necessary skills to complete the tasks to which they have been assigned should either be allocated extra time or be closely supervised.

The elements of a good assignment system include:

- Identification of measurable tasks
- Identification of project member skills
- Identification of skills needed to accomplish the identified tasks
- People assigned to each task
- Backup personnel for each task in the event that the primary person is transferred, leaves, and so on

SUPPLIES

The magnitude of supplies consumed by any one project will vary significantly. Normally, minor supplies are maintained by the department, such as coding pads, pencils, and so on. On the other hand, the project may have some valuable supplies, such as disk packs, standards and other manuals, preprinted project report forms, and so on and these should be recorded.

The elements of a good supplies record-keeping system include:

- Logging of type and quantity of supplies on hand
- One person accountable for each type of supply
- Purpose of supplies usage, if applicable
- Periodic count of supplies to ensure that they are still present

---

EDP ADMINISTRATIVE GUIDELINE 33

The project manager who keeps good records can explain what has happened and why.

PROJECT ADMINISTRATION WORKSHEETS

The systems project administration function should keep records on each of the areas being administered. This chapter identified 22 areas that the project leader should consider as part of project administration. Each of these areas, such as supplies control, will involve a series of items to be performed. It is recommended that a worksheet be maintained on each area and the administrative items in those areas be identified and controlled.

Let us look at an example of controlling project supplies. Some of the items that might need to be done are:

- Create a small supply of expendables for the project
- Contact purchasing to order special project supplies
- Maintain logs on nonexpendable supplies
- Periodically count the supplies on hand

For each of these items, some action is needed, someone should be made accountable for it, and the dates for accomplishment should be indicated. Maintaining this type of information ensures the project leader that the tasks will be done.

A sample worksheet for this purpose is illustrated in Figure 60. The example above has been included on that worksheet. The name of the area is indicated on the worksheet and all of the items are listed under the item column. If there is a contact, such as the purchasing manager, that should be indicated. The specific action or actions that have to be undertaken should be listed on the form together with the person to whom that action is assigned. The project manager should maintain the forms and indicate the day on which the assignment was made and the day on which it was completed. Room is provided on the form for any comments regarding completion or problems with the assignment.

A SYSTEMS ADMINISTRATION CHECKLIST

Administration of computer systems is a responsibility shared by the departmental administration function and the project leader. In larger departments, the centralized administration function may assume many of the tasks, whereas in smaller data processing departments the project leader will have greater administrative responsibilities. The checklist shown in Figure 61 is designed for the project leader to assess the adequacy of application system development administration. "Yes" answers, meaning the function is performed either centrally or within the project, are indicative of good administrative practices. "No" answers to the checklist should be investigated further as potential vulnerabilities regarding the performance, credibility, or success of the application system.

Item	Contact	Action Needed	Assigned to:	Dates		Comments
				Start	Stop	
1. Create supply of project expendables	Admin. function	Get standard supply set	Jim	2/10	3/1	
2. Develop contact with purchasing department to ensure that needed supplies are ordered	W. Smith	Establish purchasing contact	Martha	2/17	3/1	
3. Create and maintain a log on nonexpendable supplies	DP Std. #6310	Develop a log sheet	Bill	2/15	3/1	
4. Count nonexpendable supplies quarterly: 3/31, 6/30, 9/30, and 12/31	None needed	Conduct physical inventory using supplies log sheet	Cindy	3/31 6/30 9/30 12/31	3/31 6/30 9/30 12/31	

Figure 60 *Systems Project Administration Worksheet for the _____ Area*

Item	Response			
	Yes	No	N/A	Comments
1. Is administration and control considered part of the project manager's role?				
2. Are projects organized in a manner that recognizes the importance of project administration (e.g., making someone accountable for administration)?				
3. Is there a formal project administration interface with independent application review boards?				
4. Is there a formal project administration interface with internal auditors?				
5. Is there a formal project administration interface with the data processing security officer?				
6. Is there a formal project administration interface with a purchasing officer or other person responsible for contracting project services?				
7. Is there a formal project administration interface with system programmers?				
8. Is there a formal project administration interface with computer operations personnel?				
9. Is there a formal project administration interface with the data base administrator?				
10. Is there a formal project administration interface with the clerical support function within the data processing department?				
11. Does the project manager have a formal method of controlling project documentation?				
12. Does the project manager have a formal method of controlling utilization of the resources assigned to the project?				
13. Does the project manager have a formal method of controlling changes to the project requirements?				
14. Does the project manager have a formal method of controlling the source and object libraries?				
15. Does the project manager have a formal method of controlling data processing standards?				
16. Does the project manager have a formal method of controlling inputs to the project?				
17. Does the project manager have a formal method of controlling project deliverables?				

Figure 61 *Systems Administration Checklist*

	Response			
Item	Yes	No	N/A	Comments
18. Does the project manager have a formal method of controlling the quality factors associated with user expectations?				
19. Does the project manager have a formal method of maintaining and controlling records relating to the project schedules?				
20. Does the project manager have a formal method of maintaining and controlling records relating to the status of project completion?				
21. Does the project manager have a formal method of maintaining and controlling records relating to the time reporting of project personnel?				
22. Does the project manager have a formal method of maintaining and controlling records relating to the budgetary and accounting information?				
23. Does the project manager have a formal method of maintaining and controlling records relating to project member assignments?				
24. Does the project manager have a formal method of maintaining and controlling records relating to project supplies?				

Figure 61 *(continued)*

10

User Administration

The DP department has the mission of meeting the needs of operational management. Most data processing departments were formed to assist users in the use of a complex technology. It was believed that it was more economical to hire "experts" in computer technology than to permit all users to solve their own technological problems.

The use of "experts" is common throughout industry. Many organizations hire tax experts, legal experts, and so on. These central resources are then available when the need for those services exists. In most instances this is cheaper than, for example, to have a centralized legal department rather than attempting to build a legal staff within each area of the company.

However, the daily need for, and dependence on, the computer put this expertise in a special category. More users are beginning to take back some of the computer work that they previously delegated to the data processing department, or work that was never requested. For example, many users write programs using terminals, others are acquiring microcomputers, and still others are purchasing software from outside vendors. The role and relationship between the data processing department and the user is changing.

This chapter discusses the user/EDP interface in a changing computer environment. A continuation of the types of conflicts that have occurred in the past may potentially undermine the role and responsibility of data processing. On the other hand, through effective administration and control, data processing's role can evolve and perhaps strengthen as organizations enter an era of intense user activity with computers. The administrative solutions to user/EDP conflicts presented in this chapter are based on the concept that the user's involvement in all aspects of EDP will increase dramatically within the next few years.

THE TRADITIONAL USER/EDP INTERFACE

Developing an effective application system is a technically complex task. Business requirements must be broken down into minute tasks so that they are executable on a computer. In addition, all possible error conditions must be anticipated and corrective action determined and installed in the application system in order to minimize operational problems. In larger systems, this can take many years of effort.

The process that has evolved for systems development is one of multiple translations. First, the user translates requirements to the data processing department. Those requirements must then be translated into systems design specifications. The design specifications are translated into program specifications. The program specifications are translated into program code, and the program code is compiled (i.e., translated) into machine language. At the end of this process, an executable system exists for the user to satisfy the requirements.

The multiple translations required to go from a need to an executable system is like a party game that many have played. The host of the party writes a story on a piece of paper. The host whispers that story word by word to the first guest. That person, from memory, then tells the story to the next person. That person then relates the story from memory to the next person, and the process continues until the story has been passed to everyone at the party. The host then asks the last person to hear the story to tell it to the entire group. After that person has relayed the story to all the guests, the host reads the original story. There is normally great laughter, because the story, which has been passed through many people, no longer resembles the original story. One is always amused at what has been added to embellish the story, and some key elements of the story may have been dropped altogether.

The interface between the user and the data processing department should not turn out like the party game. Data processing should not be embellishing the system with things they believe will make the application better, nor should they exclude items important to the user. Unfortunately, many of these changes occur so subtly that neither the data processing department nor the user is fully aware of what happened until the executable system is executed, at which time the user suddenly becomes aware that the story they are hearing is not the one they told to the data processing department.

The process that has evolved in designing systems is illustrated in Figure 62. This illustration shows that the data processing department focuses all of their technology through a project leader. The project leader interfaces with a user project coordinator (or an equivalent term meaning the key contact point for the user), who is the spokesperson for the user. These two persons hold the key to a successful project.

Two problems arise from this interface relationship. First, the people may be required to spend too much time with their own departmental activity.

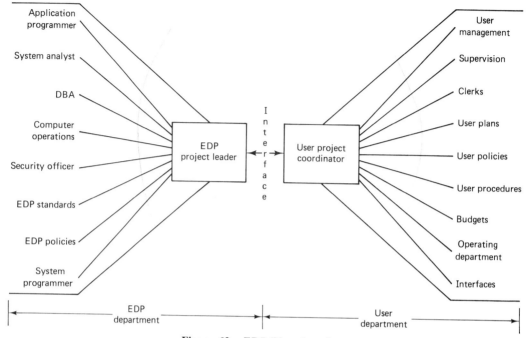

Figure 62   *EDP/User Interface*

The areas in which the project leader and user coordinator must interface are illustrated in Figure 62. This requires that a person be knowledgeable in all areas within his or her department and also understand the role, common mission, and needs of the other department. To be successful, these contact personnel must have the full respect and support of their individual departments. Generally, these positions should not be viewed as technical but rather, as administrative. Second, these people must define and ensure that the requirements are properly implemented. If they focus heavily on the full definition of requirements, their other role may suffer.

One might better describe this interface relationship as one of continual conflict—not conflict from the perspective of problems between two areas but rather, conflict in allocating time, effort, and resources among the various tasks to achieve the highest probability of success. The successful project identifies the conflicts and then develops solutions to overcome obstacles affecting the success of the project.

EDP ADMINISTRATIVE GUIDELINE 34
Failure to develop an effective interface between users and data processing personnel may cause users to seek alternative processing solutions.

AREAS OF POTENTIAL EDP/USER CONFLICT

The ideal EDP project leader and user project coordinator might be described as a ''super-person.'' If one were to list all of the attributes needed to be successful in either role, that person could probably not be found, and if found, probably could not be afforded. Thus both the user and data processing department normally must make compromises in filling the position. Depending on people's strengths and weaknesses, certain interface areas may be neglected either through lack of skills, knowledge, or time. These neglected areas can become areas of potential conflict.

The areas that have led to the most conflict in EDP/user relationships are illustrated in Figure 63 and described below (note that the rest of the chapter provides solutions to these conflicts).

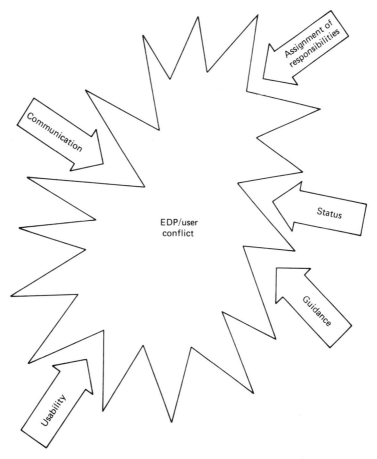

Figure 63   *Areas of Potential EDP/User Conflict*

ASSIGNMENT OF RESPONSIBILITIES

If a user purchased software from an outside vendor, the user/vendor relationship would be described with a legal contract. This would outline the responsibilities of each party. Unfortunately, when the application is developed internally, regardless of who develops the application, the relationship is more loosely defined. Although this has some advantages, it also poses a problem of certain tasks not being accomplished because each person thought the other would do it, or failed to recognize the need to have some tasks performed.

COMMUNICATION

Computer people speak computerese, and user people speak userese. Not only does this result in a communication gap, but frequently the same word is used by the parties differently. For example, the computer person may speak of a "program" as a computer program, whereas the user may refer to a "program" as an activity conducted by the user.

Occasionally, technical people become overly enmeshed in technology and forget the mission of the organization. Users are provided forms to document their needs, which they are expected to understand. Some users are intimidated by this practice and pull back, letting the data processing personnel take a dominant role. In other instances, periods of almost open hostility occur. Regardless of the cause or result, communication failures can result in system failures.

STATUS

During development, maintenance, and operation, users and project personnel need status information. Requirements change, the results of processing change, technology changes, business conditions change, and so on. If the flow of information between the two areas is inhibited, problems may result because needed information is not exchanged. For example, users must be continually aware of potential delays, and data processing people must know new requirements and changes in volume of anticipated processing. This flow of information should be easily comprehensible and consistent.

GUIDANCE

An effective interface is one in which both parties strive for the successful completion of the project. This means an environment free of fear of criticism, put-downs, and reprimands. If each group cannot freely discuss their ignorance, shortcomings, and mistakes with the other, the flow of suggestions, guidance, and synergism necessary for a successful project cease. Each group must openly solicit and genuinely want the ideas, thoughts, and constructive criticism of the other.

USABILITY

Computer systems are designed to be used by people, and for people. If systems are difficult to use, they will not be used. Programmers will not use capabilities that are difficult to understand or use. They will revert to a small subset of capabilities they are familiar with and have confidence in. Users of application systems are no different. Features which they find complex to use or difficult to understand go unused. When users must fight through complex forms or procedures, history shows that the error rates go up significantly. Errors and omissions can be attributable to either mistakes and misunderstandings by the user *or* improperly designed computer systems. All too frequently, it is the latter.

EDP ADMINISTRATIVE GUIDELINE 35
If the customer is "king," the best data processing talent should be used to interface with users.

BUILDING A USER ADMINISTRATION FUNCTION

User relationships are complex and vary from project to project. Solutions to potential conflict must be customized based on the characteristics of the project and the skills of the people involved. Data processing management should be involved in building these relationships. The following four-step process is recommended for this purpose:

1. *Identify project strengths.* The interface between the user and data processing should be built on the strengths of both. The strengths that should be considered include:

    Skill of user in EDP
    Skill of EDP personnel in user area
    Past experiences in project relationships
    Importance of the project to the organization

2. *Identify skills needed in user and EDP area to install the project successfully.* The role of project leader and project coordinator should be customized, based on the strengths of each department. Knowing these strengths, customized job descriptions for the two positions should be

developed (note that it is not necessary to write actual job descriptions, but it is important to capitalize on EDP capabilities). This will form the basis of a search for the appropriate person to fulfill each position, rather than assigning someone because he or she is available at the time.

3.   *Fill the interface roles.* The person best satisfying the interface requirements should be selected for the role. It may be better to delay the project, or even not do it, than to staff it improperly. The balanced risk portfolio concept works.

4.   *Develop project contract.* The same effort that is involved in having work performed by an outside contractor should be involved in an inside contract. This means that contractual negotiations should be undertaken by the two primary contacts. This contract will spell out what is expected of each party. Note that some of the items in the contract are normal ways of doing business and should already be included in an available document. At the conclusion of this exercise, the working relationship and DP expectations between DP and the user(s) will be defined.

Many men and women before they get married develop contracts defining each other's role, and the settlements and division of property in the event of a divorce. The beginning of a marriage, like the beginning of a computer project, is a honeymoon period. If the parties cannot contract a relationship that is satisfactory to each party at that time, things will probably never get better. The contract not only helps decide problems during the forthcoming relationship, but may during negotiations lead the parties involved to recognize that there are serious problems to be resolved before the project has any chance for success.

Among the items that should be included in a user/EDP project contract are:

- Role and responsibility of each party
- Formal methods of communication
- Methods to resolve conflict
- Access to people in the other area
- Status reporting
- Method for defining project expectations (i.e., quality of project)
- Determination of who is at fault in the event that a problem occurs, and potential resolution of problems (e.g., user does not pay for problems caused by data processing personnel)
- Schedule and deliverables
- Schedule of dates and costs
- Methods of assigning personnel to project
- Right of user to reject and/or request replacement of EDP personnel on the project
- Expected skill level of parties on the project
- Guarantees and/or service agreements

EDP ADMINISTRATIVE GUIDELINE 36
Written contracts resolve many disputes before they occur and define how to solve those that do occur.

Effective day-to-day administration between EDP and user personnel is essential to the success of a project. This administrative relationship should address the five areas of potential conflict between users and EDP personnel. The identification of specific areas of conflict, together with solutions recommended for those conflicts, follow for each of the five areas.

REDUCING COMMUNICATION CONFLICT

Users cannot be expected to be technically proficient in the computer, and computer people should not be expected to be conversant in user operations. However, the groups must converse, and those communications must be explicit and understandable. The computer cannot perform generalities; it must perform specifics.

Good communications begin with an understanding of the need for good communications. If both parties are not aware of the consequences inherent in poor communication, those problems will probably occur. Good communications begin with good listening. If both parties listen, and encourage open and free communication, the probability of achieving a communication objective is high.

Interface personnel from both the user and data processing areas should be schooled in listening and communication practices. The job description for these people should list communication skills as a prerequisite for the job. The types of practices that these people should be schooled in regarding good listening practices are listed in Figure 64. These are the type of practices that are taught in a communication course or included in communication books.

Areas of communication conflict, with the potential result of that conflict and some recommended communication solutions, are listed in Figure 65 and described below.

INTERFACE BETWEEN EDP PROJECT PERSONNEL AND USER PERSONNEL IS POOR

Users frequently accuse data processing project personnel as being technocrats. Some users state that they believe that DP's emphasis is on technology, with user needs and requirements coming second. In addition, many EDP personnel are described by users as "crude" and "blunt" in their interaction. Some

1. _Listening objectives:_ We want people to:
   Talk freely and frankly
   Cover matters concerning them
   Furnish information
   Better understand the problem we are discussing
   See causes, reasons for problems, and solutions

2. _Good listening practices:_ The listener should:
   Show interest
   Be understanding
   Express empathy
   Single out the problem if there is one
   Listen for causes of the problem
   Help the speaker associate the problem with the cause
   Encourage the speaker to solve his or her own problem
   Cultivate the ability to keep quiet
   Not argue
   Not interrupt
   Not pass judgment too quickly
   Not give advice unless requested
   Not react too directly with the speaker's sentiments
   Retain humility; don't know it all
   Listen with greater intensity
   Observe with greater acuity
   React with greater empathy
   Be more understanding—more sensitive to the speaker's actions and reactions
   Listen for more than words
   Listen for feelings, not sentiments and emotions
   Seek to distinguish differences between fact and interpretation
   Listen in terms of speaker's enthusiasm or pessimism
   Determine if reaction is automatic to previous ideas and habit patterns
   Listen in terms of meaning, not words—what is the person really saying?
   Not hear what you would like to hear

Figure 64 _Good Listening Practices_

User/EDP Conflict	Potential Result	Recommended Solution
Interface between project personnel and user personnel is poor	EDP people use jargon and are blunt in describing problems and causes—causes strained relationship	Appoint management-type person as interface
Neither group recognizes the importance of the other's problem	Each group is more concerned about its own mission—results in no real give and take in developing solution	Cross-fertilization of personnel
Users do not use important system features, or misuse them	System is underutilized, or excessive problems occur	Develop system training sessions for user personnel Develop "picture" manuals for user personnel Prompting within the system
System overengineered for user clerical personnel	System is complex to use or does not meet some clerical problems, resulting in errors or need for excessive manual processing	Provide clerical personnel system with walk-throughs during development

Figure 65   *Reducing Communication Conflict*

users feel that many DP people are not polished in the practice of business, are unable to articulate business problems, and are generally poor communicators.

The results of poor interfacing between technical people and users have hurt both the technical people and the projects. Experience shows that few data processing professionals get promoted directly from data processing into senior management. Generally, they are not viewed as team players but rather, as highly skilled technicians doing technical things. Within the projects, relations are often strained and thus good lines of communication destroyed.

One solution is to appoint a professional interface. In many instances these are not skilled technicians but rather, managerial-type communicators. The objective is to present a good image and a person who, although not able to address every issue on the spot, can make things happen.

In a new-car agency, they rarely let the customer talk to the mechanics. A service manager in a white jacket discusses the problem with the customer. The service manager then gives the work to the mechanic and explains to the mechanic what to do. When the customer returns, the service manager, using the information provided by the mechanic, explains to the customer what has been done to fix the car. This same type of solution in data processing, although it might appear costly, may be the most cost-effective method of defining requirements and getting action taken.

NEITHER GROUP RECOGNIZES
THE IMPORTANCE OF THE OTHER'S PROBLEM

It is difficult to appreciate how one feels until one stands in another person's shoes. Their problems are not my problems. Therefore, not only do I have difficulty in appreciating the other's problems, but many times I have so many of my own that I don't have the time to sit and think about the other person's problems.

Discussing how a particular discipline or principle works does not really allow someone to comprehend that idea fully. For example, we can speculate about what it must be like to fly in an airplane, and we can talk to people who have flown in airplanes, but until we experience it ourselves we do not really comprehend what it is like to look at the Earth from 30,000 or 40,000 feet above it. The same is true in the computer field. We can describe what programming is, show a picture of a program, but until someone has actually had to put instructions together, enter them into the computer, and make them work, he or she does not fully understand programming.

The obvious solution to this dilemma is to put the other person into our shoes. If the user transfers people to data processing to work as programmers and systems analysts, and data processing transfers people to the user area, these people will all understand the other's mission. This cross-fertilization can be for a few weeks or it can be permanent. Once a good understanding of the other's mission develops, a real give and take occurs in developing solutions to the project problems.

USERS DO NOT USE IMPORTANT SYSTEM
FEATURES OR MISUSE THEM

Computer systems are normally very technically complex. They include hundreds, or even thousands, of options in processing. Within any reasonable-size system, there are probably millions of paths of logic that can be used in processing data. It is a major challenge to users to understand the capabilities included within a computer system in enough detail to be able to use those capabilities effectively.

The net result of not understanding the system is an underutilization of the capabilities or excessive problems. If users do not understand the system, they will misuse the features, which can result in errors. Sometimes errors have a domino effect, in that a single small error triggers a chain reaction of errors which can be costly to the organization.

The solution to this conflict is to provide the user with a means of understanding the system capabilities. Three solutions to this conflict are:

1. *System training sessions for user personnel:* The data processing personnel understand the system capabilities. They should develop formalized

training sessions for user personnel to explain those features. These give-and-take sessions help users learn the features, which could be followed by on-the-job training given by project personnel.

2. *"Picture" manuals for user personnel:* Users work primarily with terminal screens and input and output documents. Most of the processes that they perform can be related to a specific part of an input transaction or the use of an output report. If the manuals show the documents, screens, transactions, or applicable reference to the user clerical process, capabilities can be tied to that item. For example, if the user is to complete a form, the part of the form that the user is to fill out should be circled and cross-referenced to the instructional information. These picture documents should also provide quick and easy reference to solving problems users may encounter. Primarily, users need reference manuals, not training manuals. Keying instructions to readily identifiable pieces of documents or typical problems facilitates reference.

3. *Prompting within the system:* On-line systems provide a unique instructional opportunity. The system developers can provide the system instructions tied to specific user action. If the user is having problems, the system can provide a capability, such as letting the user type "HELP" on the terminal. The request for help provides the instructional information on the terminal screen, explaining the correct way to perform the process to accomplish a desired result.

SYSTEM OVERENGINEERED
FOR USER CLERICAL PERSONNEL

Most computer system designers are highly skilled technicians. They have mastered a very complex trade through years of schooling, on-the-job experience, and personal motivation to learn. These designers represent some of the more highly skilled technicians in the organization.

These technicians design the logic to be followed by user personnel in accomplishing their mission. Frequently, these designers cannot identify with the skill and/or motivation of the people using these systems. Many of the clerical people are working to earn the money, and really do not care about the job they are performing. At the salary levels many are paid, they do not feel motivated to do a lot of thinking and research. They do the work as it comes along, no more, no less.

If the systems are designed for highly skilled technicians, they may not work effectively when operated by clerical personnel. On the other hand, the system designers may have difficulty identifying with the level of system skills for which they should be designing the system. If it is incorrectly designed, they may cause the clerical personnel to introduce errors into the system, or they may force these clerical people to search for simpler ways to accomplish the task. Generally, the clerical people will search out the simplest way, regardless of whether the method they use is effective or economical.

The solution recommended for this conflict is to force systems analysts to explain the system to the clerical personnel who will use the system. This explanation should occur periodically throughout the developmental cycle, and even during maintenance. The systems analyst should be required to review the step-by-step procedures that the clerical people will be expected to follow in performing their work.

Most clerical personnel enjoy the opportunity of embarrassing the computer people by identifying obvious system vulnerabilities. Although this exercise may be painful for the computer systems analyst, it is beneficial for the organization. This concept has been introduced in many organizations through industrial psychologists, who state that the advantages of this process are:

- It causes the clerical people to feel they are part of the developmental process, and thus the system is theirs and they should encourage its success.
- It identifies potential vulnerabilities.
- It forces the systems analyst to think through precisely how people will use the system during the developmental stages.
- It develops a systems analyst/user relationship that fosters communications within the group.

REDUCING DIVISION OF RESPONSIBILITIES CONFLICT

Senior management is responsible for accomplishing the organization's objectives, in accordance with the articles of incorporation or equivalent, and the directives specified by the board of directors or legislative body. In fulfilling that mission, senior management delegates to operating managers the authority and responsibility to accomplish specific tasks and objectives. For example, paying employees is delegated to the payroll manager; controlling the assets of the organization, to the comptroller; and producing products, to the production manager.

Operating managers can use staff functions to assist in the accomplishment of their mission, but cannot delegate responsibility for their mission. In other words, the payroll manager can use a variety of services to help prepare payroll, but cannot delegate the responsibility for the accuracy, completeness, authorization, and timeliness of the payroll process.

In the development of data processing systems, the assignment of responsibilities is frequently misunderstood. The conflicts that can result from this inadequate definition of responsibilities, and some recommended solutions, are listed in Figure 66 and described as follows.

User/EDP Conflict	Potential Result	Recommended Solution
EDP role in the project development process is not fully defined	EDP will assume too much authority or tasks will not be completed	EDP charter (defining EDP system development role)
Project personnel will not accept their role in the project	Tasks not performed by proper person	Project control responsibilities chart

Figure 66   *Reducing Division of Responsibilities Conflict*

EDP ROLE IN THE PROJECT DEVELOPMENT PROCESS IS NOT FULLY DEFINED

Data processing is generally a service group. As such, it is responsible for the effective use of automated resources, but not for the integrity of the data processed by the computer. Obviously, data processing has a custodial responsibility to safeguard the data in its trust, but cannot differentiate between good and bad data provided by the users of the system.

The solution to this is a clearly defined EDP charter. If users of computer services clearly understand the data processing mission and responsibilities, they will recognize their responsibilities for automated systems. Data processing must be careful not to exceed their mission as stated in the charter so as to lead users to believe that they have responsibilities which they do not, in fact, have.

PROJECT PERSONNEL WILL NOT ACCEPT THEIR ROLE IN THE PROJECT

Even with a clearly defined charter, there will be confusion over some of the specifics of implementing computer systems. Unless all parties in a project fully understand the role and responsibilities of themselves and other parties, some tasks may not be performed. For example, data processing may believe that the users will verify the integrity of computer processing, while the user believes that data processing will verify the integrity. The result is that no one might fulfill that testing responsibility.

Responsibility Conflict Solution

The solution to this conflict is to develop a project control responsibilities chart. This chart should indicate the detailed project control responsibilities, and then which party is responsible for fulfilling those responsibilities. A recommended control responsibilities chart for an automated system is illustrated in Figure 67. This chart identifies eight control tasks. For each of these tasks the primary responsibility for accomplishing the task, as well as the secondary responsibility, is shown for the user, data processing, and senior

Control Task	Control Responsibility[a]		
	User	Data Processing	Management
Identify risks	P	S	P
Determine acceptable level of loss	P		
Establish control objectives	P	S	
Design controls	S	P	
Implement controls	S	P	
Test controls	P	S	
Monitor controls	P	S	S
Initiate control changes	P	S	

[a]P, primary responsibility; S, secondary responsibility.

Figure 67 *Recommended Control Responsibilities in an Automated Application*

management. This concept clearly shows who has which responsibility at a sufficient low level that responsibility for the tasks is specific and measurable.

Control responsibilities in an automated application are divided among the user, data processing, and senior management. Controls can be divided into two general categories with risk being the control requirement. General controls are the primary responsibility of senior management, whereas application controls are the responsibility of the user. Data processing can help either one with the impact of automation on the control objectives.

The user has the primary responsibility for the application. Thus it is only the user who can determine the acceptable level of loss, which then becomes the control objective. For example, if the risk is uncollectible accounts, and the user states that 1 percent is a reasonable loss, the control objective becomes to build a system that will collect 99 percent of the receivables. Data processing has the responsibility to design and implement the controls in the automated system to achieve those objectives. Once designed and implemented, the user then has primary responsibility to verify that the controls are in place and working, both prior to and after implementation. If the controls fail to work properly, it is the user's responsibility to initiate changes. Obviously, the user and data processing work as a team, so that if one has the primary responsibility, the other should be attempting to assist.

Senior management is responsible for control. Therefore, they have a secondary responsibility to ensure that application controls function. This responsibility is normally fulfilled in larger organizations by internal auditors, and in smaller organizations by the external CPA.

REDUCING STATUS CONFLICT

Good decisions require good data. If managers do not know the exact status of a project, they may make decisions that result in poor utilization of resources or people conflicts. Success of a computer project is important to many people. Therefore, if it appears that the project is failing, people begin to build alibi files. Frequently, this leads to the self-fulfilling prophecy, in that if enough people believe that a project is failing, it will fail.

The user/EDP status conflicts are listed below, together with recommended solutions (see Figure 68 for a synopsis of these conflicts).

PARTIES DISAGREE ABOUT WHAT IS TO BE ACCOMPLISHED

It is always amusing to observe two people arguing about an issue when neither has the correct facts. Frequently, people argue more dramatically when there is an absence of facts. This is because it is difficult to argue over an event when the facts are known. Once they are known, discussions tend toward solutions and away from attempting to define the problem.

Successful computer projects depend on contributions from both the user and the data processing department. It is important that these responsibilities be defined and the deliverables identified in detail. This is best accomplished through a "living" contract. The living aspect of a contract means that it is defined as well as possible when the project begins, and then continually amended to the satisfaction of both parties. It is better to have a disagreement in the planning stage over who is to perform a task than at the point where the task should be completed but is not.

User/EDP Conflict	Potential Result	Recommended Solution
Parties disagree about what is to be accomplished	Arguments over who is to do what	Project contracts
Parties disagree about the quality of the work performed	Arguments over the intent of requirements	Quality standards
User-noted problems are not corrected	User dissatisfaction with EDP project	RAPP form (to permit user to formally report problems)
One party does not know what the other party did	Delays in implementing requirements or taking action	Formal status reports

Figure 68   *Reducing Status Conflict*

PARTIES DISAGREE ABOUT THE QUALITY
OF THE WORK PERFORMED

Quality, unlike beauty, should not be in the eyes of the beholder. Quality should be identified and stated in measurable terms. If the quality factors are quantified and measured against standards, there will be no argument over whether or not the quality of the project has been achieved.

USER-NOTED PROBLEMS
ARE NOT CORRECTED

One of life's frustrating situations is to identify a problem, ask someone to correct that problem, and then get burned shortly thereafter because the problem has not been corrected. In the eyes of many people, this is an inexcusable situation. Normally, the reason it happens is oversight. The solution is to document and control user-identified problems.

Control over user-identified problems is best achieved through a numbered problem-reporting form. Such a form is illustrated in Figure 69, a RAPP Form (Reporting Application Potential Problem Form).

The form is completed as follows:

- *Application:* The name of the application.
- *RAPP No.:* A sequential control number.
- *Reported by:* The name of the person who identified the problem.
- *Date:* The date on which the problem occurred.
- *Report(s) Affected:* The report, screen, or other output from the computer system on which the problem was identified.
- *Data Affected:* The file, record, and/or data elements associated with a problem.
- *Description of Problem:* A brief narrative description explaining the problem in the user's words.
- *Impact of Problem:* The effect that the problem has on the user's business. This should be quantified, if possible.
- *Recommended Solution:* The user's suggestion for fixing this problem.
- *Needed by:* The date by which the problem should be corrected.
- *EDP Action Requested:* An indication as to which of the following actions the user wants performed:

> The problem should be fixed as soon as possible (ASAP).
>
> The problem should be discussed with the user.
>
> Data processing should provide an estimate to fix the problem.
>
> The problem should be considered in a future change to determine if it can be economically incorporated at that time.

Application:		RAPP No.:
Reported By:	Date:	
Report(s) Affected:		
Data Affected:		
Description of Problem:		
Impact of Problem:		
Recommended Solution:		
Needed by:		

EDP Action Requested:
- ☐ Fix ASAP   ☐ Provide estimate to fix
- ☐ Discuss   ☐ Consider with future change

Figure 69 *RAPP Form (Reporting Application Potential Problems)*

The primary objective of the form is to force meaningful discussion with the user. It also makes a formal record of the problem so that any future discussion of the problem will be based on the documented evidence included on or attached to this form. Data processing departments that use a RAPP or equivalent form find that user satisfaction increases because their problems are stated more specifically, and there is no question as to whether or not a problem has been reported to data processing.

ONE PARTY DOES NOT KNOW
WHAT THE OTHER PARTY DID

Duplication of work can normally be reduced by good status reports. This involves each party keeping the other advised as to the actions being taken by the other party. Obviously, actions that do not affect the other party need not be reported. On the other hand, providing each other with good status information usually has a positive effect on the morale and success of the project, because informed people tend to make good decisions.

REDUCING USABILITY CONFLICT

Data processing capabilities are designed to be used. Resources acquired or developed that are not used represent wasted corporate resources. Examples of wasted resources include:

- System features built and not used
- Microcomputers acquired and not used
- User terminals installed and not used
- Software purchased and not used
- Answers to information-processing problems available in a centralized data processing function but not used (in other words, the organization pays to have the users acquire knowledge that has already been bought and paid for by the organization)

The types of usability conflicts that occur and some recommended solutions to those conflicts are illustrated in Figure 70 and explained below.

SYSTEM MESSAGES
NOT ACTED UPON PROPERLY

Most computer system messages are detective controls. These controls are effective only when they are acted on. The reason users may not act on computer-produced messages are:

- Messages are not understood.
- Messages arrive in large quantities.
- Users are not instructed on the importance of the messages.
- Users do not know what action to take (and thus take no action).

The solution to these dilemmas is twofold. First, specific action should be defined, listing the precise steps that should be taken by the user. This solves the problem of what to do when the message occurs. Assigning priori-

User/EDP Conflict	Potential Result	Recommended Solution
System messages not acted upon properly	Problems and losses that should be investigated may not be investigated	Message priorities
Users do not fully utilize system data analysis capabilities	Information that could be easily produced by the computer is prepared manually or not used at all	Inquiry systems
Problems occur that should have been anticipated	The problems result in unnecessary losses or expenditure of effort	Anticipation controls
System not used by user management	User performance, productivity, and profitability may be reduced	Management information reporting system

Figure 70   *Reducing Usability Conflict*

ties to the messages tells users the importance of the message. This solves the problem as to whether or not the user should take action on the message.

USERS DO NOT FULLY UTILIZE SYSTEM DATA ANALYSIS CAPABILITIES

Computer systems are information systems. They provide users not only with the specified reports, but also with access to information needed for purposes such as:

- Following up on transaction problems
- Determining the magnitude of a problem
- Providing information for managerial decisions

The solution to this conflict is to provide inquiry systems. Data base management systems normally have inquiry systems associated with them. Other systems can develop inquiry systems through the use of utility programs and/or development of simple report writers that can restructure and reformat data files. The costs of these inquiry systems are normally offset manyfold by the increased capabilities provided by the system.

PROBLEMS OCCUR THAT SHOULD HAVE BEEN ANTICIPATED

Most of the problems that occur in computer systems are ones that people say could not happen. Unfortunately, most of the things that could not happen do happen. If the computer personnel take the extra time and effort to build in warning messages that anticipate these types of problems, the life of the user may be made considerably easier. Anticipation controls should look for:

- Orders or transactions that vary significantly from the normal transaction for that type of user or event
- Overflow conditions, such as numbers too large for the size of the field
- Space management problems (in other words, the space allocated for a specific purpose is almost consumed)
- Timing problems

SYSTEM NOT USED BY USER MANAGEMENT

Most computer systems are designed for and used by clerical personnel. At best, first-line supervision gets actively involved in the use of the system. However, user management may not take advantage of system capabilities.

Systems should be able to produce information of value to the management of the user area. The reason information may not be used is that it was not specified by the user, or offered by the data processing group. This weakness can be overcome by discussions with user management regarding the type of information they need to manage their department.

An example of the type of management information analysis that can be provided by a billing system is illustrated in Figure 71. This shows for six different sales offices the percent of products returned per $1000 of sales. This type of information may be valuable to user management in assessing the effectiveness of the six different sales offices. The profitability and productivity of user areas may be increased through making secondary uses of information in the computer system for managerial planning and decision-making purposes.

REDUCING GUIDANCE CONFLICT

Information processing is no longer restricted to the data processing areas. Distributed processing, communication systems, microcomputers, and office automation equipment are a few of the capabilities that are pushing users into the information processing age. These new systems promise to break any processing backlog and at the same time offer new uses for the computer.

Data processing has two choices with user-directed computer processing. First, they can take a hands-off attitude and hope the user fails, as may be the case. Second, they can become an active participant and counselor in helping the user use processing capabilities more effectively. While the short-term effect may be loss of business in the data processing department, the

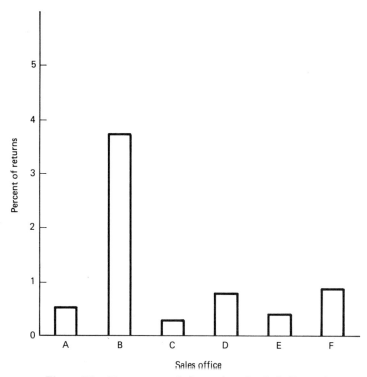

Figure 71   *Management Information Analysis Example*

long-term effect is more effective information processing by the organization.
 The type of conflicts that arise when users get more actively involved
in their own computer processing, and some recommended solutions, are illustrated in Figure 72 and described below.

User/EDP Conflict	Potential Result	Recommended Solution
User attempts an EDP task and fails	Wasted resources	Information center
Procedures good for the organization may in- convenience some users	Wasted resources	User group
EDP policies and procedures are inconsistent with the desires of users	User dissatisfaction with EDP	User group
Methods of interface are restrictive	Ideas do not flow freely	Quality circle (adjust process) Review board (improve product)

Figure 72   *Reducing Guidance Conflict*

USER ATTEMPTS AN EDP TASK AND FAILS

The first attempt with any new technology is difficult. The less the user knows about that technology, the higher the probability of failure. If users fail in microcomputer applications, for example, the result is wasted corporate resources.

The solution is to have the data processing personnel provide guidance. The suggested method for doing this is through an information center. Some of the tasks of that information center might include:

- Recommending hardware and software to acquire
- Operating a computer store (in other words, purchasing hardware and software through the data processing department and then reselling it to users)
- Operating a hotline for guidance and advice
- Providing temporary assistance in the event that there is turnover in the user department
- Helping users get out of trouble
- Providing corporate standards, procedures, and guidelines regarding information processing in the corporation

PROCEDURES GOOD
FOR THE ORGANIZATION MAY
INCONVENIENCE SOME USERS

Information processing is a part of the responsibility of operational areas. Although it may be advantageous to establish central corporate direction, it can be difficult to enforce those procedures. If a manager is given responsibility to run an area, it is hard to state that he or she can run that area *except* in the use of data processing.

The attempt to control information processing centrally is further complicated by how that direction affects individual users. For example, a policy that might be advantageous to the corporation may not be for some users. One user may benefit from the policy, whereas for another user extra effort is required to comply to the policy. For example, the organization may standardize on Apple computers, which because of a large contract provides low-cost hardware and software to the entire organization, but because Apple does not have a specific type of computer package, a single user may have to develop that in-house rather than purchasing it.

The solution to this problem is the formation of a user group. Data processing is in a no-win situation in these circumstances. If they recommend Apple computers, some users will be unhappy with them. On the other hand, if a user group is formed and they select that computer, even though it may be based on a data processing recommendation, the users then "own" the decision and tend to be happier with it.

EDP POLICIES AND PROCEDURES ARE INCONSISTENT WITH THE DESIRES OF USERS

Data processing establishes policies and procedures to facilitate their work. Many of these procedures directly affect users, such as system development methods, system maintenance methods, request forms to be completed for new projects, changes to projects, or other types of assistance. If users are unhappy with these procedures, they tend to make life miserable for the systems analysts and programmers.

A solution to this is the formation of user groups. If these groups disagree with a particular policy or procedure, they can work with the data processing department to instigate new procedures. Because all of the users have a say in this change, the new policy, even though it may not be significantly different, will be more acceptable to the users.

METHODS OF INTERFACE ARE RESTRICTIVE

Frequently, the procedures established for communicating between users and data processing personnel have the net result of limiting communication. For example, clerical personnel in the user area may not be able to communicate directly with data processing personnel. On the other hand, programmers may have to go through a project manager to ask a question of the user. Although these procedures were established to improve the flow of communication, they may have exactly the opposite effect.

Two solutions to increasing the flow of ideas between users and data processing personnel are:

1. Quality circles when used to adjust the process
2. Review boards when used to improve the product

Both quality circles and review boards involve the same type of people. Under the quality circle concept they are free to explore any area that inhibits good relationships. In other words, quality circles tend to work on the interface process. On the other hand, review boards are designed to evaluate the products produced by the project. Because these bring together all the parties involved, they can increase the flow of information and ideas on improving specific deliverables, such as project reports.

A USER ADMINISTRATION CHECKLIST

One systems analyst stated that "data processing would be fun if there weren't any users." This type of comment emphasizes the importance of user relationships as well as the problems many data processing people have in building effective relationships. The checklist shown in Figure 73 is designed for the project leader to use to assess the adequacy of relationships with the user. "Yes" answers, meaning that there is good communication interface between the user and data processing project team, are indicative of good practices. "No" answers to the checklist should be investigated further, as potential problems in successful computer projects.

Item	Response			
	Yes	No	N/A	Comments
1. Are the persons who interface with users trained in how to perform that interface?				
2. Is good communication skill a required characteristic for persons who interface with users?				
3. Are the responsibilities for both user personnel and EDP personnel clearly defined in each project?				
4. Are the relationships between user and EDP varied on the strengths of the project relating to the other area?				
5. Are interface people carefully selected because they complement the characteristics of the other area?				
6. Are the roles and responsibilities of each group put in writing?				
7. Is the opportunity taken to cross-train personnel in the other area wherever practical?				
8. Do data processing project personnel develop easy-to-use training material and train users in how to use new and changed features of computer systems?				
9. Are the skills of user personnel taken into consideration in the systems design?				
10. Is there an EDP charter which fully defines the EDP systems development and maintenance role, and is that charter available to users?				
11. Have the project control responsibilities been identified and assigned to the appropriate party?				
12. Are quality standards established for each project to predefine what the project must do to be successful?				

(continued)

Figure 73   *User Administration Checklist*

	Response			
Item	**Yes**	**No**	**N/A**	**Comments**
13. Are users provided a means, such as a RAPP form, by which to document and present problems to the data processing group?				
14. Do data processing project personnel have the opportunity to document and present system problems to the users? (Note: The same form could be used for both purposes.)				
15. Are formal status reports prepared by both users and data processing personnel on the project?				
16. Are messages and reports requiring user action prioritized to indicate the importance of those messages?				
17. Do computer projects contain anticipation controls so that problems can be detected as soon as they occur?				
18. Do the data processing people work with users to develop inquiry systems to the computer files?				
19. Does the project team work with user management to ensure that management provides the type of information they need to manage their area properly?				
20. Has data processing established an information center to assist users in utilizing information processing more effectively?				
21. Has data processing formed a users group so that they can mutually agree on their needs and pursue the solution to those needs?				
22. Are quality circles established, comprised of both users and data processing personnel, and charged with developing better means to work together?				
23. Are review boards established for each major project to provide an independent assessment of the performance of the project?				
24. Are review boards established for each major computer project to ensure that all parties have an opportunity to input to the system as it is designed?				

Figure 73 *(continued)*

Chapter

11

Vendor
Administration

The success of the data processing function is partially dependent upon the successful use of vendor services and products. At a minimum, the data processing department acquires hardware from outside vendors. At the opposite end of the spectrum, some corporations contract their entire data processing services through an outside vendor.

The acquisition of a service or product from an outside vendor should be considered a project. To be successful, it requires the same level of commitment and management as any other data processing project. Once considered a project, the same life-cycle controls supplied to any other project can be adapted to vendor-acquired products.

This chapter describes the administrative aspects of a vendor life cycle. The vendor life cycle begins when a need is recognized and does not terminate until the vendor product is no longer useful. In addition, the chapter describes how to evaluate individual vendors to ensure that the vendors delivering high-quality products are reused, whereas vendors whose products are problem plagued are eliminated from future consideration.

CONTRACTING VERSUS IN-HOUSE-DEVELOPED PRODUCTS

In the early days of data processing, organizations acquired their computer hardware from vendors but created everything in-house. The not-invented-here syndrome (NIH) was prevalent. Of course, the poor quality of vendor software encouraged many corporations to create their own software.

As the quality of vendor-produced products increased, it became more difficult to substantiate the not-invented-here philosophy. Organizations began to evaluate vendor products on their own merits. Those products that could be acquired more economically through vendors were acquired through vendors, leaving in-house personnel free to concentrate on products that were unavailable commercially or could be developed more effectively in-house.

The most common reasons to acquire software products and services from outside vendors are:

- *Lower in cost:* A vendor organization may offer a needed product at a lower cost than the cost to develop the product in-house. In most instances the vendor can amortize the cost of the product over many customers, and thus no one customer must pay the full cost to develop the product. In other instances, the vendor can use either better methods for developing software, or more efficient or lower-cost personnel. The net result is a savings to the organization acquiring the product or service.
- *Developed more quickly:* Many vendor-produced products are on the shelf and available when needed. For example, if an organization decided that they needed an inventory management system, they could approach a vendor who had such a product already available. Thus the product might be acquired months or even years earlier than it could be developed in-house.
- *Unique product (skills to develop not available in-house):* The product offered by a vendor is one that was not conceived in-house. This includes most of the operating software and many of the specialized applications. For example, to do effectively, a lens design program or automatic inventory replenishment system may require special algorithms or background that may not be available in-house.
- *Resources not currently available in-house:* The application may be one that could be developed in-house, and perhaps even at a lower cost than through a vendor, but the resources needed to do it are not currently available. Thus, rather than delay the project or change priorities for existing projects, the product is acquired through a vendor.

COMMONLY USED CONTRACTUAL SERVICES

The range of services available through vendors is extensive. The spectrum of services ranges from acquiring hardware to subcontracting the entire data processing function. In between are a wide variety of products and services.

The areas of vendor support can be divided into hard products, soft products, and services (see Figure 74). Hard products relate to computer hardware, associated services, and supplies. Soft products are the software and associated support services, while the services category represents buying knowledge from outside vendors.

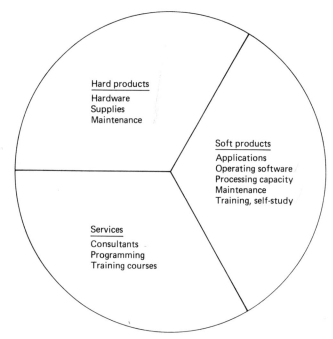

Figure 74   *Areas of Vendor Support*

Most organizations contract for hard products. These normally include the computer hardware, printer paper and other media, plus maintenance of the hardware systems. These products are generally recognized as products that cannot be produced in-house. Data processing organizations have been contracting for these products for years and know how to do it.

Organizations may or may not need to contract for soft products. Those vendors that unbundled their software make it necessary for their customers to contract for much of the operating software. However, outside vendors may be able to offer better software at lower prices, making operating software acquirable from vendors other than the one that manufactured the hardware. The acquisition of applications from vendors is growing in acceptance. Many industries, such as banking, may actually acquire more application software from vendors than they produce in-house. However, organizations have been less successful in satisfying their expectations with vendor software than they have with hardware.

Some organizations use outside vendors (i.e., service bureaus) to perform much of their computer processing. The options include service center processing, time sharing, or even the complete takeover of the data processing mission. In some instances, only processing resources are acquired, but in many instances, the vendor provides both the application system and the resources to process that application.

The contracting of consulting, programming, and training services evokes strong options for and against by many organizations. Some believe they can do anything better in-house than can be performed by vendors, whereas others use vendors regularly to supplement their in-house staff. The degree of satisfaction in contracting for services is dependent on the reputation of the vendor and the effort put into developing good contractual specifications.

The key to successful vendor negotiations is a systematic process for dealing with vendors. This process can best be described as a vendor life cycle. Like a system development life cycle, it provides the framework and controls necessary to ensure that the product will meet specifications.

EDP ADMINISTRATIVE GUIDELINE 37

Acquiring a vendor product is a data processing project that requires a vendor life-cycle methodology.

THE VENDOR LIFE CYCLE

People repeat the same basic steps each time they deal with a vendor. One can see that in each vendor negotiation the needs must be explained, and the vendor who bids on the work must be evaluated, as well as types of guarantees and commitments the vendor will make. The end result of the negotiation is a contract. Observing the common elements of this process, one can subdivide the process into phases to produce a life-cycle methodology for dealing with vendors.

The advantage of a life-cycle methodology is the thoroughness by which it reaches a conclusion. Experience has shown that in systems development there is a considerable payback to this initial thoroughness. Doing the job right the first time is significantly cheaper than correcting and recorrecting errors made throughout the process.

A six-phase vendor life cycle is illustrated in Figure 75. This figure shows the six phases of the life cycle, together with the administrative and control concerns in each phase. The methodology developed must deal with those administrative and control concerns to ensure that the vendor produce meets specifications.

The six phases are described briefly below and discussed in detail in later sections:

developed in
↑ Requirements

Life-Cycle Phase					
Requirements	Vendor Identifi- cation	RFP	Acceptance	Test	Maintenance
Administrative and Control Concerns					
Adequate definition Measurable Contract- able Constraints Cost/bene- fit analysis	Extensive Qualified Available Reputable	Bidder quality control Guarantee Mainte- nance Enhance- ments Require- ments/ terms	Select best vendor Acceptable terms Training material	Meets require- ments Compatible Necessary skills acquired	Service Enhance- ments Training updated Enforce contract

Figure 75   *Vendor Life Cycle*

1. *Requirements:* Defining the desired product plus the intention to consider an outside vendor to develop or produce the product.
2. *Vendor identification:* Investigative process to determine which vendors should be considered as potential candidates for bidding on the desired product or service.
3. *Request for proposal (RFP):* A solicitation to one or more vendors to bid on the project.
4. *Acceptance:* The selection process used to narrow down to the vendor that will be awarded the contract.
5. *Test:* Assurance that the winning vendor's product meets the contractual specifications. (Note: In many instances, the acceptance and test phase will occur simultaneously, as organizations will test products before they accept them.)
6. *Maintenance:* Assurance that the product continues to perform as specified, that any necessary corrections or enhancements are made, and that the contractual provisions are enforced.

It is recommended from an administrative and control perspective that the vendor life cycle be formalized. Individuals negotiating with vendors should be instructed as to their role and responsibility in each phase, together with how to perform that phase. The remainder of this chapter is designed to fulfill that purpose.

PHASE 1: REQUIREMENTS

A vendor project, as with all other projects, begins with the requirements phase. Once the needs have been established, a determination can be made as to how best to satisfy those needs. In many instances the requirements are defined long before it is determined whether or not an outside vendor will be used to satisfy those needs.

The administration function in data processing has two acquisition responsibilities: first, to develop an acquisition process, or to understand and utilize the organization's acquisition process; and second, to oversee and control the acquisition of vendor products. This is necessary to ensure that the procedures are followed properly and that the organization is protected against poor vendors and poor products.

The most common pitfalls in acquiring vendor products are:

- The product fails to meet specifications.
- The product is not delivered on time.
- Inadequate training is provided on how to use the product.
- The product does not work.
- The product costs more than the purchaser believed it would.

Many of these faults are attributable to poorly defined requirements. As in systems development, this is the key step for ensuring success of the project. As we explore this and the other phases of the vendor life cycle we need to answer the following three questions:

1. What are the objectives of the phase?
2. Who is responsible for the phase?
3. How is the phase performed?

The emphasis in this chapter will be on the administration and control of the contracting process. Thus the materials will concentrate more on the process than on the specific product. Knowing that the product achieves the objectives is the responsibility of the person desiring the product. The administration and control function is concerned that that need is appropriately documented, that a reasonable process is followed to select the best vendor, that the installed product meets specifications, and that the contractual obligations of the vendor are fulfilled.

What Are the Objectives of the Phase?

The requirements phase must define the product in sufficient detail that a vendor can understand and deliver the desired product. If the following two general rules are followed in developing these requirements, they are usually satisfactory to ensure getting the desired product:

1. Define requirements in measurable terms so that it can be positively determined whether or not the requirements met the objectives.
2. The requirements should be written in sufficient detail so that test conditions can be developed from those requirements to test whether or not the product meets the specifications.

The vendor bidding process can be used to decide whether the product should be developed in-house or acquired from an outside vendor. When this is done, it is extremely important that the requirements be specified in a manner that is compatible with in-house development. For example, in-house software development may be required to comply with documentation and other standards. If a vendor can develop a product without meeting those standards, obviously the vendor could produce the product at a lower price because it is not the same product. Therefore, it is essential in the administration and control of requirements that the specifications be stated in a manner that is consistent with what would be developed if the contract was awarded in-house.

The considerations that should be evaluated in writing requirements include the need to specify the:

- Compatibility with other existing products.
- Compliance to in-house standards and procedures.
- Method of training people in using the package.
- Types of documentation required.
- Length of time that the product will be needed. (It is desirable to include the right to cancel any contract if the product is not needed that long. Note that the vendors may not agree to this type of restriction without a price penalty.)
- Skill level of people who will be using the product.
- Projected changes in in-house products that may affect these requirements.
- Method for ensuring that the product remains usable as the organization's requirements change.
- Amount of effort required to use the package.
- Desired level of reliability expected from the product.

Who Is Responsible for the Phase?

The user has primary responsibility for the requirements phase. The user is the one who is requesting and will be accountable for the installed product. However, other parties have a vested interest in this phase, including:

- *Accountants:* Ensuring that any cost and benefit considerations are stated properly and in accordance with any financial procedures

- *EDP administration:* Ensuring that the process has been followed and that the RFP resulting from the requirements phase contains all the information needed
- *Management:* Deciding whether or not the project should be approved and, if so, whether an outside vendor should be considered to accomplish the project

How Is the Phase Performed?

The general requirements process for a vendor product is basically the same as for an in-house product. However, in actual practice if an outside vendor is involved, the requirements tend to be more detailed and specific. The general rule of contracting is: "What you request is what you get." Although some vendors may do more work than is necessary for fulfilling the contractual obligation because they want to get additional work, there is no obligation for the vendor to do it, and in many instances they may refuse unless they are adequately compensated for the extra work.

The steps that should be followed in completing this phase are listed in Figure 76. This is a worksheet that can be used by either the project leader or EDP administration to ensure that the process is adequately followed. The

Program Step	Objective of Step	Who Performs?	Dates		Comments
			Start	Complete	
1. Define specifications of item	Develop basis for vendor bid	User			
2. Define specifications in measurable terms	Develop basis for evaluating delivered item	User			
3. State desirability of using vendor	Decide if can complete using vendor	User			
4. Define vendor constraints	Identify conditions to be included in RFP	User/administration			
5. State benefits and cost considerations	Put estimate on maximum amount of contract	User/accountants			

Figure 76   *Requirements Phase Program*

worksheet is designed so that it can be indicated on the worksheet who performs each step, and when it is started and completed. The "who performs?" column is completed in Figure 76 using generic titles. In actual practice, the name of the specific person should be entered on the worksheet. In addition, the comments column is provided to describe any problems, or to reference or amplify the results produced by the step.

An explanation of each of the five steps in the requirements phase follows:

1. *Define specifications of item.* The attributes and/or processes to be completed must be defined. These specifications should indicate the criteria that must be accomplished for the project to be successful.

2. *Define specifications in measurable terms.* Communication problems occur when specifications are stated in general terms. This can result in the user expecting one set of criteria while the vendor is building the product to another set of criteria. When the criteria are put in measurable terms, it improves communication and increases the probability that the desired product will be built.

3. *State desirability of using vendor.* Some products need to be developed in-house because of special skills or confidentiality; other products must be purchased outside because it is either uneconomical or unfeasible to develop the product in-house. However, many situations are unclear and the user of the product should state in the development of the requirements whether or not vendors should be considered.

4. *Define vendor constraints.* It is generally impractical to offer the world the opportunity to bid on a product development. The number of potential bidders should be restricted to those whose probability of success is high. For example, vendors who have failed to deliver high-quality products in the past will probably not deliver them in the future and should be excluded from the bidding process.

5. *State benefits and cost considerations.* It is a good business practice to go through a cost/benefit evaluation on acquired products. Obviously, this must be consistent with the organization's procedures, but even if not required, it is a healthy exercise for data processing personnel. If the necessary skills to perform this evaluation are not present in the data processing department, they should use their organization accountants to help with this process.

At the end of this phase, all of the information needed to go out and discuss the requirements with the vendor will be documented. It is generally a good idea to use the same procedure for documenting vendor project requirements as for in-house requirements. In many instances the same forms and processes can be used.

EDP ADMINISTRATIVE GUIDELINE 38

The product you get from contracting is the one you specify—so be sure when you develop your written specifications that they are for the product you want!

PHASE 2: VENDOR IDENTIFICATION

Finding the right vendor to develop the needed product can be a time-consuming and frustrating exercise. On the other hand, the process is also a diversion from normal work and may be undertaken as a challenge by the data processing staff. Enjoyable or not, it can be a costly process for a data processing department and should be controlled.

Organizations can approach the identification of vendors in any of the following three ways:

1. *From a preferred vendor list:* The organization predetermines which vendors can be included in bidding.
2. *Through open solicitation:* A public solicitation for interested vendors is made through newspaper advertisements and the like.
3. *Through research:* The organization, through publications, contracts, or consultants, determines which vendors are applicable to be included.

It is sometimes good practice to write a large number of vendors to determine if they are interested in bidding on the project. This letter can invite vendors to indicate their willingness and ability to produce the desired product within the time frame specified. In many instances, the vendors who can satisfy a contract may not easily be known, but through a public solicitation their interest and/or abilities to produce a certain product can be made known.

What Are the Objectives of the Phase?

The objective of this phase is to identify the most qualified vendors to perform a service. Depending on the number of projects contracted through vendors, this function may be centralized in the purchasing department.

During the bidding, many vendors make themselves "a pain in the neck" through continuous phone calls and inquiries. When there is a good possibility of landing a contract, marketing people can become overly aggressive. Therefore, it is helpful to intersperse EDP administration, or a formal purchasing function, between the vendor and the person who requires the product.

Some of the methods that have proved effective in harnessing vendor aggressiveness include:

- Requiring vendors to make all contacts through the administration function.
- If vendors get overly aggressive, notifying them that unless they stop specific tactics, they will be excluded from bidding on a project. (Note that it is more advisable to let vendor management harness their own aggressive sales people than to request that a specific sales person be taken off the account. The punishment of not dealing with that vendor is usually sufficient.)
- Notifying company officers which vendors are currently involved in negotiations with the organization. This is done so that if the vendor should contact a member of senior management in an attempt to acquire preferential treatment, that manager can warn the vendor of unethical practices. It is important that senior management know so that if a potential vendor makes a contact in an ethical manner, they not receive the same reprimand as the overly aggressive salesperson. Direct all unsolicited sales solicitations to administration personnel.

Who Is Responsible for the Phase?

The EDP administration group should accept responsibility for this phase. It behooves an EDP administrative group to maintain lists of good vendors in different areas. These lists can be formal or informal. The most logical sources of good vendors include:

- Updating and rating services such as AUERBACH and DATAPRO
- Analysis of previous dealing with vendors
- Recommendations by organizations using vendors
- Analysis of professional publications and vendor material

How Is the Phase Performed?

There are many poor vendors in the data processing area. It is generally a good rule not to deal with unproven vendors, and not to acquire an unproven product. It is normally better to let your competitors debug vendor products and then use them.

The golden rule of contracting is to require the vendor to demonstrate how they ensure they can deliver a high-quality product. In many instances, this may involve the vendor documenting how they test the product to ensure that it meets specifications. For example, the quality control program for a vendor might be evaluated before they are invited to bid on a project.

The steps that should be followed in the vendor identification phase are listed in Figure 77. This worksheet is for use by the person controlling this phase. A discussion of each of the four vendor identification phase steps follows:

1. *Identify as many potential vendors as practical.* Vendors considered for a project should have the appropriate credentials and resources to satisfy the requirements.
2. *Verify qualifications to bid on this item.* Vendors should be required to substantiate how they will ensure that the product delivered meets specifications. This is primarily their program of quality control.
3. *Determine availability of vendor to do item.* Through investigation or inquiry, a determination should be made as to whether the vendor has the appropriate resources to complete the project within the scheduled time frame.
4. *Verify reputation of vendor to perform specifications.* In most instances, this will require "testimonials" from previous customers. It is good practice to ask a vendor for a complete customer list so that the persons selected for a testimonial are at the organization's discretion, not the vendor's. If the vendor objects, that objection can usually be overcome by stating to the vendor that no contact will be made with one of the vendor's customers until the vendor has been notified. It is even reasonable to have the vendor make the initial contact.

Program Step	Objective of Step	Who Performs?	Dates		Comments
			Start	Complete	
1. Identify as many potential vendors as practical	Ensure that qualified vendors are given the opportunity to bid on the item	Administration			
2. Verify qualifications to bid on this item	Limit vendors to the most qualified for this item	Administration			
3. Determine availability of vendor to do item	Limit vendors to those who can perform item	Administration			
4. Verify reputation of vendor to perform specifications	Limit vendors to the most reputable	Administration			

Figure 77 *Vendor Identification Phase Program*

At the conclusion of this step, the categories of or specific bidders should be known. Note that in some instances this step is pre-performed through an approved vendor list. In other instances, the phase can be quite extensive and complex.

PHASE 3: REQUEST FOR PROPOSAL (RFP)

The request for proposal (RFP) phase involves the formal requests to the vendor for proposals to complete the project. The proposal returned should include an agreement to perform the specification and then give the terms for that effort. In some instances, the vendor may require clarification of some of the criteria before the final proposal can be submitted.

In returning the proposal, the vendor might do any of the following:

- Accept terms and state price.
- Modify criteria and propose terms. In many instances, the vendor may not be able to achieve the criteria specified but may be able to offer an acceptable product.
- Offer alternative proposals. In some instances, these will be additional features which could be included, or entirely different products for accomplishing what the vendor believes to be the objectives.

This phase can be used by an organization as an information-gathering process. For example, the organization may not know exactly what they want. For example, they can generally outline the area they would like in an inventory management system. General specs are included in the RFP and then the vendor is encouraged to propose whatever they perceive would accomplish the job most effectively. When this approach is taken, the requirements phase is much shorter, as the vendor will do most of the work.

What Are the Objectives of the Phase?

The objective of this phase is to gain a commitment from one or more vendors to deliver the desired product and to state the cost of their effort. From an administrative perspective it is important that the quotation fully define all of the vendor deliverables and support services. For example, it is important to know the type of guarantee the vendor gives on a product, how they will maintain and enhance it, and the terms of the contract.

In many instances, it is the vendor who will provide the contract. In this instance, one can be assured that the contract will be favorable to the vendor. On the other hand, unless the organization is very large, it may not be profitable to the vendor to negotiate an individual contract with an organization. Therefore, it can be important that the organization know specifically what terms they can and cannot accept before beginning detailed negotiations. The RFP from the vendor should indicate those terms.

Who Is Responsible for the Phase?

The primary responsibility for this phase resides with EDP administration. It is their responsibility to ensure that the RFP going to the vendor is complete, and that the vendor addresses all of the criteria in the RFP. If a central purchasing function exists, they will become involved in the terms of the contract and probably will handle the contractual negotiations. However, this does not exclude administration from representing the data processing function in these contractual negotiations.

How Is the Phase Performed?

It is desirable to establish firm ground rules for vendor bidding. Skilled marketeers can dazzle the uninitiated with a variety of features neither wanted nor useful. Think how often you were able to predetermine the exact automobile you wanted and then buy it.

A good marketing person will attempt to "hook you" on the product before they describe its deficiencies. Once they have convinced you that they have the product you want, you become blinded to the problems. You have been sold and then begin to rationalize the unimportance of any problem. The bidding process should avoid that wherever possible.

The steps to be followed in this phase (see Figure 78) are:

1. *Require vendor to substantiate quality control program.* The proposal received from the vendor should include material substantiating how the vendor will ensure the quality of the product. For personal services, this is best done with testimonials. For software, a testing/quality program could be included, and for hardware, the reliability specifications should be provided.

2. *Request guarantee statement.* This should basically state the quality level the vendor expects, and if it fails to achieve that quality level, what the vendor will do to remedy the situation.

3. *Request maintenance statement.* Most data processing products require maintenance to correct defects and to ensure that they remain technologically current. The vendor's program to do this should be included in the RFP.

4. *Request enhancement program.* Vendors should be asked to include a statement as to what enhancements they expect to include in the product within the next year or two. If firm enhancements are known, they

Program Step	Objective of Step	Who Performs?	Dates		Comments
			Start	**Com-plete**	
1. Require vendor to substantiate quality control program	Ensure that the item is subject to a quality control program	Adminis-tration			
2. Request guarantee statement	Determine vendor's action if item fails to work	Adminis-tration			
3. Request maintenance statement	Determine item repair procedures	Adminis-tration			
4. Request enhancement program	Determine vendor plans to improve or replace item	Adminis-tration			
5. Request proposal on requirement and items	Solicit bid from vendor	Purchasing			

Figure 78   *Request for Proposal (RFP) Phase Program*

should be stated. In addition, it is desirable to get the vendor to commit their intentions in the proposal, even though this does not require them to produce the enhancements.

5.   *Request proposal on requirement and terms.* A formal written proposal should be obtained from the vendor outlining the information above in addition to the product they expect to deliver.

At the conclusion of this phase, the vendor is committed to deliver a specified product at a predetermined price. At this point, the organization must begin to narrow down the vendors to the best or best few choices in order to economically select the winner.

PHASE 4: ACCEPTANCE

In many organizations, the acceptance phase and the test phase are conducted simultaneously. This is because until the organization tests and verifies a product's performance, they may not desire to accept a vendor and assign a contract. On the other hand, many organizations select the winning vendor and then verify that that product meets the contractual specifications. There are advantages and disadvantages to both approaches.

We will discuss the acceptance phase as if it were a separate phase from testing. This is to emphasize the different aspects of each, but recognizing that in fact the two may be performed simultaneously. However, it should be noted that the responsibility for the formal acceptance of the vendor is normally performed by a group different from that which tests the product to ensure that it satisfies requirements.

Ideally, the acceptance criteria should be predetermined. If they are not, the user may easily be swayed by unimportant criteria. Again, good marketing personnel can make you think you want something which you really do not, and you don't recognize it until after you have bought the product.

What Are the Objectives of the Phase?

The objective of the acceptance test phase is to predetermine the acceptance criteria and then evaluate the RFPs against those criteria. Generally, criteria can be divided into the following three categories:

1. *Mandatory requirements:* If the vendor product does not include these requirements, the vendor will be excluded from the bidding.
2. *Desirable criteria:* These are criteria that the user would like but are not essential. In most instances, these are the accessories that would be nice if available. These are the criteria that are normally used for tie-breaking.
3. *Unexpected but desirable features:* The vendor may have features that the user never considered but when exposed to them, considers to be desirable. These, too, should be considered tie-breakers.

A major risk is acquiring a product based on category 3 features, because you may be swayed by something that you really do not need. Therefore, they should carry considerably less weight than the desirable features in tie-breaking. Ideally, a predetermined weighting scheme would state the value assigned to these category 3 criteria.

A suggested vendor selection worksheet is provided as Figure 79. This should be completed before the RFPs are returned from the vendor. The user should indicate on the worksheet all of the essential selection criteria.

The Vendor Selection Worksheet

Organizations need a method to determine the winning vendor scientifically as opposed to judgmentally. When judgment takes hold, the decision may be made on irrational criteria. The vendor selection worksheet (see Figure 79) provides a scientific method for determining the winning vendor. The worksheet is divided into essential and tie-breaking criteria. Those items that fail to meet the essential criteria should be deleted from consideration.

Item Needed _____

No.	Essential Selection Criteria	Vendor Satisfies				
		1	2	3	4	5

No.	Tie-Breaking Criteria	Maximum Points	Vendor Award				
			1	2	3	4	5
	Total Points						

Figure 79   *Vendor Selection Worksheet*

The tie-breaking criteria are used when two or more vendors meet the essential criteria. However, one vendor may far exceed the essential criteria and thus even though two or more vendors meet the criteria, it is obvious which should be selected. For example, if one of the selection criteria is that the item must be priced less than $15,000, and one product is priced at $15,000 and the second at $10,000, it would be obvious that the second would be selected on that criterion alone, assuming that all other essential selection criteria have been achieved.

This form should be completed prior to completing the bidding process. All of the essential and tie-breaking criteria are recorded on the vendor selection worksheet. The points allocated to the tie-breaking criteria are also included. In the event that a vendor proposes new criteria, they can be considered, but should not carry nearly as much weight as the predetermined tie-breaking criteria. Some organizations allocate only one point for any criterion that arises during the selection process. Note that at this point these category 3 criteria are not known.

As each vendor's RFP is received, that information is recorded on the vendor selection worksheet in the "vendor satisfies" columns. In the essential criteria column, a check mark can indicate that the essential selection criteria have been met, and a plus sign (+) can be put next to the check if the criterion is exceeded. In our example of the price, the product that came in at $10,000 would receive a check mark indicating that it met the $15,000 criterion, and a plus sign indicating that it exceeded the selection criteria.

The tie-breaking criteria should also be recorded after reviewing each RFP. The maximum points for each tie-breaking criterion should be indicated on the form. The person doing the selection would then allocate points up to the maximum number of points on how well the vendor satisfied the criteria. For example, if adequate documentation was a tie-breaking criterion and 10 points allocated, each vendor would be awarded from 0 through 10 points. If the documentation for a package contained everything that might be expected in documentation, it would be allocated 10 points. If no documentation was provided, 0 points would be awarded that vendor. As documentation moves from none to everything needed, the number of points awarded increases from 1 through 10.

After all the vendor RFPs have been received and recorded, the selection process begins. It proceeds as follows:

1. All of the vendors that fail to meet the essential selection criteria are deleted from the selection process.
2. If one vendor far exceeds the other vendors in meeting the essential selection criteria (given the most pluses), that vendor is selected.
3. If two or more vendors are approximately equal in the essential selection criteria, the number of points allocated to each vendor for the tie-breaking criteria are accumulated. The vendor with the most tie-breaking criteria points is awarded the contract. Note that if the number of points is approximately equal (e.g., within plus or minus 10 percent of one another), the tie-breaking criteria may also be considered equal.
4. If the essential and tie-breaking criteria are approximately equal for two or more vendors, the award should be based on (and in that order) (a) price, (b) expected future service, (c) previous dealings with the vendor, and (d) projected future enhancements.

Who Is Responsible for the Phase?

EDP administration should have primary responsibility for the acceptance phase. This does not mean that they evaluate the product and allocate the points based on how well it satisfies the user but rather, that they should direct the selection process. Administration should ensure that the selection criteria are predetermined before the RFPs are returned. When this happens, there is a significantly greater probability that the selected product will meet the true needs of the organization.

How Is the Phase Performed?

Most of the effort expended during the acceptance phase will be involved in evaluating the product to determine how well it satisfies the acceptance criteria. Again, it may be necessary to enter the test phase in order to acquire some of the acceptance criteria. However, it may be more economical to have the vendor provide that information in the RFP so that only minimal effort is spent in testing.

The steps that should be followed in determining the most acceptable vendor(s) (see Figure 80) involve:

1.   *Use a selection criterion to select qualified vendors.* The process outlined in Figure 79 accomplishes this step. In the case where two or more vendors are considered equal, tie-breaking procedures must take effect.

Program Step	Objective of Step	Who Performs?	Dates Start	Dates Complete	Comments
1. Use a selection criterion to select qualified vendors	Select best vendor	Administration			
2. Determine that vendor terms are acceptable	Select acceptable vendor	Administration			
3. Determine that personnel can use product	Select usable product	Administration			

Figure 80   *Acceptance Phase Program*

Normally, the tie-breaking criteria will serve this purpose. Where these do not, the tie-breaking criteria discussed previously should be used.

2. *Determine that the vendor terms are acceptable.* Even though the product is the best, the terms offered by the vendor may make that vendor unacceptable. For example, the vendor may want to sign a long-term contract and will not offer the desired price for a shorter term. Thus, equally important with the requirements are the terms and conditions imposed by the vendor.

3. *Determine that personnel can use product.* The final payoff of the product will be its use in the organization. If it is overengineered for the staff that will use the product, it may be an undesirable product. The acceptable vendor must offer a fit with requirements, price, contractual terms, and usability of the product.

At the end of this phase, a vendor and a product have been selected. The contract can then be negotiated, with the final acceptance being dependent on the implemented product meeting the contractual specifications. If the product is already available, the testing may have been done during this phase. On the other hand, if the product has to be developed or is not readily available, testing will occur in a separate phase.

PHASE 5: TEST (comes out of requirements, if specified well)

The test phase is designed to ensure that the product delivered by the vendor meets the contractual specifications. These contractual specifications should be the requirements established by the user in the first phase of the vendor life cycle. The methods of testing vary depending on the type of product.

Specifications defined in measurable terms become good test requirements. On the other hand, the more general the specifications, the more difficult the test phase becomes. Like the acceptance phase, it is important that the test criteria be established before the phase begins.

An effective method for conducting the test phase is to acquire the vendor's test conditions. For software, the vendor should have developed test conditions and predetermined the results from those conditions. If this criterion is acceptable, the organization can use the same test data to evaluate the product prior to acceptance. Again, a good-quality control program by the vendor will provide high assurance that the delivered product will meet the specifications.

Testing is no more enjoyable with a vendor product than it is with an in-house product. However, once the product has been accepted by the vendor, the cost of correcting may be considerably greater than if the defect were uncovered prior to acceptance. As long as an organization is withholding funds pending meeting certain criteria, the vendor is going to be much more willing to make changes than after the product has been paid for.

It is generally a good rule to withhold approximately 25 percent of the purchase price pending successful completion of the test phase. It is fairly common in the industry and should not be objected to by vendors. Some sort of club to hold over the vendor helps ensure that the contract *will* be fulfilled.

What Are the Objectives of the Phase?

The objective of testing is to ensure that the acquired product meets the user requirements. If acceptance and testing are combined, this phase will have been performed before the product is accepted. On the other hand, this may not be practical in some acquisition procedures: for example, if a product is being specifically constructed for the organization. In these instances, the contract will be signed long before the product is developed. In other instances, even when the product is pretested as a prototype, the organization may still wish to verify the acceptability of the delivered product.

Testing of an acquired product is basically the same task as testing a product developed in-house. It begins with the establishment of a test plan. The plan must then be converted into a reality through the preparation of test conditions. The results expected are predetermined. The product is then subject to testing to determine that the test conditions produce the desired results. If so, the product is acceptable. If not, it must be determined whether the test conditions or the product has failed.

It is desirable not to pay for a product until it has satisfactorily passed a test. However, many vendors may require an advance payment before they deliver the product. This is particularly true if the product is to be custom made. In those instances, it is common practice to withhold some percent of the purchase price pending successful completion of the test.

Who Is Responsible for the Phase?

Testing is the responsibility of the user or requester of the product. This does not mean that processing is not involved in the test. It means that the user must make the final decision as to whether or not the product has satisfactorily passed the test. At a minimum, this means that the user should be involved in determining the test conditions and then reviewing the results of testing.

Although many users do not want to get involved in this phase, the contracting process should insist on it. Two of the strongest tools that can be used to ensure success are accountability and responsibility. When the user is responsible for testing and accountable for the correctness of the product, they do become involved in testing.

How is the Phase Performed?

The performance of the test phase requires the user to define how the product will be used in the vendor's business. Once this has been determined, the test conditions necessary to ensure that the product will meet those requirements become obvious. Ideally, the test conditions would be constructed during the requirements phase and executed during the test phase.

The steps that should be followed in executing the test phase (see Figure 81) include:

1. *Verify delivered item meets requirements.* The specifications defined during the requirements phase must be turned into test conditions. This is done most easily when the specifications are measurable. As previously stated, good specifications form the basis for test conditions. These conditions must be the broadest possible conditions. Not only should they verify what the system can do, but must verify that it can protect itself against invalid transactions or operating conditions. For example, in applications this might mean entering invalid transactions, and for hardware it might mean testing that it can protect itself against surges in electrical power.

2. *Verify that item is compatible with operating environment.* Rarely does one product operate independent of all other products. For example, a software package must interface with an operating system, and hardware components must interface with other hardware components. It is important to verify that compatibility exists between the new and existing products.

    This type of testing normally involves interconnecting the new product with existing products. The operation is then run to determine compatibility. It is generally a mistake to assume compatibility. If com-

| | | | Dates | | |
Program Step	Objective of Step	Who Performs?	Start	Com-plete	Comments
1. Verify that delivered item meets requirements	Ensure that product satisfies requirements	User			
2. Verify that item is compatible with operating environment	Ensure that item works in operating environment	User			
3. Verify that staff can operate item	Ensure that staff is adequately trained	User			

Figure 81   *Test Phase Program*

patibility is assumed, testing might occur in an environment other than the one in which the product will run. Unfortunately, experience has recorded many disasters, in that once delivered, the product did not run. Some of these are still sitting on the shelf waiting for the operating environment to change. These types of tests include:

Product is compatible with existing hardware and operating software.

Data flowing to and from this product to other products are compatible.

The speed of processing is compatible with the speed of other processing units.

Error tolerances are compatible with environmental quality standards.

3.   *Verify that staff can operate item.* The final test of any product occurs when people begin to use it for its intended purpose. In many instances, highly trained technicians under controlled conditions can operate the product successfully. On the other hand, that same product, used by less motivated personnel in the hustle-bustle of the real world, fails.

It is good practice to test products by having the people who will use them operate them. In computer operations, this means that normal operators will utilize the product from vendor-produced documentation. For software, it means that the clerical personnel will interact with the package following the vendor instructions. If the product can operate under these conditions, it is probably an effective product. This assumes that prior to this time, it has been verified that it meets the requirements and is compatible with the operating environment. It would be a mistake to use the time of the operations and clerical personnel to debug the package other than from an operational perspective.

At the end of this phase, a vendor product will be ready to be installed to meet operational needs. A contract has been signed with the vendor and production is ready to begin. The life cycle now moves into the final maintenance phase.

PHASE 6: MAINTENANCE

Organizations live with acquired projects long after the acquisition date. The maintenance phase is the management of the acquired product in a production status. It is during this phase that the data processing personnel must keep the product in synchronization with the changing needs of the organization.

Maintenance is a phase frequently overlooked in contractual negotiations. The greatest emphasis is placed on getting the product that meets the specifications and ensuring that it works. People sometimes forget that that product may be in use for two, five, 10, or even 20 years. The life of many data processing products that were believed to be five years or less has extended to 20 years and more.

One only need think back to the technological and administrative changes over the past 20 years to visualize what might happen in the ensuing 20 years. Technological advances that have not even been conceived will occur. Products purchased today must be adaptable to many of the new changes.

It is impossible to predict all of the maintenance requirements during the life of an acquired product. However, what is possible is to recognize that maintenance will be needed and to plan for it as best as possible. Primarily, this involves ensuring that both the organization and the vendor are in agreement that maintenance will be necessary.

Unfortunately, many organizations consider the vendor life cycle concluded when the product is accepted and installed. In actual practice, it just begins. The administration and control of a vendor contract is an important aspect of the vendor life cycle.

The following three conditions are necessary to make the maintenance phase work:

1. One person should be assigned accountability for each vendor contract (i.e., product).
2. The accountable person should be supplied with a copy of the contract.
3. The contract should be reviewed periodically to ensure that the vendor is complying with the provisions of the contract.

It is surprising how frequently vendor contracts are stored in the purchasing or other central area. The person working with the vendor does not have a detailed knowledge of the contract and in fact may have never seen it. On the other hand, that person is supposed to ensure that the vendor lives up to the contract—impossible situation!

What Are the Objectives of the Phase?

Maintenance encompasses all those activities that occur after the successful product is installed. Maintenance encompasses the correction of problems, technological updates, documentation changes, product enhancements, and any other activity necessary to extend the useful product life.

The performance of the maintenance will vary by product and contract. In some instances, the vendor will retain full maintenance responsibilities, which may be a separate contract and fee. In other instances, the purchasing organization will assume full responsibility for the maintenance of the product.

Software products can be maintained either around or through the product. Around-the-product maintenance can involve the development of manual procedures, preprocessors, or postprocessors. Through-the-product maintenance involves changing the product to correct defects or meet new requirements.

The general rule for maintaining vendor products is: "Don't change vendor products." Violations of this rule normally result in more extensive costs than those associated with not changing the product. Invariably, as new versions are released, organizations are locked into older versions or extensive maintenance charges.

Who Is Responsible for the Phase?

The EDP administration group should have oversight responsibility for maintenance. Naturally, they do not perform the maintenance on EDP products, but they may have accountability for the product. This means that administration becomes the interface between the user and the vendor to ensure that the contractual provisions are performed properly. Administration retains copies of the contract, monitors the contract, and should interview users periodically to ensure that they are receiving the appropriate services. Users not receiving the appropriate services should be instructed to call EDP administration to remedy such a situation.

How Is the Maintenance Phase Performed?

Maintenance of vendor products normally falls into one of the following four categories:

1. *Maintenance provided automatically by the vendor:* This can be routine maintenance, enhancements, or correction of defects.
2. *User-detected defects:* Problems encountered by the user in the normal course of operation should be brought to the attention of the vendor or the person responsible for maintenance for correction.
3. *Technological enhancements:* As other aspects of the operating environment are technologically upgraded, it may also be necessary to upgrade other vendor products accordingly.
4. *Product enhancements:* Features that were not available when the product was contracted for may become available through vendor initiative or user request. In either case, these involve modification of the product. Note that in some instances they will be entirely new versions of the product.

As the product is maintained, it must be subject to testing. It is generally the responsibility of the user to ensure that the operational proficiency of the product is maintained. If good test criteria were established when the product was acquired, those same criteria can be reused to test the correctness of maintenance. Note that some criteria may have to be modified or added but that the general test conditions may be reusable.

The steps to be executed during the maintenance phase are illustrated in Figure 82. This worksheet can be used to administer the maintenance phase. Note that as the contract is reviewed, a new worksheet may be needed. The program steps that should be taken to ensure that the product stays in synchronization with the needs of the organization are:

1. *Ensure that vendor provides needed service.* The vendor's long-term interest in a product should be assessed. Obviously, this should occur during contractual negotiations. What needs to be done during maintenance is to ensure that those services are provided. This means that someone should be assigned accountability to ensure that service happens. This person should be provided with a copy of the contract and have a work program designed to ensure periodically that the service specified in a contract is, in fact, provided.

2. *Ensure that needed enhancements are requested and acquired.* Most organizations have established procedures to assist users in requesting

			Dates		
Program Step	**Objective of Step**	**Who Performs?**	**Start**	**Complete**	**Comments**
1. Ensure that vendor provides needed service	Monitor execution of vendor contract	Administration			
2. Ensure that needed enhancements are requested and required	Monitor execution of vendor contract	Administration			
3. Ensure that training program is updated with changes to item	Monitor execution of vendor contract	Administration			
4. Enforce contract provisions	Ensure that vendor fulfills contract provisions	Administration			

Figure 82 *Maintenance Phase Program*

changes. Frequently, a form is prepared which becomes the basis for driving change. Unfortunately, many organizations do not have the same type of procedure for changes in acquired software and hardware products. Without such a procedure, needed enhancements and corrections may not be documented. Without documentation, they may be lost. Procedures need to be established that collect, record, and pursue with vendors needed changes and enhancements. Someone should be assigned accountability for this task, and should provide regular reports to users on the status of changes and enhancements.

3. *Ensure that training program is updated with changes to item.* Acquired items should be updated and enhanced as the product is changed. This includes training and instruction manuals. The person responsible for the product should ensure that any training sessions, or operator or user manuals, are updated to coincide with changes to the software package.

4. *Enforce contract provisions.* Well-negotiated contracts cover a variety of clauses and situations. As stated many times previously, these negotiated provisions should be enforced. The benefits of contractual negotiations are lost if the contract is forgotten after the product is installed.

The EDP administration function should assume responsibility for the maintenance phase. This does not mean that they perform all of the program steps but rather, that they ensure that the program steps are followed. EDP administration should perform the following for each acquired product:

- Ensure that one person is accountable for the maintenance of that product.
- Ensure that one person is accountable for enforcing the contract provisions.
- Provide the person accountable for enforcing contract provisions with a copy of the contract.
- Develop administrative procedures such that the people accountable for maintenance know what is expected of them.
- Ensure that each vendor is evaluated on the type of service and maintenance they provide.
- Ensure that the accountable and responsible personnel fulfill their assigned tasks.

EDP ADMINISTRATIVE GUIDELINE 39

Marketing's oldest rule is: "Let the buyer beware." Positively reworded for EDP administration, it should state: "Let the buyer enforce contractual provisions."

KEEPING SCORE ON THE VENDORS

Organizations are involved with a large number of vendors. These vendors may contact employees in different departments at different times. In many instances, the vendors may not be known, or their dealings with the organization may not be known.

There are two unfortunate situations that can occur in dealing with a single vendor. The first is that the vendor provides unsatisfactory service and yet at another time the organization again contracts with that vendor. In most instances, the same poor service is received a second time. Second and equally unsatisfactory is the situation in which a vendor provides outstanding service and yet is not considered for another contract in the vendor's area of expertise.

The solution to this dilemma is to keep records on the results of vendor contracts. These records should be referred to in determining what vendors should be asked to bid on future contracts. The record should also be reviewed before any contracts are made with the vendor. This relatively inexpensive but effective method will improve the quality of vendor contracts.

Each interaction with a vendor should be evaluated. Even if the vendor is not the successful bidder, it is valuable to keep records on the negotiations with that vendor. This should not include casual discussions with vendors but rather, interaction with serious contenders for a contract.

EDP ADMINISTRATIVE GUIDELINE 40

It is a shame to deal with a poor vendor—it is a sin to deal with that vendor more than once.

A vendor scorecard (see Figure 83) is provided for vendor evaluation. The scorecard is designed primarily for vendors winning contracts, but can also be used to evaluate vendors seriously evaluated in the contractual negotiations. When vendors have not won the contract, that should be clearly noted on the scorecard.

The vendor scorecard provides for seven evaluation criteria. It is not meant to be a complex form but rather, one that takes only a few minutes to complete. It is normally completed by the person accountable for the contract. That person rates the vendor in the following seven categories:

1. *Satisfaction of requirements:* The vendor met the needs of the organization.
2. *Fulfillment of contract terms:* The vendor stood behind and performed all of the contractual provisions.
3. *Quality of item:* The product delivered met the quality expectations of the organization.

Vendor Name _____		Item _____				Vendor No.: _____	

		Rating					
Evaluation Criteria	N/A	More Than Ade-quate	Fully Ade-quate	Less Than Ade-quate	Unac-cept-able	Comments	
1. Satisfaction of requirements							
2. Fulfillment of contract terms							
3. Quality of item							
4. Adequacy of training							
5. Adequacy of maintenance							
6. Availability of promised enhancements							
7. Overall support of item							

Would you recommend vendor? ☐ Yes ☐ No   Why? _____

Rated by _____   Dept. _____   Date _____

Figure 83 *Vendor Scorecard*

4. *Adequacy of training:* The vendor provided sufficient training so that the organization could use the product successfully and kept the training up to date as the product changed.

5. *Adequacy of maintenance:* The vendor product provided the level of service that was expected, either through excellence of product and/or adequacy of the vendor to maintain the product or provide the capabilities of maintenance.

6. *Availability of promised enhancements:* Those extensions that the vendor agreed would be provided were, in fact, provided.

7. *Overall support of item:* In general, the vendor was attentive to the needs of the organization.

Each of these seven items should be rated to the degree of satisfaction. This is attitudinal as opposed to factual. We are looking for vendors that satisfy people. In some instances, it may be desirable to have the rating made by two or more people.

Each of the seven evaluation criteria should be rated in one of the following categories:

- *More than adequate:* Exceeds contract requirements
- *Fully adequate:* Met contract requirements
- *Less than adequate:* Did not meet all contract requirements
- *Unacceptable:* Failed to meet contract requirements

If the evaluation criteria are not applicable, the N/A column should be checked. If it is advantageous to explain the rating, a comments column is provided for that purpose. Comments generally are helpful.

The key question on the form is at the bottom. This question asks whether the rater would recommend the vendor for future contracts. This is answered with a simple yes or no answer, but the rater is asked to explain why. This question really sums up the entire evaluation and hopefully the evaluation will support this recommendation.

A VENDOR CONTRACTUAL CHECKLIST

The material in this chapter is designed to assist in the administrative aspect of vendor negotiations. The vendor life cycle covers negotiations with the vendor from the development of requirements to the point where the vendor product is no longer needed. However, this discussion has not provided a detailed analysis on evaluating vendor contracts.

In most instances, the vendor provides the contract. One must be aware that a vendor-developed contract will be favorable to the vendor. In dealing with large organizations such as IBM, it may be difficult to get contractual concessions. On the other hand, it is the obligation of the organization to provide the maximum protection for the organization. At a minimum, this means a detailed scrutiny of the contract to ensure that the provisions are fair.

It has been recommended that any contract be reviewed by the organization's legal counsel. The objective of the legal counsel review is to ensure that the legal provisions are acceptable to the organization. The lawyers may not be able to determine that the product considerations in a contract are fair. This function of the contractual review should be performed by the EDP administration function.

The vendor contractual review checklist shown in Figure 84 is designed to assist EDP administration in fulfilling their review function. The checklist is designed so that "yes" answers are desirable attributes of contracts from the organization's perspective, and "no," undesirable. Those areas checked "no" should be reviewed with legal counsel and the potential user of the product to ensure that the provision is acceptable. If not, EDP administration should either have the provision changed or eliminate that vendor from contention. Note that in some instances, when a vendor knows they will be eliminated from consideration due to contractual provisions, they may change those contractual provisions.

EDP ADMINISTRATIVE GUIDELINE 41

A good contract is a fair contract to both parties. EDP administration should be equally concerned when a vendor contract is overly favorable to one party.

	Response			
Item	Yes	No	N/A	Comments
1. Does the contract specify the requirements in sufficient detail so that acceptability of the delivered product can be measured?				
2. Has the delivery date of all deliverables been specified in the contract?				
3. Has the price to be paid for each deliverable been specified in the contract?				
4. Does the contract specify the vendor's obligations in the event that the product fails to meet specifications?				
5. Does the vendor warrant the reliability tolerances of the product to produce accurate and complete results?				
6. Does the contract indicate what the vendor will do (i.e., quality control procedures) to ensure that the product works as specified?				
7. Has the vendor's responsibility for installation been specified?				
8. Has the customer's responsibility for installation been specified?				
9. Has the location where the product will be installed been specified?				
10. Does the contract indicate the type of operating environment in which the product will work?				
11. Is the organization permitted to move the product from location to location?				
12. Does the contract provide for withholding of funds until the organization is ensured that the product works as specified?				
13. Have the methods of payment been specified?				
14. Have the dates of payment been specified?				
15. Does the vendor agree to upgrade the product in the event that the operating environment changes?				
16. Have the vendor's maintenance requirements been specified?				
17. Has the cost for maintenance been specified?				
18. Has the caliber of vendor personnel who will provide maintenance been specified?				
19. Has the location where maintenance will occur been specified?				
20. If the contract is for hardware, does it permit foreign attachments?				
21. If there are multiple vendors involved in the operating environment, do the contracts specify problem identification responsibility?				

Figure 84 *Vendor Contractual Checklist*

	Response			
Item	Yes	No	N/A	Comments
22. If there are multiple vendors involved, does the vendor accept responsibility for making their product operational?				
23. Has the life of the contract been specified?				
24. If it is a lease contract, will part of the lease amount go toward purchase?				
25. If it is a lease contract, has the purchase price been specified?				
26. Have the dates of any desired enhancements been specified?				
27. Has the cost for future enhancements and services been specified?				
28. Does the vendor agree to stock parts and/or maintain a cadre of qualified maintenance personnel in close proximity?				
29. If the vendor goes out of business, do all product rights revert to the organization (i.e., source code listings, copyrights, etc.)?				
30. If the vendor goes out of business, is the method of transferring spare parts, source listings, etc., specified?				
31. If the vendor goes out of business, does the organization have the right to reproduce training manuals, etc.?				
32. If the vendor discontinues service on this product, do the same rights revert to the organization as if the vendor had gone out of business?				
33. Has the length of vendor support for the product been specified (i.e., minimum length)?				
34. Has the method of determining whether or not the product is acceptable been specified?				
35. Has the place and time where acceptance testing will occur been specified?				
36. Is the contract fair from the vendor perspective?				
37. Is the contract fair from the customer perspective?				
38. Has the contract been reviewed by the organization's legal counsel?				
39. Has the method of training organization personnel been specified?				
40. Has the training material for organization personnel been specified?				
41. Has the operator/clerical training material been specified?				
42. Has the method of training operation/clerical method been specified?				
43. Does the system contain adequate controls so that the functioning of the system can be determined?				

Figure 84 *(continued)*

287

Item	Response			
	Yes	No	N/A	Comments
44. If special part/forms, etc., are needed, does the vendor supply them?				
45. Is the location and method of acquiring supplies specified in the contract?				
46. Can the organization terminate the contract provided that they give reasonable time notice?				
47. If the organization cannot terminate the contract during the life of the contract, has a method been specified for breaking the contract?				
48. Are the penalties for breaking the contract reasonable?				
49. Can the organization duplicate the product, assuming that it is software, for use throughout the organization?				
50. If the product cannot be duplicated, does the contract provide for reduced prices for additional copies?				
51. Are the vendor's rights governing access to the organization's premises and records specified?				
52. Has the state and/or country whose laws govern the contract been specified?				
53. Has the organization had satisfactory relations with this vendor in the past?				
54. Does the vendor have sufficient resources to stay in business for the life of the contract? (For example, review the vendor's financial statements to ensure that the vendor has the probability of staying in business.)				
55. Have other users of this product been contacted to determine the performance of the contract?				
56. Have other customers of this vendor been contacted to ensure that the vendor is reliable?				
57. Does the organization have the right to cancel the contract in the event that the vendor fails to deliver the product at the specified time or cost, or if it does not include all the deliverables?				
58. Does the organization have the right to cancel the contract in the event that the contractual product specifications are not achieved?				

Figure 84 *(continued)*

CONTROLLING ADMINISTRATION

Control is the totality of methods, procedures, and tools used to ensure administrative procedures and performed in accordance with the intent of management. Good control makes good EDP administration.

Chapter

12

The Quality
of Administration

EDP administration is normally viewed as an overhead function. In fact, in many organizations it is viewed more as a necessary evil than as a productive part of the data processing department. One project leader described administration as "another impediment by management to stop me from doing my job on time."

If EDP administration is viewed as a profit center within a profit center, the view of both the people within administration and those using it will change. Administrative functions that are detrimental will be eliminated, leaving those functions that are necessary to get the job done. Generally, no one disagrees that some administration is necessary; it is usually the extent and how administration is performed that is debated. These are measures of the quality of administration, and as the quality improves, so does the approval of the staff being administered.

This chapter discusses the impediments to high-quality administration and how to overcome those impediments. The previous portion of the book explains what administration should do. This chapter explains how to do it in a manner that is productive through the use of quality concepts. The most difficult part of administration is going from a concept that people like to an implementation that is equally likable.

IMPEDIMENTS TO QUALITY ADMINISTRATION

EDP administration tends to fail because it falls short in the following eight areas. (Note: As you read these impediments try to put yourself in the shoes of the EDP staff; or visualize yourself trying to return a product in a department store to a disinterested clerk abiding exactly by the rules.)

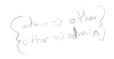

1. *Administrative response time:* The administrative function does not provide the data processing staff with the needed information at the time it will be of most value to the project. In addition, administration is frequently lax in advising data processing personnel of the need for administrative data. In many instances, the staff is pressured to supply administrative information quickly when, in fact, they could have been notified much earlier and provided that information at their leisure.

2. *Accuracy of output:* Administrative data are frequently viewed as second-class information. For this reason, they may be perceived as inaccurate and unreliable. For example, the time-reporting system accounts for an individual's workweek, but rarely do people believe that the system provides data with a high degree of accuracy. Thus the information is of minimal value because people recognize that it is only an approximation of the real world, not what is really happening.

3. *Timeliness of output:* The administrative data may have a low priority for processing. Even some administrative groups do not believe that they should be high-priority processing. Reports frequently lag weeks, or even months, after the events have occurred. Information processed this late may not be of the value it could have been in making decisions.

4. *Response to problems:* Needs of project personnel may take a low priority in respect to other administrative duties. For example, a project may need clarification on a particular point before people can understand the report; they may also need a breakdown in order to make a good decision, but have difficulty getting the administrative group to act on their specific problem.

5. *Attitude and cooperativeness:* Administrators may feel that "they don't have no respect" from their peers. This may be a direct result of an uncooperative attitude on the part of administrators. Administrators may express the attitude that the staff will do it "my way." While data processing is geared up to be of service to users, administrators are not always geared up to be of service to the data processing staff.

6. *Meeting schedules:* Meeting schedules is frequently viewed as the responsibility of the staff, not the administrators. This may be partly due to the fact that administration is not viewed as essential, and therefore gets accomplished on an "as time is available" basis. Some of these attitudes on the unimportance of administration reflect through all of these attributes.

7. *Usefulness of output:* Data processors frequently survey their users on the value of output reports. Administrators rarely survey their users on the value of administrative output. It does not matter whether the data are good or bad if they are viewed by the users of administrative data as worthless information. Perhaps if it serves no purpose, the administrative reports should be stopped, just as data processing frequently stops issuing reports which they recognize are no longer useful.

8. _Distribution of output:_ Good channels of distribution for administrative reports may not be established. Sometimes an insufficient number of copies are distributed, or they may be distributed to the wrong people.

Some administrative functions are excellent; others are true elephant graveyards. If administration is viewed as a profit center and charged with justifying the function, these impediments seem to disappear. On the other hand, when administration is relegated to a necessary evil, the impediments grow.

DEFINING QUALITY ADMINISTRATION

Quality means compliance to standards. If any project can meet the standards established for that project, it should be considered a quality project. Therefore, quality administration by definition means compliance to the administrative standards.

Standards in administration are the measure of how well administration is doing. These are the goals and objectives established for administration. If these goals and objectives can be stated in measurable terms, administration can strive to achieve those goals and objectives and become a quality administrative function.

Let us look at how we might establish an administrative standard in the eight quality areas described previously as impediments. (Note: These are only examples of one of what might be many standards.)

1. _Area:_ Administrative response time
   Administrative standard: Personnel will be given at least five working days to respond to all requests.
2. _Area:_ Accuracy of output
   Administrative standard: Administrative reports should be accurate within plus or minus 1 percent.
3. _Area:_ Timeliness of reports
   Administrative standard: Reports will be issued within 24 hours after the input has been received.
4. _Area:_ Response to problems
   Administrative standard: Any request for information or clarification received by 3 P.M. will be responded to that day; and detailed reports issued within two days 90 percent of the time.
5. _Area:_ Attitude and cooperativeness
   Administrative standard: The data processing staff will be surveyed annually about the attitude and cooperativeness of the administrative group and on a rating scale of "uncooperative," "cooperative," and "more

than cooperative." The desired rating should be "cooperative" or "more than cooperative."

6. *Area:* Meeting schedules

   Administrative standard: On a yearly basis, 95 percent of the projects will be met on or before the scheduled date.

7. *Area:* Usefulness of output

   Administrative standard: Data processing personnel will be surveyed yearly and on a usefulness of output rating scale of "not useful," "useful," and "very useful." The administrative reports should achieve an overall rating of "useful" or better.

8. *Area:* Distribution of output

   Administrative standard: On a yearly basis, the administrative reports should reach the right person 98 percent of the time.

Quality does not just happen; it must be a goal of the administrative function in order for it to happen. Either the administrative manager or a staff assistant in a larger organization must have the quality of administration as one of that person's responsibilities. This means that that person must look objectively at the administrative process to ensure that it provides a high probability of producing quality output, and then look at the products produced by administration from a quality control perspective to ensure that they meet the administrative quality standards.

There are three general approaches to the administrative function. These are quality, productivity, and control. The three are illustrated as a quality triangle in Figure 85. Note that these concepts are not mutually exclusive, but one must be dominant.

The administrative manager must make a basic decision about which of the three quality triangle philosophies are to be emphasized. If control is emphasized, the underlying philosophy is to follow the process. The administra-

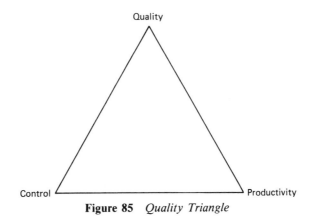

Figure 85 *Quality Triangle*

tive manager will develop procedures, forms, and methods, and require that the data processing staff follow those procedures precisely. The concept is that if the procedures are followed, the proper results will occur. Productivity emphasis attempts to accomplish the work as fast as possible. Emphasis is on achieving the numbers. This means doing the work faster, which may be accomplished only by allocating a predetermined time to the administrative function. The underlying philosophy here is that if people work harder, more work will get done in a given period of time. The last concept is quality. This says that the most important aspect of work is how well the work is done. The staff is asked to produce the best possible product that they can deliver. Again, quality is defined as compliance to standards, so the best possible work they can deliver is that which complies to standards.

Generally, the control and productivity emphasis leads to unsatisfactory results. Emphasizing control results in the forms being completed, but the data may be no good. This has been shown to happen over and over again when people are forced to follow a method which they do not believe is the best method. When productivity is emphasized, people tend to work faster. The philosophy is to finish on schedule, write more lines of code per hour, and so on. What tends to happen when this philosophy is emphasized is that more bad products are produced per hour. This philosophy was predominant in a lot of American automotive manufacturers. Their concern was to get the car off the production line every 43 seconds and not worry about one or two missed steps. These could always be corrected by the dealer, or recognized by the customer, who would return it to the dealer for correction. How well this philosophy worked can be stated in a new advertising slogan by one American automotive manufacturer, which is: "Quality is number one."

The quality emphasis works. Once quality becomes the overriding issue, the guidelines or standards for quality must be established. In order to achieve those standards, controls must be put into place. As soon as effective controls are in place directed at producing quality products, productivity goes up dramatically. This has been the experience of many Japanese organizations. Unfortunately, quality concepts usually take time to develop. The turnaround of a poor-quality administrative group into a high-quality group may take 18 to 36 months. This means that not only must the administrative management want quality, but senior data processing management must also support that concept.

EDP ADMINISTRATIVE GUIDELINE 42

It takes less time to do it right the first time than to correct it after it has been done wrong.

THE EDP ADMINISTRATION/STAFF
QUALITY PARTNERSHIP

Quality administration occurs when the administrative function and the staff develop an effective working relationship. In other words, administration needs accurate data and cooperation from the staff in order to produce the type of administrative reports needed to manage projects. Neither administration nor staff can decide independently to increase the quality of administration.

The responsibility for initiating a quality program resides with the administrative manager. This person must recognize the need to improve quality and take the steps necessary to improve quality. It is an everybody wins situation, but only happens when one person acts as the quality catalyst to make it happen.

The administration/staff quality partnership is illustrated in Figure 86. The figure shows quality occurring through an objective cycle. As the quality of output from administration improves, the desire to provide quality input increases. As the quality of input increases, the quality of output further increases and the process continues with an ever-increasing degree of quality.

The steps EDP administration can take to improve quality output include:

- *Giving ownership of administrative reports to the user:* The reports generally are not prepared for administration. Once the users of the report

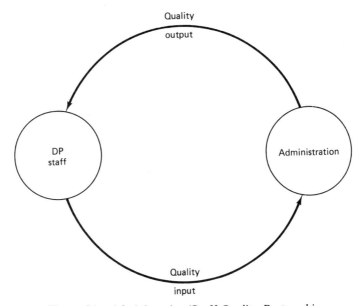

Figure 86   *Administration/Staff Quality Partnership*

recognize that they belong to them, that they can improve them, and that their input makes them better, quality will improve.

- *Assigning quality accountability:* One person should be accountable for the quality in each administrative product. For example, if there is a time-reporting system, one person should be accountable for the quality of that report.
- *Making people responsible for the quality of the work they perform:* Each person should be responsible for his or her part of the administrative process. EDP administration should not be checking the work of the staff personnel, nor should the staff personnel be checking the work of EDP administration.
- *Training the staff in performing the administrative function:* Do not assume that the staff or administrative personnel know how to do specific functions. Ensure that they are trained in that function and conduct sufficient evaluations to ensure that they have mastered those skills. Once a person has been taught a function, and it has been demonstrated that the person has mastered those skills, the person should be expected to produce high-quality work. If that person cannot perform at the quality level for which he or she has been trained, the person should be moved to another job.
- *Providing the staff tools to measure the quality of administrative work:* People can assess the quality of their own work only when they are given the appropriate tools. For example, time-reporting sheets that are self-checking (e.g., total across and down to determine accuracy of reporting) provide a tool for a person to assess the mathematical quality of administrative data.

The EDP staff can improve the quality of the administrative process and reports by:

- *Recording information on a timely basis:* People should not rely on their memory to store administrative data. For example, monthly time reports that are prepared on the last day of the month are much less reliable than when that information is entered daily.
- *Alloting adequate administrative time:* Administration is an important tool in improving the quality of data processing work. However, like any other function, if sufficient time is not allocated to perform it, it will not be done, done well, or done on time.
- *Suggesting areas for improvement:* The staff should not complain about poor administration, or gripe about procedures they do not like but rather, should be encouraged and provided with a method for making suggestions as to how to improve those processes.
- *Creating administrative quality circles:* Personnel should participate in quality circles designed to improve administrative productivity. (Note: Quality circles are discussed in this chapter.)

THE STEPS FOR BUILDING ADMINISTRATIVE QUALITY

The administrative baseline profile established using the procedures in the beginning of this book are valuable in assessing the effectiveness of quality. Quality cannot be improved until it is measured. The administrative manager must have reliable information about the quality of administration in order to improve it.

The administrative manager has three basic options available to measuring and improving the quality of EDP administration. These are:

- Self-evaluation and improvement
- Task force assessment and recommendation
- Administrative quality circles

These options are not mutually exclusive. The manager may use any or all of the options singly or in combination. Which process is selected is not important; what is important is that the administrative manager take action to measure and improve quality where necessary. The options are discussed individually below.

Self-Evaluation and Improvement

Good managers can study their own function, interview people affected, identify problems, and initiate actions to improve areas of weakness. This is typical of the functions performed by a systems analyst. Since many administrative managers have been systems analysts in the past, they may be effective in assessing needs and developing solutions.

The administrative manager may decide to use outside assistance in this assessment. The manager could ask the organization's auditors to perform an operational audit of administration, hire consultants, or ask one of the systems personnel to perform this study. The process may look at all or at parts of the administrative process.

Many quality improvements can be made by automating parts of the administrative function. Ideas for automation may come from attending conferences with administrators, review of the literature, or discussion with vendors of automated administrative products. The objective is to develop better quality methods of performing administrative work.

Task Force Assessment and Recommendation

A one-time task force of personnel affected by administration could be convened to help improve the quality. This is a relatively low-cost, but frequently very effective method to kick off a quality campaign. The objective is to involve people affected by the quality of administration in developing quality action plans.

The task force process is initiated by the administrative manager. It generally takes only a few hours of key people's time. The task force approach is a four-step approach, performed as follows (see Figure 87 for an overview of these four steps).

Step 1. Organize Task Force

The administrative manager should organize a task force of people representative of those dealing with EDP administration. Ideally, all of the major areas and projects within data processing would be represented. On the other hand, the task force should probably not exceed six to nine people or it becomes unwieldy.

The type of people selected would be:

- Project managers
- Data base administrator
- Standards manager
- Operations manager
- Security officer
- Manager, technical support
- One or more members of senior data processing management

The task force would be asked to spend one to three hours to assess the quality of administration. The task force would not be asked to develop specific plans, because the administrative manager must stay in charge of administration. Advice can be solicited, but the control of the department should not be delegated to a task force. Note that if the task force makes specific recom-

Step	Objective
1. Organize task force	Assemble those concerned or affected by administration
2. Discuss quality factors	Explain the eight impediments to quality administration
3. Rate and rank quality factors	Ask the participants to rate and rank the quality factors
4. Build a quality plan of action	Improve quality weaknesses

Figure 87 *Quality Building Steps*

mendations, and the administrative manager chooses to ignore those recommendations, relationships may suffer more than if the task force was never convened.

Step 2. *Discuss Quality Factors*

The administrative manager should discuss the eight quality factors discussed previously in this chapter. If there are other factors that are important to the administrative manager, they can be added to the list of factors. The discussion should not be permitted to degenerate into a complaint session but rather, should attempt to scope each of the quality factors and the aspects of those factors that are important to the task force.

A member of administration should act as a recording secretary for this meeting. Generally, it is not advisable to tape-record the session because that tends to inhibit people's involvement in the discussion. On the other hand, many good ideas and concerns will be raised, which should be recorded for future analysis.

Step 3. *Rate and Rank the Quality Factors*

This is a two-step process. First, the attendee rates administration on how well they are doing; and then second, ranks the eight factors in importance to the success of administration from one through eight.

Each attendee of the task force meeting rates the performance of EDP administration on the five-point scale for each of the eight quality factors. The rating scale is:

- Very poor performance (in conducting the administration function)
- Poor performance (in conducting the administration function)
- Average performance (in conducting the administration function)
- Good on performance (in conducting the administration function)
- Very good performance (in conducting the administration function)

Where appropriate, the rater should be asked to comment on the rating. Although this is optional, it is very helpful and valuable information to obtain. The comments should be designed to cite good and bad administrative practices.

The task force members next rank the eight quality factors. The ranking is to indicate which they perceive to be the most important factor for administration, the second most important, through the eighth most important. For example, if they believe accuracy of output is the most important it would be ranked 1, and if they believe meeting the schedule is the least important it would be ranked eighth.

A rating worksheet for this purpose is provided in Figure 88. This work-

Quality Factor	Rank	Rating					Comments
		Very Poor	Poor	Avg.	Good	Very Good	
1. Administrative response time							
2. Accuracy of output							
3. Timeliness of output							
4. Response to problems							
5. Attitude and cooperativeness							
6. Meeting schedules							
7. Usefulness of output							
8. Distribution of output							

Rated by _____   **Date** _____

Figure 88   *EDP Administration Quality Evaluation*

sheet lists the eight quality factors, and provides space to rank and rate each of the factors, and a column for including comments. Although the form provides space to indicate who it is rated by and the date, this can be left as optional. On the other hand, it is helpful to know which area or person provided a rating, because they may help understand the rating or improve the quality, and it also provides an opportunity to go back to that person to discuss specific ratings or comments if it seems appropriate.

At the conclusion of the ranking and rating of the quality factors, the task force should be dismissed. This provides the type of information that is needed to address administrative quality problems. The task force should be thanked and dismissed. Although there is a quasi-obligation to advise the task force as to what factors will be addressed for quality improvement, nothing should be promised.

The administrative manager is warned that this process builds expectations. If no action is taken after this exercise, the attendees will feel cheated. On the other hand, if action is taken, the attendees will feel partly responsible for the improved quality. This ''ownership'' of improvement is a very positive factor in making quality happen.

Step 4.   Build a Quality Plan of Action

The rating and ranking exercise provides two pieces of information. First it indicates which factors appear to be most important to the users of administrative data (i.e., the ranking exercise). The high-ranking areas are the ones that should be addressed first if improvement is needed.

The rating exercise provided each of those factors indicates the amount of effort that should be expended on the factor. Obviously, those factors rated very good would require only minimal or no effort for improvement even though they ranked high in importance, whereas if high-ranked factors rated poor or very poor, they should get immediate and perhaps extensive attention.

The comments frequently provide insight into the rating. If the administrative manager receives a poor rating but is uncertain, additional investigation should be undertaken. This is best performed by personal visits to the task force members.

Administrative Quality Circles

Quality circles are a concept perfected by the Japanese and were discussed earlier in the book. It is a variation of participative management. It provides the opportunity for employees to improve the work effectiveness, productivity, and quality of the activities in which they are involved.

An administrative quality circle would be a group of people, normally peers, who are involved in or affected by data processing administration. Although it would include administration personnel, it should include a representative sample of the data processing department members.

The quality circle and the task force differ in one very important aspect. The task force or committee concept is management directed. In other words, in the previous process a task force was formed, given an assignment to do by the administrative manager, and then dismissed. The quality circle decides what tasks it will work on, works on those tasks, and develops a recommendation through democratic action without intervention by management.

The operation of the quality circle can best be explained by reviewing the rules for quality circle operation, which are:

1. *Membership is voluntary.* No one is appointed to a quality circle. Management agrees to the concept and then explains to eligible candidates that a quality circle is being formed. The ground rules, objectives, and obligations of membership are explained. The persons eligible then determine whether or not they want to be on the quality circle. If they desire to join the quality circle, they volunteer; if they decide not to join the quality circle, there is no pressure placed on anyone by management. Membership must be voluntary.
2. *One hour per week is allocated.* Management's only commitment is one hour per week per member of the quality circle. Normally, the members can select the hour that they want.

     Like all other quality circle functions, the selection of when it meets is done on a democratic basis. Quality circles do everything by vote, one vote per person. Note that although the time per week is limited, there are no time constraints on the number of weeks that it can take to accomplish a task.

3. *Management provides a facilitator.* One person should be appointed a quality circle facilitator. Normally, this is a member of management who has been trained in the operation of quality circles. This person has two primary roles. The first is to communicate to the quality circle those tasks which management is interested in and that have a high probability of suggestions being accepted versus those tasks on which management would frown if the quality circle should study them. For example, normally, it would not be prudent for the quality circle to study the salary structure of the data processing department, as that is a management prerogative. The facilitator should advise members of these facts. Second, the facilitator should be knowledgeable in the tools and techniques that make a quality circle work. If the members get off base or need assistance, the facilitator should be available. On the other hand, the facilitator is not a member of the quality circle, and in fact may not meet with the quality circle. Many facilitators who meet with the quality circle do not sit in the circle but rather, are outsiders and respond only when called upon.

4. *Quality circles select the topics.* What the quality circle will work on is the prerogative of the quality circle. Normally, the circle goes through a brainstorming or green-lighting session, identifying the types of topics that they believe should be addressed. Through discussion and other quality circle techniques, the group votes on which topics they want to discuss. The topic that gets the most votes becomes the first topic for discussion. The circle will continue to work on this topic until they have a solution to present to management.

5. *The quality circle is a unit.* No individual member in the quality circle should be given or attempt to get credit for quality circle recommendations. The objective of the quality circle is not to improve the reputation of a single person but rather, to improve quality and productivity. On the other hand, quality circles are an excellent training ground for management, and good work done by individual quality circle members is normally recognized.

6. *Management retains approval rights.* After the quality circle concludes the study, they present their recommendations to management. Management then decides whether to accept, reject, or accept with modification the recommendation of the quality circle. What makes the concept so powerful is that if management accepts the concept and implements it, the quality circle members are obligated to support it. It is not management's idea; it is their idea.

Although many of the quality circle recommendations are small in scope, they each tend to improve the quality and productivity of administration. As stated previously, quality is not a short-term concept but a long-term concept. It is through the continual improvement and bootstrapping of ideas like those produced by quality circles that administration is improved.

QUALITY ASSURANCE VERSUS QUALITY CONTROL

The improvement of administration involves both a quality assurance and a quality control function. Normally, these are not full-time functions but rather, duties assigned to people in the administrative area. Quality assurance is a function that evaluates the administrative process, and quality control evaluates the products produced by administration.

Both functions are necessary to ensure the increasing quality of administration. Good products cannot be produced by a bad system. If the system is bad, it is the assessment of the quality of the system through a quality assurance function that adjusts the process. The self-assessment, task force, and quality circle methods discussed previously are all designed to improve the quality of the process and thus could be viewed as quality assurance functions.

Quality control, as stated previously, is the responsibility of the people performing the work. These people need the standards and assessment tools if they are going to measure quality to ensure that it exists. This process requires that the administration function establish an administrative quality hierarchy.

The Administrative Quality Hierarchy

Quality control flourishes in a structured environment. For administration, the structure is represented by a hierarchy of policies, procedures, standards, and guidelines. Without such a hierarchy, it is difficult to instigate an effective quality control program.

This book has proposed numerous areas for administrative policies. Administrative management, through the establishment of a set of policies, creates the framework for building a quality environment.

Policies explain the objectives and intent of data processing management. Procedures explain how that policy will be executed. Standards define what management expects, and guidelines or recommendations on how to accomplish the standards.

This administrative quality hierarchy is illustrated in Figure 89. The hierarchy shows that it begins with a policy, moves downward to procedures, then standards, and finally, guidelines. The hierarchy is structured much like a system or program. The policy is at the top of the structure, which may be supported by one or more procedures. These procedures, in turn, are measured

Hierarchy   **Example**

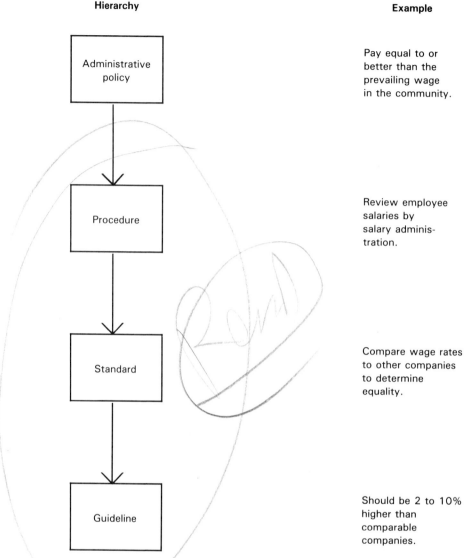

Pay equal to or
better than the
prevailing wage
in the community.

Review employee
salaries by
salary adminis-
tration.

Compare wage rates
to other companies
to determine
equality.

Should be 2 to 10%
higher than
comparable
companies.

Figure 89   *Administrative Quality Hierarchy*

by compliance to one or more standards. The guidelines follow the standards as the lowest level in the administrative quality hierarchy.

An example of the administrative quality hierarchy is also illustrated in Figure 89. This shows a data processing administrative policy which is to "pay equal to or better than the prevailing wage in the community" for data processing personnel. Obviously, in data processing the community is national and the wages paid are to be on a par with wages paid for comparable people in comparable positions. This policy needs procedures explaining how the policy is to be accomplished. One of the procedures is shown in the example, which is to establish a salary administration group to review employee salaries. This is to ensure that data processing salaries stay competitive with other companies over a period of time. Organizations need standards so that they can measure whether or not the policy is being achieved. The one standard included in the example is to compare the wage rates of the data processing professionals within the company to the wages paid by other companies to determine the quality of salaries for comparable positions. If the company salaries are equal to or better than the other prevailing wages in the community, the standard of comparison to like companies will demonstrate that the policy is being achieved. The standard also explains what is expected by management for compliance to the policy. Finally, a guideline is provided which states that wages should be 2 to 10 percent higher than comparable companies. This is not a standard but merely a suggestion (i.e., guideline) to ensure that the policy is achieved. The totality of all these represents one small hierarchical structure in the administrative quality hierarchy. Obviously, in practice there would be more procedures, standards, and guidelines to ensure that this policy was achieved.

It is the responsibility of the administrative manager to ensure that the appropriate administrative policies, procedures, standards, and guidelines exist within the data processing area. The administrative manager will not initiate all policies but should play an active role in the development of this hierarchy. It is "the" building block in assuring not only quality administration, but quality data processing.

KEY ADMINISTRATIVE PRINCIPLES
THAT PROMOTE QUALITY

The administrative rules presented throughout this book are designed to highlight key administrative principles. Following these principles appears to have a high correlation with a quality administrative function. Obviously, no single organization follows all of the principles, but those data processing organizations that do follow many of these principles tend to have high-quality administration and data processing.

Some of these principles are more helpful in creating a high-quality administrative environment than others. The key principles that seem to be present in the most successful data processing installations are:

- *Separate status reporting from pay reporting*. Those organizations that couple the reporting of status and administrative information with pay information tend to receive less accurate information.
- *Minimize administrative requests*. Data processing personnel should not be burdened with administrative overhead. The administration function

should determine that each piece of information they collect is essential and know exactly how that information will be used to improve the quality of data processing.

- *Collect administrative data as a by-product of other systems.* The best administrative systems use other systems to collect administrative data. For example, collecting billing information from automated job accounting logs eliminates the need for operators to record data manually. These concepts not only improve the quality of data collected, but eliminate the administrative burden placed on people.

- *Report meaningful data.* Data processing staff and management personnel should not be burdened with large numbers of cumbersome-to-use reports. The information contained within the reports should be minimized to those data essential to the operation of the department. Wherever practical, the administration should be presented in pictorial format, as that is normally easier to interpret than are lists of numeric data.

- *Emphasize quality in the administrative process.* An everyday responsibility of the administrative function should be to emphasize the need for quality in the administrative process. It must not be considered a routine after-the-fact function but rather, one that is essential to the operation of the data processing department.

- *Establish an administrative quality assurance and quality control function.* Quality does not improve unless the responsibility for quality and quality improvement is clearly placed. The administrative manager should have the quality assurance responsibility, and the entire data processing staff should be responsible for the quality control of administrative data and supply the tools and techniques for them to measure and ensure that quality administration occurs.

THE TEN COMMANDMENTS OF EDP ADMINISTRATION AND CONTROL

Properly practiced EDP administration is the glue that holds data processing together. Quality concepts are what turn an average administrative function into an outstanding administrative function. Another way of describing what makes administration work is to list the 10 commandments of a good administrative function, which are (see Figure 90):

1. *Administration is people.* People make administration work and they are the essential ingredients in a successful administrative environment.
2. *Administration must originate from the top.* Administration is the guardian of data processing policies, procedures, standards, and guidelines. This hierarchy must begin with senior data processing management and the establishment of effective data processing policies.

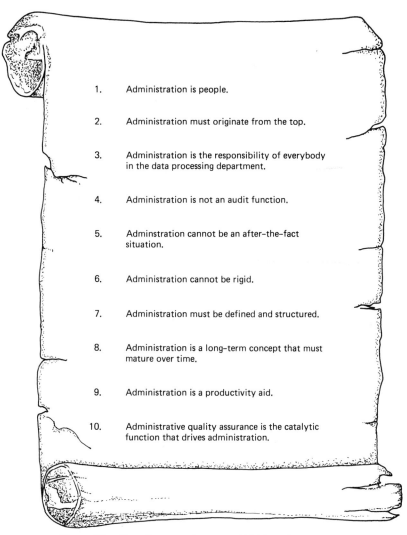

1.   Administration is people.

2.   Administration must originate from the top.

3.   Administration is the responsibility of everybody
      in the data processing department.

4.   Administration is not an audit function.

5.   Adminstration cannot be an after–the–fact
      situation.

6.   Administration cannot be rigid.

7.   Administration must be defined and structured.

8.   Administration is a long–term concept that must
      mature over time.

9.   Administration is a productivity aid.

10.   Administrative quality assurance is the catalytic
      function that drives administration.

Figure 90   *Ten Commandments of EDP Administration*

3.   *Administration is the responsibility of everybody in the data processing department.* The administrative function performs the day-to-day work administrative tasks, but the success of EDP administration is the responsibility of everybody in the department. Otherwise, it doesn't happen.

4.   *Administration is not an audit function.* The administrators are not designed to check on how well the other people do their work but rather, to perform those types of tasks that are necessary to support the data processing mission and to provide the information needed to make good business decisions. Administration should be part of the solution, not part of the problem.

5. *Administration cannot be an after-the-fact situation.* People must be involved in administrative activities throughout the workday. Administration cannot be put off until the other work tasks are finished. When administration is a second-class citizen, it shows in the quality of the administrative products.

6. *Administration cannot be rigid.* Everything worth administrating is not worth administrating well. There must be room for quick and dirty administrative procedures, and in other instances it must be very rigid and precise.

7. *Administration must be defined and structured.* Good administration will not happen unless there are good procedures to follow and standards to measure performance by. People should not have to guess whether administration has been performed properly, but should have the tools and techniques to know whether or not the job has been done well.

8. *Administration is a long-term concept which must mature over time.* The administrative process is one that must be continually improved. It must be recognized that data processing is new, and thus administration of data processing is new. Management must recognize that continual research and evaluation of the function must occur so that it can be improved continually.

9. *Administration is a productivity aid.* Good administrative procedures improve the productivity of the performance of the data processing mission. It should not be looked at as an impediment but rather, as a tool for improved productivity.

10. *Administrative quality assurance is the catalytic function that drives administration.* Administrative quality assurance is not essential, but unless there is a guardian for improving the quality of administrative practices, it may not happen. Just as it is not necessary to have a manager of standards to have good standards, it is not necessary to have a person responsible for administrative quality assurance. On the other hand, it is unusual for an organization to have good standards without a standards manager; similarly, it is unusual for an administrative group to be enthused and aggressive over quality without someone being accountable for administrative quality assurance.

EDP ADMINISTRATIVE GUIDELINE 43

Administration should be part of the solution to effective data processing—not part of the problem!

Chapter
13

Controlling and Measuring the Administrative Function

Visualize for a moment a golfer standing on the first tee of a golf course. It is a picturesque day as the golfer tees off. The ball goes straight down the fairway. The golfer calculates the distance to the green and then selects the appropriate club and hits again. This time the ball drops into the sand trap. Not to be dismayed, the golfer again selects a club and chips out of the sand onto the green. Lining up the putt, the golfer taps the ball and sinks it for a par 4. The golfer smiles and moves on to the next hole.

Now visualize that same golfer standing on the same first tee, but this time it is foggy. The golfer tees off, but is not sure of the direction of the hole. In addition, the golfer cannot see where the ball goes. The golfer becomes frustrated as he searches for the ball. Finding the ball, the golfer is uncertain what club to use next because the direction and distance to the green are not known. Again, confusion.

In the first instance the golfer can measure the distance to the hole, assess how well the last shot has been made, and make any necessary adjustments. In the second instance the golfer did not know where the ball went, had to search for it, and then was uncertain how far the hole was. In our second instance the golfer could not make adjustments because the golfer could not measure how far he had gone or how far and what direction he should go in order to sink the shot.

EDP administration is similar to the golfer in one aspect. If administration cannot measure where they have come from, and do not know where they are going, they cannot select the right club (i.e., procedure, method, etc.) to fulfill the data processing mission. In other words, administration without control and measurement can lead to frustration and confusion.

This chapter suggests methods for measuring and controlling the EDP administration function. The chapter attempts to tie together some of the assessment principles presented earlier in the book. In addition, methods for measuring and controlling the effectiveness of administration are proposed.

EDP ADMINISTRATIVE GUIDELINE 44

What you cannot measure, you cannot control.

THE NEED TO STABILIZE THE ADMINISTRATIVE ENVIRONMENT

The first step in improving control in administration is to stabilize the environment. This means that the administration process is structured. Once structured, the effect of establishing, operating, and changing a control within that structure can be identified and measured.

In the early days of data processing, system development was unstructured. This meant that each project leader could make individual decisions on how they wanted to create a new system. When the data processing department began to introduce procedures and standards (i.e., controls) into this unstructured environment, the effect of those procedures and standards could not be measured. The result was that very few felt that standards were important because they were not convinced that they could not do as well or better than the way proposed by the standard.

As the developmental and maintenance environment becomes more structured, the effect of new standards and procedures can be more clearly measured. For example, many departments can demonstrate the reduced cost in developing and maintaining systems when they move to a more structured or stabilized environment. The same principles need to be applied to EDP administration.

The difficulty in controlling data processing is that data processing has been viewed as being more of an art than a science. It is difficult to apply control to an artistic environment because we are looking for creativity, which is difficult to control. On the other hand, if data processing is viewed as a scientific environment, controls can be used effectively. Once properly controlled, one of the desirable by-products is an increase in productivity (assuming, of course, that doing quality work is the major thrust).

The effect of control as experienced in a move from an unstructured to a structured development environment can be measured. Many organizations have publicly stated reductions in the maintenance cost of those systems of up to 50 percent. Although the reduction is important, it is also important that the change can be measured. In this example, the change is adding a control.

Once the administrative environment is stabilized, changes in that environment can be measured. Once this happens, improvements in productivity and quality should be dramatic. Like the golfer, once the distance, direction, and obstacles in the way to sinking the golf ball in the hole are known, the game can be won on skill. On the other hand, on a fog-strewn golf course, skill may not be the deciding factor as to who wins.

CONTROLLING THE ADMINISTRATIVE FUNCTION

The objective of control is to prevent losses. "Losses" is used in the broad sense here to mean any unfavorable act. This can be the loss of assets, loss of time, or loss of credibility.

The first step in any control design process is to identify the source of losses. These are frequently referred to as risks. Once the source and magnitude of the risk has been determined, controls can be designed to reduce that risk.

Many of the administrative risks were described in the preceding chapter as impediments to the successful operation of the administration function. Chapter 12 suggested that these impediments or risks be ranked, which is a method of indicating the magnitude of the risk. Ideally, the risks would be quantified, but that may be impractical for many administrative groups.

The following questions must be answered in developing a system of administrative control:

1.   What needs to be controlled?
2.   How much does it need to be controlled?
3.   How should it be controlled?
4.   Are the implemented controls effective?

If these four questions can be answered satisfactorily, the administrative environment should be considered adequately controlled. On the other hand, if the administrative manager cannot answer those questions, a control study should be undertaken. Each of the questions is discussed individually below.

What Needs to Be Controlled?

All of the events that can negatively affect the administrative group may need to be controlled. The challenge for the administrative manager is to identify those potential negative events. The more specific the manager can be in identifying those events, the easier they will be to control. This book should be considered your checklist for identifying problems. The questionnaires at the end of each chapter in Section II should be an invaluable aid to the administrative manager in identifying potential control problems.

How Much Does It Need to Be Controlled?

It is normally either impossible or impractical to reduce losses to zero. In most situations, it is cheaper to incur losses than to attempt to stop them completely. An easy-to-understand example is key entry. It is basically impossible to stop all key entry errors from occurring. Even with several different key verification processes, a few errors are likely to remain.

If losses cannot be reduced to zero, two options occur. One is to establish "zero defects" as an objective and strive to achieve that objective even though it is impossible. The other option is to establish standards of performance (i.e., controls) and then establish controls to meet those standards.

The differences in the two options should be clear. The one that strives for perfection will fall short, so that the true effect of the control is difficult to measure. In that case, any defect is considered a control failure. The second option has goals or targets to achieve and the controls can be adjusted if the target is missed on either side.

The reason one would not want to stop all defects is that it may not be cost-effective. Obviously, zero defects is a good goal. However, as stated previously, it may not be the most practical control objective.

The cost-effectiveness curve of controls is illustrated in Figure 91. This shows that as the amount of losses decreases, the cost of controls increases. Since the only purpose for control is to reduce the losses, the cost of control must be considered part of that loss. In other words, the total value of the loss is the loss that occurs plus the cost of the controls designed to prevent that loss. It is essential to understand that if it were not for the potential loss, there would be no need for control.

The cost-effectiveness curve of controls shows us that after a specific point it costs more to reduce the loss than the loss itself. On the overcontrolled side of the curve, for each control dollar expended, losses will be reduced less than $1. On the undercontrolled side of the curve, each dollar spent on control will result in more than $1 reduction in the loss. At the point where the lines cross, $1 expended on control will reduce losses exactly $1. This is the optimum point of control. Practically speaking, it is difficult to achieve, but it should be a goal in control design.

EDP ADMINISTRATIVE GUIDELINE 45
Overcontrol is not cost-effective; thus from a business perspective both under- and overcontrol are undesirable.

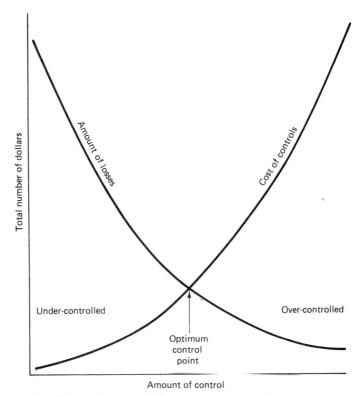

Figure 91   *Cost-Effectiveness Curve of Control*

How Should It be Controlled?

There are three general categories of control:

1. *Preventive controls:* Controls that stop an undesirable event from occurring
2. *Detective controls:* Controls that uncover the fact that an undesirable event has occurred
3. *Corrective controls:* Controls that provide the needed information or materials to remedy an undesirable event

Let us examine a situation in order to explain the three types of controls. Assume that a fire was the unfavorable condition or risk that needed to be controlled. A firewall that could stop the fire from spreading or occurring is a preventive control. A fire alarm is a detective control in that it announces that a fire has occurred; and a fire extinguisher is a corrective control in that it can put out a fire once it has been detected.

The administrative manager can select any of these three categories of controls to reduce an identified loss. The manager must answer the questions:

- Do I want to prevent the event from occurring? If so, I need a preventive control.
- Do I want to detect when an unfavorable event has occurred so that it will be brought to my attention for potential action? If so, I want a detective control.
- Do I want to detect that an undesirable event has occurred and take a predetermined action whenever it occurs? If so, a detective control with corrective countermeasure is wanted.

The criteria by which a control will be selected include:

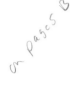

- Cost of control
- Impact of control on people and system as a motivator or demotivator
- Strength of control
- Time to execute control
- Knowledge of people in exercising control (note that some controls may be exercised through automated software packages)

The strength of administrative controls can be determined by analyzing the type of control used and the method of implementation. The strength of controls as they relate to one another is illustrated in Figure 92. This lists two methods of implementation. These are the manual implementation of controls and automated controls implemented through software packages or other automated devices.

Automated controls are generally stronger than manual controls because one can place more reliance on the control being exercised. A machine will repeat the same events every time, whereas a person may not.

Of the three types of controls, detective with planned corrective countermeasures are the strongest. These are followed by preventive controls, with detective without planned corrective countermeasures the weakest. The detective controls without planned corrective countermeasures are weak because there is no guarantee that action will be taken after the undesirable event has been detected.

Method of Implementation	Type of Control		
	Preventive	Detective without Planned Corrective	Detective with Planned Corrective
Manual	Average	Very weak	Strong
Automated	Strong	Weak	Very strong

Figure 92 *Control Selection Table (Relational Control Strengths)*

One of the most serious control problems in data processing is the failure to follow up on undesirable events that have been detected. Examples abound in the industry of computer-produced warning messages that are never acted upon or control indicators which are ignored. Administrative managers should place special attention on ensuring that preplanned corrective countermeasures are included in the control design process as often as possible.

Are the Implemented Controls Effective?

Controls are effective when they are well synchronized and cost-effective. Visualize for a moment attempting to cross a large city at the rush hour without traffic lights. It would be chaos. On the other hand, if traffic lights are unsynchronized, they may not lessen the chaos much.

Controls are like a set of traffic lights. As long as they are synchronized and directed toward the appropriate purpose, they are effective. On the other hand, if they are not regularly adjusted, traffic will back up in one direction while it flows free in the other. In many situations, this may make things worse than if there were no traffic light at all.

The message is that controls need to be adjusted. They cannot be designed, implemented, and forgotten. Assessment and adjustment must be continuous if the controls are to be effective.

The administrative control cycle is illustrated in Figure 93. This cycle explains the process of measuring and adjusting controls. The cycle begins and ends with the definition of effective administrative controls.

When controls are established, there is no guarantee that they will work, and if they work, there is no guarantee that they will be effective. When one designs controls and one designs systems, one hopes that they will work. The end product is normally the best judgment and creation of the designer.

The control cycle starts with the designer's best judgment. When put into practice, it is measured periodically. This occurs through the use of feedback mechanisms. A feedback mechanism is a mini-report writer designed to collect information about the effectiveness of an implemented control. For example, a feedback mechanism is a report showing the actual versus budgeted cost for a project as a measurement of the effectiveness of the budget process. Note that budgeting is a control.

Once measured, the effectiveness of controls must be evaluated. In our budgetary example, we said that the variance between actual and budget would be a measurement of the effectiveness process. The questions that must be asked are:

- How effective is the budgetary process?
- Should it be adjusted?
- Is greater budgetary precision cost-effective?
- Is greater budgetary precision needed for decision-making purposes?

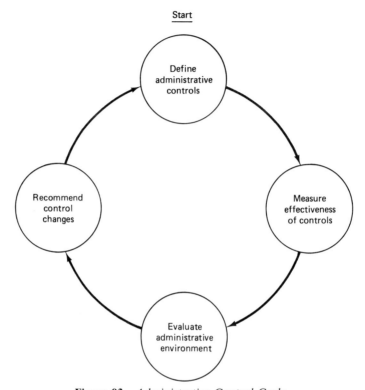

Start

Figure 93   *Administrative Control Cycle*

   The answers to these questions will determine the effectiveness of the control, or in our example, the budgetary process. If the control is deemed to be effective enough for the purpose for which it is designed, no additional action need be taken except to remeasure the effectiveness periodically.

   The fact that a control is effective today does not mean that it will be effective three months from today. If the control does not appear sufficiently effective for the purpose for which it is designed, changes to the control should be recommended. This is the last step in the control cycle. The recommended changes redefine the administrative controls. As these new controls are implemented, or existing controls modified, they must be measured as the control cycle continues.

   Failure to follow the control cycle steps results in controls getting out of synchronization with the needs of the organization. For example, when traffic lights through a city are unsynchronized, traffic becomes snarled and delayed. The same negative result can occur from ineffective controls. Since administration is heavily control oriented, understanding and living by control cycle principles are important for the effectiveness of the total administrative process.

EDP ADMINISTRATIVE GUIDELINE 46
Failure to adjust administrative controls may result in the staff circumventing many administrative controls.

METHODS TO MEASURE THE EFFECTIVENESS OF ADMINISTRATION

Everybody is capable of measuring administration. All one needs to do is ask another person how administration is doing and they can provide the answer. Thus it is not measurement that is the problem but rather, acceptance that the measurement is good.

Measurement by an independent party has more credibility than by an involved person. This means that in administration the function could be difficult to measure by either those within the administrative group or those served by the group. Neither are independent in the assessment process. However, with the proper tools, either of these parties could measure the effectiveness of the administrative process.

The credibility of the assessment increases in two instances. First, the person making the assessment is highly creditable, and thus whatever that person says is believable. Second, the assessment is factual as opposed to an opinion assessment, and thus becomes more believable.

The recommended assessment process for EDP administration is a factual assessment. This means that the measurement criteria must be very specific and nonargumentative. For example, if the quality of administration is measured on a number of reports issued on time, that analysis is factual and cannot be disputed. Although one might argue the merit of the assessment criteria and the meaning of the criteria, the factual information is nonargumentative.

The four methods that are used to judge the effectiveness of the EDP administration function are:

1. Judgment
2. Administrative criteria
3. Baseline change
4. Attribute change

Each of these methods is individually discussed.

Judgment

Of all the assessment methods, judgment is the easiest to use. One must only decide how good or bad EDP administration is and that becomes the assessment. Judgment is the most widely used method of assessing the adequacy of EDP administration.

The value placed on the judgment is related directly to the credibility of the person making the judgment. The better accepted the person making the judgment, the more people rely on the judgment. Using a team of people who come to a common judgment increases the credibility of the judgment.

The disadvantage of this method to the EDP administration group is that it is an after-the-fact method of judging. EDP administration may have met what they believe to be their objectives but the judgment may be based on other criteria. It is helpful when using the judgment method to state the criteria on which administration will be judged.

Administrative Criteria

Each profession develops a series of criteria measurements that are deemed reliable for assessment purposes. These criteria are normally factual and non-argumentative. Therefore, they meet the objective of being a good assessment method.

Let us look at how various professions use these measurement criteria. Accountants evaluate the functioning of an organization through a series of assessment relationships. Among the most common are gross profit, net profit, inventory turnover, return on investment, and comparisons between years. The medical profession uses such measurements as blood pressure and height-to-weight tables. Engineers use stress factors and load factors.

The group involved in measurement can use these factors in assessing the effectiveness of the work under its control. Unfortunately, EDP administration has not yet developed a generally agreed upon set of criteria. On the other hand, many managers use criteria as a basis for measuring the effectiveness of EDP administration.

Suggested administrative evaluation criteria are listed in Figure 94. This figure lists the types of criteria used in evaluating EDP administration and the purpose for which they are used. A more detailed description of each of the criteria listed in Figure 94, together with its advantages and disadvantages, are included in Appendix A.

INTERPRETING THE ADMINISTRATIVE EVALUATION CRITERIA

The criteria produced by themselves may have little meaning without interpretation. These are merely factual relationships that must be interpreted. It is the interpretation that determines the assessment of the EDP administrative function.

Evaluation Criteria	Purpose
1. Administrative costs/total DP costs	To measure the productivity of the administrative staff
2. Administrative staff/total DP staff	To measure the productivity of the administrative staff
3. Administrative staff/1,000 lines of operational source code	To measure the effectiveness of administration as related to the work performed by the data processing department
4. Administrative staff/million dollars processed by computer	To measure the effectiveness of the administrative staff as related to the work produced by the data processing department
5. Administrative staff growth/DP staff growth	To measure the growth of administration as related to the growth of the department
6. Staff administrative time/staff production time	To measure the administrative burden placed on the technical staff
7. Administrative staff/number of changes to DP systems	To measure the effectiveness of administration as related to the administrative burden placed on the technical staff
8. Administrative budget/actual administrative expenditures	To measure the effectiveness of the use of administrative resources
9. Average days of variance from administrative schedule	To measure the effectiveness of administration in meeting their schedules
10. Percent of DP plan accomplished in the past 12 months	To measure the effectiveness of administration in developing and administering data processing plan
11. Average days to respond to an administrative request	To measure the responsiveness of the technical staff to administrative requests
12. Average days given staff to respond/ average days to process requested data	To measure the effectiveness of administration in responding to requests by the technical staff
13. Nonresponses to administrative requests/ total administrative requests	To measure the effectiveness in the administrative staff in receiving information from the technical staff
14. Number of procedures created or revised during the past 12 months/total number of procedures	To assess the effectiveness of the administration in keeping administrative practices current with the changing requirements of data processing
15. Number of administrative forms/total DP staff	To measure the administrative burden placed on the technical staff
16. Total number of forms completed during the past 12 months/total DP staff	To measure the administrative burden placed on the technical staff

Figure 94   *Administrative Evaluation Criteria*

The first criterion listed in Figure 94 was the ratio of administrative costs to total data processing costs. If we assume that the total data processing budget was $500,000, and that the administrative costs for that department were $50,000, the criterion produced would be 1/10 or 0.1. This criterion (sometimes called a ratio or metric) must then be interpreted. The evaluator must determine whether or not it is desirable for 10 percent of the data processing budget to go into administration. In one organization it might be a very good ratio, whereas in another it would be very poor.

Let us look at an example of interpreting one of these criteria. If we were to look at the accounting profession, our ratio of concern might be net profit. If we were to look at the automotive industry during a downturn in automotive sales, 2 percent net profit might be outstanding, while if, at the same time, one of the high-technological companies made only a 2 percent net profit, we would consider it one of the poorer companies in the industry. Our 10 percent ratio for administrative costs must be interpreted similarly.

The most common ways to interpret the meaning of one of these criteria are:

1. *Comparison to national norm:* If there is an industry-wide norm for one of these criteria, an administrative group can compare its ratio to the industry norm. For example, if the average data processing organization spent 7.5 percent of their budget for administration, a group spending 10 percent would be considered above norm and ineffective.

2. *Comparison to industry norm:* Industries are different in the way in which they use the computer. For example, it may be difficult to compare the banking industry to the heavy manufacturing industry. For example, the banking industry might show a 12 percent ratio of administrative cost to total DP cost, whereas the heavy manufacturing industry would show only 8 percent. In this instance, our 10 percent would be considered good if we were in a banking industry, and poor if we were in a heavy manufacturing industry.

3. *Trend over time:* Each criterion can be evaluated through its change over a period of time. For example, if last year, administrative costs had been 12.5 percent and were down to 10 percent this year, we could assume that the administrative group had been very effective based on that one criterion.

The final assessment of all four methods is judgment. However, the difference is how the judgment is made. In the judgment method, the judgment cannot be supported. In the other three methods, factual and attitudinal information is gathered and quantified as a support of the judgment. The more factual the criteria, the easier it becomes to support the assessment of the EDP administrative function.

Baseline Change

At the beginning of the book, it was suggested that the administrative manager develop a baseline for the function. This baseline was comprised of both factual and attitudinal information. The objective of the baseline was to assess the functioning of the baseline at the current time.

The objective for establishing the baseline was to identify areas of potential administrative weakness. Once these weaknesses had been identified, it was suggested that a plan of action be developed. The plan of action was designed to correct the weaknesses.

If a baseline has been established, it can be used for evaluation purposes. This requires that the current baseline be identified. The difference between the two baselines is then the evaluation of the effectiveness of the administrative function. It also becomes an evaluation of the implementation of the administrative plan of action.

The administrative baseline is described in Figures 12 and 13. Figure 12 is a factual baseline, and Figure 13 is an attitudinal baseline. The factual baseline normally covers a period of time, such as 3, 6, or 12 months. The attitudinal baseline is taken at a specific point in time.

When the baseline method is used, a 6- or 12-month spread between baselines is advised. It is difficult to measure change in many of these criteria in a smaller amount of time. For example, a one-month change in baseline information may be more indicative of a few specific events than of a long-range trend. If the administrative group made a "goof" within the last week or two, it could significantly affect the attitudinal baseline information.

The suggested method for showing changes in baseline is as follows:

- *Factual baseline:* Show the percent increase or decrease from the previous baseline period. For example, the first baseline item shows the relationship between the percent of administrative employees and total employees in the data processing department. The assessment would then show the change in this percentage between the periods. For example, if the ratio during the first baseline was 10 percent, and the ratio at the second baseline period was 8 percent, the change would be a 20 percent reduction in this factual baseline criteria. Each factual baseline criterion can be listed and the percent change shown.
- *Attitudinal base line:* This baseline criterion shows the attitudes of people for nine different areas. However, rather than pure attitude, these are based on preestablished criteria. Thus it is not pure attitude but rather, attitude based on preselected criteria. This information can then be shown on the graph in Figure 13. This assessment will show the attitude bars at the two points in time. The bars should either be shown in different colors, or one shown as an open bar and the other penciled in black to show the two periods of time.

Attribute Change

This method is a personal assessment of the effectiveness of the administrative group. It is frequently employed by users of administrative services based on evaluation criteria. The users of administrative services are asked to evaluate the function based on how they believe it is doing. This might be known as a "how are we doing" user survey.

This type of assessment is subject to personal bias. If people like the administrative group, they tend to rate it higher, whereas if they do not like the group or perhaps the people in it, they may rate it low. For this reason, some surveys throw out the one or two best ratings and one or two poorest ratings. It is felt that the remaining ratings are more representative of the actual functioning of the group.

It is recommended that this type of survey be taken annually. However, some data processing organizations conduct the survey monthly. They use the survey for two purposes: first, as an opportunity to meet with users and discuss administrative services—this becomes a mini-quality circle concept, and second, to develop a continuous assessment of the functioning of the administrative group. They argue that the frequent surveys help them make on-the-spot adjustments. As such, the group can be more responsive to its users.

This information should be displayed in graphical format using bar charts. The two periods should be shown as different colored bars. This enables a quick visual assessment of the change in attitudes by administrative users between two different time frames. A case study of this method is described in Figure 95.

IF WE KNOW WHERE WE HAVE BEEN, WHERE SHOULD WE BE HEADING?

Data processing continues to undergo significant technological changes. While each technological advance brings huge productivity increases, it also creates huge problems. The administrative function must be able to adapt to these technological changes.

The first generation of data processing applications were oriented toward control of operations (see Figure 96). During these early days of data processing, the systems installed were order-entry systems, billing systems, payroll systems, airline seat reservation systems, and so on. The objective was both to reduce operating costs and to improve the day-to-day operations of the business. In most organizations, these systems justified the use of the computer. On the other hand, in many organizations there was little change between the manual system and the automated system.

These operation control systems took advantage of technology wherever applicable. For example, most began as tape batch computer systems and then

BANK IMPROVES QUALITY OF SERVICE VIA MONTHLY USER SURVEYS*

Bank increases quality of DP report distribution by 50%.

In 1980, Rhode Island Hospital Trust National Bank, a $2 billion commercial bank located in Providence, set as an objective to improve the quality of their DP operations and to build the credibility of the department with its users. During that year, Mark Marcantonio was selected to head the bank's DP department.

During early 1982, the bank began using a monthly user survey tool enabling DP management to increase communications with its users, obtain objective reports of performance, document problems, and provide comparisons of performance with other organizations. The survey was based on quantifiable standards of performance covering the following criteria:

1. Accuracy of output
2. Distribution of output
3. Timeliness of output
4. Quality of output
5. On-line availability
6. Response time
7. Systems development schedules
8. Response to problems
9. Attitude and cooperativeness (a qualitative measure)

The process entails the documentation of problems and the reporting of satisfaction reflecting users' assessments of the level (on a scale of 1 to 5:1 = unsatisfactory and 5 = exceptional) of DP service they are receiving. Input from users is reviewed monthly by Louis Buonaiuto, assistant vice-president and head of computer operations at the bank, to confirm the ratings prior to compiling the data for analysis. Louis was chosen for this role because he not only could see a direct payback in terms of objective reports (of problems) versus subjective ones, but was also in the position of initiating corrective action quickly in response to most legitimate complaints expressed by users.

Prior to initiating the monthly survey, an Improvement Opportunities Survey was made to reflect the existing performance of the DP department, thus providing a base for later measurements in the use of the service.

The survey revealed that the performance criteria receiving the highest number of complaints by users (in sequence of importance) were:

- Response time
- Timeliness of reports
- Distribution problems
- Response to problems

To improve its communication with users, specific technical support personnel at the bank were assigned to individual applications, and individual systems analysts/programmers were designated as "owners" of the application systems for given users. These personnel, as well as appropriate representatives from the user departments, were instructed on how to facilitate communications between DP and its users.

*This case study is based on services provided the bank by Dick Mathews of Mathews and Company.

Figure 95 *Case Study*

Review of Monthly Reports

As the survey process was implemented, the reports produced by the service were routinely reviewed at monthly meetings. Personnel attending these meetings included representatives from applications support, systems development, and the primary user contact for each department.

Major agenda items acted on at these meetings included issues outstanding from previous meetings, matters impacting the efficiency of the user's operation, criteria showing low levels of performance, and assignment of responsibility for the resolution of identified problems.

Results of Implementing a User Survey

Figure 1 shows the bank's overall monthly performance for seven months commencing in April 1982. Each area is individually analyzed. For example, Figure 1 reveals that *Distribution of Output* averaged 2.2 for the seven-month period compared with a low of 1.8 which was reported during the first two months. The increase of 0.4 on a rating scale beginning with 1.0 is equal to 50 percent compared to a bank's goal of 10 percent. Based on the results reported by users, Louis has taken steps to further improve the quality of the report distribution function—as well as the timely receipt of output— by purchasing a software package that is designed to help correct existing problems. Also, DP's results in increasing communications with users can be seen by observing the high ratings given to the **Response to Problems** and *Attitude and Cooperativeness* criteria which showed average ratings of 4.6 and 4.2, respectively.

Summary

Mark Marcantonio said about the user survey technique:

The most significant thing this "management tool" does is to force communication between DP and users. In the process, it helps solve the biggest problem, which has to do with DP's understanding of the customer's business and the customer's understanding of our capabilities and limitations.

From Louis Buonaiuto's position as the bank's liaison officer, he says:

Improving the quality of DP's services is easy to say but difficult to achieve. With the monthly survey, we now have a management process to foster DP's quality. It allows us to focus on the real problems within the data center, and our performance is no longer a subjective process. As a side benefit, our communication with users is improved.

Figure 95 *(continued)*

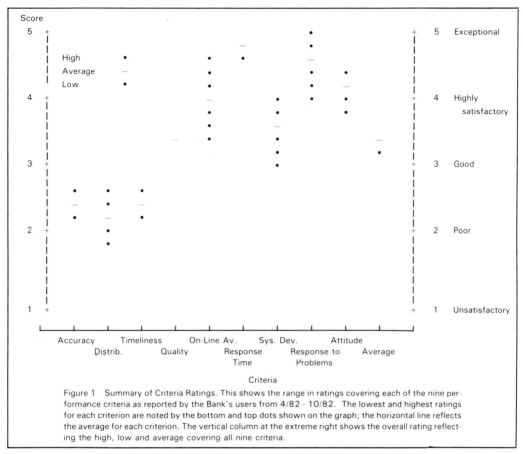

Figure 1   Summary of Criteria Ratings. This shows the range in ratings covering each of the nine performance criteria as reported by the Bank's users from 4/82 - 10/82. The lowest and highest ratings for each criterion are noted by the bottom and top dots shown on the graph; the horizontal line reflects the average for each criterion. The vertical column at the extreme right shows the overall rating reflecting the high, low and average covering all nine criteria.

Figure 95   *(continued)*

moved to on-line systems when the technology became cost-effective. From a management perspective, the objectives of the operation control systems are well known, making the problem one of implementation and not comprehension.

The second generation of application systems were management control systems. These are more complex systems requiring a better understanding of the needs of the organization. Examples of management control systems include general ledger systems, job status systems, budgeting systems, and inventory replenishment and management information systems.

Many of the management control systems were developed by incorporating judgment into the system. For example, a production control department would try to anticipate sales and schedule production to meet those trends. These systems use information available from other systems to perform a variety of complex analyses to develop a production schedule.

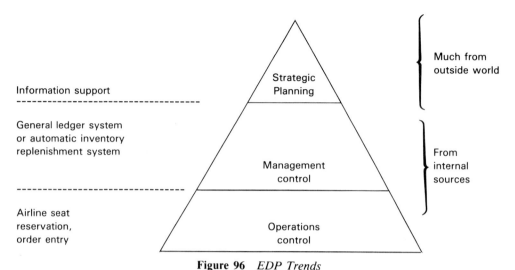

Information support

General ledger system
or automatic inventory
replenishment system

Airline seat
reservation,
order entry

Strategic
Planning

Management
control

Operations
control

Much from
outside world

From
internal
sources

Figure 96   *EDP Trends*

The management control system poses an administrative challenge. Management control systems involve management as users, as opposed to first-line supervisors who were the users of the operational control systems. In addition, although the operational requirements were well known, the management requirements were not. This frequently resulted in poor information being produced by the system. For example, products were ordered that were not needed.

Organizations are now beginning to move into the third generation of application systems. These are the strategic planning systems in which information is used to establish the direction and plans of the organization. Although the operational and management systems use internally generated information, the strategic planning systems also use information from outside sources. Examples include economic models, competitive analysis, financial analysis, and planning systems. This use of the computer normally involves interaction with planning personnel and the use of some sophisticated mathematics or planning algorithms.

The change from operation control to management control to strategic planning has a maturity cycle associated with it. As each phase begins, there is an initiation of new developmental, technological, and planning processes. As these processes begin, there is a period of excitement, followed by one of concern and sometimes disillusionment. Most administrators have lived through these cycles and are familiar with many of the negative side effects. The two that have seemed to have caused the most problems are the inability to complete projects within budget and on time. These have affected the credibility of the data processing department negatively.

As the use of the new technology expands, the lack of control over that technology becomes readily apparent. For example, as data base technology expands, we are experiencing problems with data definition, data consistency, and controlling data redundancy. To restore confidence in data processing and technology, controls must be installed.

We have experienced this cycle during the operation control and management control phases. We are now reexperiencing it as we begin the strategic planning phase. This phase is coupled with the use of data base and data communication technology. Most organizations are still searching for ways to control this current phase as its use expands.

Application and Technological Trends

The following trends can be expected in data processing:

- *Explosion of microcomputers:* The microcomputer will become as common as the telephone. Most management and professional staff will have their own microcomputers or access to a microcomputer. This will increase the need to provide more technical guidance and support throughout the organization, as opposed to having that administrative support limited to the data processing department.
- *Retrofitting older systems:* The systems developed in the 1960s and 1970s will need to be rebuilt. In many instances, it will not be practical or economical to discard those systems and rebuild them from scratch. Techniques will need to be developed to rebuild the older systems, either piece by piece or with a long-range retrofitting plan.
- *Acceleration of data base technology:* Data base is coming. It will probably be a relational data base, providing almost unlimited processing capabilities but posing some administrative challenges. The need for strategic planning systems will accelerate the use of data base.
- *Large integrated networks:* There will be more coupling of terminals, microcomputers, and office automation to the centralized computers and data bases. This will necessitate better documentation, design concepts, and intercoupling of software and methods.
- *Improved emphasis on quality:* Systems that come close to meeting user needs will no longer be good enough. The concept of heavy maintenance and inflexible design must be changed. Data processing organizations must learn how to build systems right the first time.
- *Better design methodologies:* The monster systems created in the past will become obsolete. The design of systems must be downgraded so that smaller stand-alone modules can be developed faster. The inflexibility and time spans coupled with the very large systems of the 1960s and 1970s will not meet the needs of the 1980s and 1990s.

The Future Role of EDP Administration and Control

The key to EDP administration control in the 1980s and 1990s is that of putting it all together. Data processing is comprised of many pieces. Frequently, these pieces are disjointed and competitive. For example, the standards being developed by one group are not being taught to new people by the training group. There is a lack of commonality of purpose.

EDP administration and control is the glue that must hold all the pieces together. Projects can no longer be developed by a single group. One can project based on the trends that in the future more groups will be involved in building systems. One such group will be data base administration. What is needed is to assemble all of the individual pieces and make them work.

The pieces needed to make a project work are illustrated in Figure 97 as a puzzle. This puzzle shows EDP administration and control in the center, holding the other pieces together. If EDP administration and control can direct all the pieces toward a commonality of purpose, the function will be overwhelmingly successful in accomplishing its mission.

EDP ADMINISTRATIVE GUIDELINE 47

No greater compliment could be paid to EDP administration and control than to state that it is the function that holds together the various parts of data processing and directs them toward a commonality of purpose.

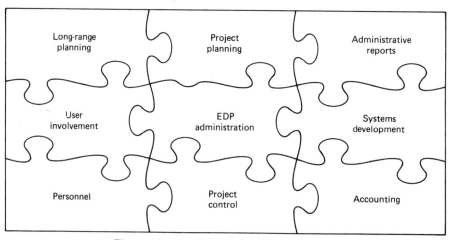

Figure 97   *Putting All the Pieces Together*

A

Administrative Measurement Criteria

CRITERION *Administrative costs/total DP costs*	*NUMBER* *1*

DESCRIPTION OF CRITERION

The total dollar costs of performing the administrative activities in a data processing department should be related to the total data processing department cost. The administrative costs can be either the budget of the administrative group or, if budgetary collection processes permit, all of the administrative costs of the department.

HOW TO COLLECT

The cost should be collected through the normal departmental time-reporting and/or budgetary accounting system. If formal records are not maintained, people costs can be used in estimating the cost of the people associated with administrative activities.

HOW TO INTERPRET

A good measurement would be a low percent of administrative costs to total data processing costs. A suggested rule of thumb is that 5 percent or less of the data processing resources should be allocated to administration. The measure can be evaluated at a single point in time, but may be more valuable interpreted as a trend over a period of time to ensure that the trend is not upward.

ADVANTAGES

This measure provides an indication of the resources consumed for non-productive purposes. The advantage of measuring it is that it can be controlled only when it is measured.

DISADVANTAGES

The definition of administration may vary from company to company and person to person. The validity of the measurement is impaired as the definition of administration becomes less rigid.

CRITERION	*NUMBER*
Administrative staff/total DP staff	*2*

DESCRIPTION OF CRITERION
This criterion measures the total number of full-time people devoted to administrative activities in relationship to the total DP head count. Full-time people can in fact be full-time people or the total of parts of individual people whose job function is partly administrative.

HOW TO COLLECT
The full-time people can be determined through analysis of the organizational chart of the data processing department. Part-time allocation to administrative activities should be acquirable through a time-reporting system or interview. Note that this does not include the administrative time spent by technical people in the performance of their job.

HOW TO INTERPRET
This measure needs to be interpreted two ways. If the administrative head count is too low, the administrative burden is shifted to higher-priced technical people. On the other hand, a high administrative head count may waste resources. The actual measurement will vary based on the amount of paperwork that needs to be performed by people versus the amount of paperwork that is automated in a data processing department. A suggested measurement would be in the range 1:5 to 1:20 administrative head count to total staff.

ADVANTAGES
This measure assesses the adequacy of administrative staff in relationship to the technical people who are supported by that staff. The measure can tell whether there is too much or too little administration.

DISADVANTAGES
This measure does not take into account the automation of the administration function, the specific needs of the technical staff, or the effectiveness of the people in administration.

CRITERION	*NUMBER*
Administrative staff/1000 lines of operational source code	*3*

DESCRIPTION OF CRITERION
This measure equates the ability of the administrative staff to support the creation and maintenance of source code.

HOW TO COLLECT
The total number of executable operational source codes are counted. These are the executable statements for the programs on the source master that are being run in an operational environment. Only the operational version of each program should be counted. The administrative staff is the total number of full-time people working in administration. (Note: A full-time person can be comprised of parts of numerous people.)

HOW TO INTERPRET
This measure is stating the number of lines of source code that are supported by one administrative person. The measure is attempting to equate administrative services to some measure of the work performed by the data processing function.

ADVANTAGES
Much of the current mission of data processing is managing operational applications. Thousands of lines of source code provides a measure of the magnitude of the maintenance effort. This metric relates administration to an operational characteristic of data processing.

DISADVANTAGES
Source code may not be an effective measure of data processing effort. The amount of staff required to maintain 1000 lines of source code varies according to the complexity of the code and the generation and documentation of the code.

CRITERION	*NUMBER*
Administrative staff/million dollars processed by computer	*4*

DESCRIPTION OF CRITERION
This criterion measures the total number of dollars processed by the computer supported by a single administrative staff member.

HOW TO COLLECT
The total administrative staff count comprises the equivalent full-time people whose primary responsibility is administration. It does not include time spent by the systems and programming staff for administrative purposes. The dollar amount of transactions processed by the computer will need to be collected from the control reports produced by those computer systems.

HOW TO INTERPRET
The objective of this metric is to demonstrate the contribution that the administrative staff is making to the business. The interpretation that should be used is to show that a large volume of processing of business dollars can be supported by a small administrative staff in data processing. The greater the number of dollars, the greater the measure.

ADVANTAGES
This measure attempts to put data processing administration in a relationship of value to the business. Without data processing, these dollars would be processed by people who would have to be supported by an administrative staff. Thus the EDP administrative staff is put in the business of supporting the value of business transactions.

DISADVANTAGES
This measure may not be valid because it will depend on the average dollars processed by a single transaction and/or the degree of automation of those applications.

CRITERION	NUMBER
Administrative staff growth/DP staff growth	5

DESCRIPTION OF CRITERION

This criterion compares the growth of EDP administration to the growth of the total data processing staff.

HOW TO COLLECT

It is suggested that this be an annual administrative metric. The percent change in administrative staff should be calculated using full-time equivalents, and the percent of the total data processing staff excluding the administrative staff should be calculated as a percent. The two percentages should then be used to produce a metric.

HOW TO INTERPRET

It is reasonable to expect that administration should grow in approximately the same percent as the technical staff. If it is growing faster than the technical staff, that is indicative of poor performance, and indicates that Parkinson's Law does work. If the administrative staff is increasing at the same ratio or less, that would be indicative of good administrative performance.

ADVANTAGES

This metric is effective in assessing the growth rate of EDP administration. It puts that growth rate in perspective to the growth of the data processing function in the organization.

DISADVANTAGES

This metric does not take into account the administrative work load. It is possible through automation or change in responsibilities that the work of administration is increasing or decreasing faster than the growth rate of the data processing department. This metric would not indicate that work growth.

CRITERION	*NUMBER*
Staff administrative time/staff production time	*6*

DESCRIPTION OF CRITERION

This metric measures the amount of time that the technical staff spends on administrative matters versus the amount of time they devote to technical matters.

HOW TO COLLECT

A definition must be developed defining what is administrative work and what is production technical work for the technical data processing staff. The staff must then record the amount of time they spend in each of these functions. That time should be reportable through the normal time accounting system in a data processing department.

HOW TO INTERPRET

This metric shows the percent of time that is spent on administrative matters. It is generally assumed that the lower this metric, the better. The suggested rule of thumb was that administrative matters should take about 5 percent of the total workday. However, what might be more important is a trend as opposed to the precise measure. If the amount of time spent on administration is increasing over a period of time, that is cause for alarm unless there are significant new administrative tasks being given to the production people.

ADVANTAGES

This metric provides a good measure of the amount of productive time that is being used for administrative purposes. This enables management to assess the value that they are getting out of administrative information in comparison to the cost of that data.

DISADVANTAGES

This metric by itself does not indicate the value received for administrative services. A high metric for this measure should not be considered poor without interpretation. Value for time spent must be considered.

CRITERION	NUMBER
Administrative staff/number of changes to DP systems	*7*

DESCRIPTION OF CRITERION

This measure relates the number of administrative full-time equivalents to the total number of changes made to data processing systems. This comprises changes to both systems under development and systems in maintenance.

HOW TO COLLECT

The full-time data processing administrative equivalents comprise the total number of people working in administration plus the total fractions of people working on administration which total full-time people. The administrative effort expended by technical people is not included in this count. The number of changes to systems should be those changes documented on request forms as changes to operational changes or changes to developmental systems.

HOW TO INTERPRET

This measure shows the number of system changes supported by one administrative person. The measure attempts to equate the value of administrative staff with work load placed on the technical staff. A good metric is one which demonstrates that a single administrator can support a large number of system changes.

ADVANTAGES

Data processing provides services to users. One measure of that service is the number of change requests processed by the department. The advantage of this administrative measure is that it equates administrative effort within the data processing department to work load within the department.

DISADVANTAGES

There may not be a valid relationship between administrative support and system changes. The services supplied by administration may not vary in direct proportion to the number of changes, and thus the measure may not be a realistic measure.

CRITERION	*NUMBER*
Administrative budget/actual administrative expenditures	*8*

DESCRIPTION OF CRITERION
This criterion compares the budgets provided for the functioning of the administrative group to the actual dollars expended by the group in administrating the function.

HOW TO COLLECT
The information needed from this measure should be readily available from the organization's budgetary system. The metric can be used in any accounting period. The total dollar budget is compared to the actual dollars expended.

HOW TO INTERPRET
This metric measures the ability of administration to operate within its budget. Most organizations permit a reasonable variance from budget. A large variance either over or under budget would be indicative of poor management.

ADVANTAGES
This is a measure frequently used by management to assess the performance of operational units. The budget is normally tied to a plan, so that variance from the budget may be indicative of variance from the plan.

DISADVANTAGES
The expenditure, lack of expenditure, or overexpenditure of funds may not directly reflect the performance of the administrative group.

CRITERION *Average days of variance from administrative schedule*	NUMBER *9*

DESCRIPTION OF CRITERION

This criterion measures the average variance in days from the planned schedule for achieving an administrative event from the actual date on which the event was completed.

HOW TO COLLECT

Most administrative events are dictated by schedule. These should be available from the administrative group. To collect this information, the actual date of completion of each event must be recorded and the number of working days should be calculated as a plus or minus figure. Minus means completed ahead of schedule; plus, behind schedule. An arithmetic average should then be calculated.

HOW TO INTERPRET

The ability of an administrative group to meet its schedules improves its credibility. Knowing whether the administrative group is ahead, on, or behind schedule represents the ability of the group to perform its work on time.

ADVANTAGES

This measure shows how well the administrative group was able to meet its planned schedule. Because administration expects the technical people to perform work by schedule, this measures them on the same performance as the one with which they often measure the technical staff.

DISADVANTAGES

Completing administrative work behind, on, or after schedule may not be under the control of the administrative staff. For example, if the technical staff does not provide them with data until after the scheduled completion date, they, in turn, cannot do their work on time.

CRITERION	*NUMBER*
Percent of DP plan accomplished in the past 12 months	*10*

DESCRIPTION OF CRITERION

The data processing plan contains the tasks and milestones to be accomplished during the year. This measure determines the number of those events and milestones that have been accomplished over a 12-month period. Twelve months is used because it coincides with most planning periods. Also, it is long enough to measure a track record of accomplishments.

HOW TO COLLECT

The information should be available from planning status reports. Because there are normally a large number of tasks, the measurement should be on whether a task is completed or not completed. Partially completed tasks should be considered not completed.

HOW TO INTERPRET

The administrative staff is supportive of the technical staff. The ability of the technical staff to perform their work should be at least partially dependent on the resources provided by the administrative staff. Therefore, the more items completed in the data processing plan, the more effective the administrative group should have been in supporting the technical staff.

ADVANTAGES

The mission of the data processing department is to complete data processing tasks, not administrative tasks. This measures the end result of the work performed by the data processing department, and a high completion rate should reflect credit on the administrative staff for its support function.

DISADVANTAGES

There is no assurance that the administrative group made a positive contribution toward the completion of technical data processing projects.

CRITERION *Average days to respond to an administrative request*	NUMBER *11*

DESCRIPTION OF CRITERION

This measure determines how long in days it takes the technical staff to respond to administrative requests.

HOW TO COLLECT

The administrative group should maintain records as to when they send a request to the technical staff and the number of days to respond to the technical staff. If the requests are limited, this can be measured in the number of individual requests; if there are a large number of requests, it may be advisable to group the requests and indicate only when all the responses have been returned.

HOW TO INTERPRET

Interpretation of this measure should be twofold. First, it is indicative of how effective the administrative group is in getting the technical staff to respond to their request; and second, it should be measured against the number of days given to respond. For example, if the technical staff is given 10 days to respond and they responded in 10 days, that would be considered to be commendable practice in getting responses on time. The longer it takes to get administrative responses, and the number of days behind schedule in getting responses, are indicative of an administrative group that does not follow up on its requests.

ADVANTAGES

This measure shows the ability of administration to collect the type of data it needs to perform the administrative mission.

DISADVANTAGES

This ability to collect information on a timely basis may not be within the authority or ability of the data processing administrative group. Possibly no amount of persuasion can force a technical staff to provide information, because the administrative group does not have supervisory authority over the technical staff.

CRITERION	*NUMBER*
Average days given staff to respond/ average days to process requested data	*12*

DESCRIPTION OF CRITERION
This measure shows the relationship between the number of days the administrative group takes to respond to a request for information, and the number of days it takes administration to process and issue the data.

HOW TO COLLECT
The average number of days per administrative request can be determined from memos and instructions given the technical staff. They would have to maintain records as to how long it took from the day they received the data until they issued a report.

HOW TO INTERPRET
This metric indicates the need to push the technical staff for information. For example, if the ratio worked out to 1, it would be that the administrative staff did their work in the same amount of time that they gave the technical staff. On the other hand, if the technical staff had a significantly shorter time frame than the administrative staff, it may mean that an unrealistic burden is being placed on the technical staff.

ADVANTAGES
This measure is designed to assess the need to press the technical staff for information.

DISADVANTAGES
This measure does not take into account the amount of time and effort required by each group to perform their part of the work.

CRITERION *Nonresponses to administrative requests/total administrative requests*	NUMBER *13*

DESCRIPTION OF CRITERION
This measure records the responsiveness or nonresponsiveness of the technical staff to administrative requests.

HOW TO COLLECT
Administrative staff should keep records as to how many of the technical staff do not respond to their requests for information. This is then compared against the total number of requests to develop either a responsiveness or an unresponsiveness measure.

HOW TO INTERPRET
This measure indicates the willingness of the technical staff to provide administrative data, and assesses the ability of the administrative group to collect the data they need to do their job.

ADVANTAGES
This metric partially assesses the reliability of the administrative data. If a significant portion do not contribute, the administrative data collected may not be representative of what is happening in the department.

DISADVANTAGES
The ability to collect or not to collect data may not be under the control of the administrative group.

CRITERION *Number of procedures created or revised during the* *past 12 months/total number of procedures*	*NUMBER* *14*

DESCRIPTION OF CRITERION
This measure identifies the changes to administrative procedures and/or additions or deletions to administrative procedures as a percent of the total number of administrative procedures.

HOW TO COLLECT
The administrative group would need to maintain records on the total number of procedures utilized in the data processing department, and on how many of those have been added, deleted, or modified in the past 12 months.

HOW TO INTERPRET
This metric indicates the responsiveness of the administrative group to changing conditions. If the administrative procedures are not changing, it may be indicative that they are unresponsive to the changing needs of the data processing department.

ADVANTAGES
This measure assesses administration's responsiveness to changing data processing conditions by changing and maintaining the effectiveness of the administrative procedures.

DISADVANTAGES
There may not be a correlation between the number of changes and the effectiveness of those changes.

CRITERION	NUMBER
Number of administrative forms/total DP staff	*15*

DESCRIPTION OF CRITERION

This measure compares the total number of administrative forms used in the data processing department to the total DP technical staff.

HOW TO COLLECT

The administrative group should maintain an inventory on the number of administrative forms used, and should be able to collect the number of technical staff from the organizational chart.

HOW TO INTERPRET

This measure shows how efficient the administrative staff is in collecting administrative information. The fewer number of forms per person, the less training required and the ease and probably the reliability of data collected.

ADVANTAGES

The number of forms is a measure of the complexity of the administrative function.

DISADVANTAGES

The value of the information received and its usefulness to the department may not be related directly to the number of forms.

CRITERION	*NUMBER*
Total number of forms completed during the past 12 months/total DP staff	*16*

DESCRIPTION OF CRITERION

This criterion shows the relationship between the total number of administrative forms completed within the course of a year by the technical staff and the total size of the technical staff.

HOW TO COLLECT

The administrative group must keep records on how many administrative forms have been completed. The size of the technical staff should be available from the organizational chart.

HOW TO INTERPRET

This measure is indicative of the amount of administrative time spent by the technical staff on administrative matters. The larger the number of forms completed per person, the greater the amount of administrative effort required by the technical staff.

ADVANTAGES

This measure shows the burden being placed on the technical staff by EDP administration.

DISADVANTAGES

This measure does not indicate the value of the administrative material produced as a result of having the forms completed.

Appendix

B

EDP Administrative Guidelines

Chapter Number	Guideline Number	Guideline
1	1	Whatever can go wrong in EDP will go wrong—and at exactly the worst moment.
1	2	The concept of fit is like teamwork; when all forces pull together in the same direction, the company wins.
1	3	Learn the language of senior management and then discuss EDP in that language.
1	4	Poor administrative practices comprise one of the greatest obstacles to improving productivity within the data processing function.
2	5	Administrative improvements are rare when based on generalities, but common when based on specifics.
3	6	Lack of action is the direct cause of most failures. It is the predominant error made by people in every walk of life.
3	7	Do not neglect to involve senior data processing management in administrative strategy decisions.
3	8	The administrative group that ignores the complaints and suggestions of users may find itself ignored by senior data processing management.
3	9	Establishing administrative priorities based on the return on investment will also return a credibility dividend to the administrative function.
3	10	Limit alternatives considered to no more than four choices; rarely will anyone ask for more.
3	11	It takes fewer resources to do it right than to explain why you did not.
3	12	People, not functions, accomplish objectives. Appointing a ''sponsor'' responsible for the accomplishment of administrative objectives improves significantly the probability of that objective being accomplished.

Chapter Number	Guideline Number	Guideline
3	13	There is no greater finale to a person's efforts than the simple words: "It is done and it works."
4	14	Planning is the function for which there never seems to be enough time—and there never will be unless the department plans ahead.
4	15	A good data processing plan is one that is in step with the organization's plan.
4	16	In deciding how much planning information to collect, make your error on the side of collecting too little information—time spent in collecting unwanted information is time lost forever.
4	17	It is best to begin with too little administration and control, and then expand as necessary—but only a little at a time.
4	18	Developing a plan means signing an undated resignation. Failure to accomplish a plan may mean your job.
5	19	Estimates are only as good as the credibility of the estimator. The only method to improve the credibility of the estimator is to make good estimates.
6	20	Using a priority system for data processing that is consistent with the mission of the organization puts data processing in step with senior management.
6	21	You cannot manage what you cannot measure. By measuring the skill level, departmental managers can manage the skill levels of their staff.
6	22	Planning for unplanned work is a good plan.
7	23	If management treats subordinates as responsible people and works to help them, not criticize them, communications will open up.
7	24	Good supervisors cause good systems to happen.
8	25	Customers will flock to the business that provides the best service at the lowest cost (or at a reasonable cost).
8	26	Everything worth doing is not worth doing well.
8	27	People are upset when their work is late, but the pain of tardiness can be relieved by being informed of the approximate length of the delay sufficiently in advance of the time scheduled.
8	28	The bitterness of poor quality remains long after the sweetness of meeting the schedule has been forgotten.
8	29	Accounting training for the data center manager will not only result in lower data center costs, but will teach that manager the language of management—which is accounting.
9	30	You cannot manage what you do not know—project administration tells you what you need to know in order to manage properly.
9	31	Do not assume that the other person will do his or her job—if you want to be sure it is done, check on it!
9	32	If it is worth doing, it is worth controlling.
9	33	The project manager who keeps good records can explain what has happened and why.
10	34	Failure to develop an effective interface between users and data processing personnel may cause users to seek alternative processing solutions.
10	35	If the customer is "king," the best data processing talent should be used to interface with users.

Chapter Number	Guideline Number	Guideline
10	36	Written contracts resolve many disputes before they occur and define how to solve those that do occur.
11	37	Acquiring a vendor product is a data processing project that requires a vendor life-cycle methodology.
11	38	The product you get from contracting is the one you specify—so be sure when you develop your written specifications that they are for the product you want!
11	39	Marketing's oldest rule is: "Let the buyer beware." Positively re-worded for EDP administration, it should state: "Let the buyer enforce contractual provisions."
11	40	It is a shame to deal with a poor vendor—it is a sin to deal with that vendor more than once.
11	41	A good contract is a fair contract to both parties. EDP administration should be equally concerned when a vendor contract is overly favorable to one party.
12	42	It takes less time to do it right the first time than to correct it after it has been done wrong.
12	43	Administration should be part of the solution to effective data processing—not part of the problem!
13	44	What you cannot measure, you cannot control.
13	45	Overcontrol is not cost-effective; thus from a business perspective both under- and overcontrol are undesirable.
13	46	Failure to adjust administrative controls may result in the staff circumventing many administrative controls.
13	47	No greater compliment could be paid to EDP administration and control than to state that it is the function that holds together the various parts of data processing and directs them toward a commonality of purpose.

Index